DISCARDED BY
MEMPHIS PUBLIC LIBRARY

**Alhaji Usman Danga**
Paramount Ruler
Emir of Zuru
*(Installed 1964)*

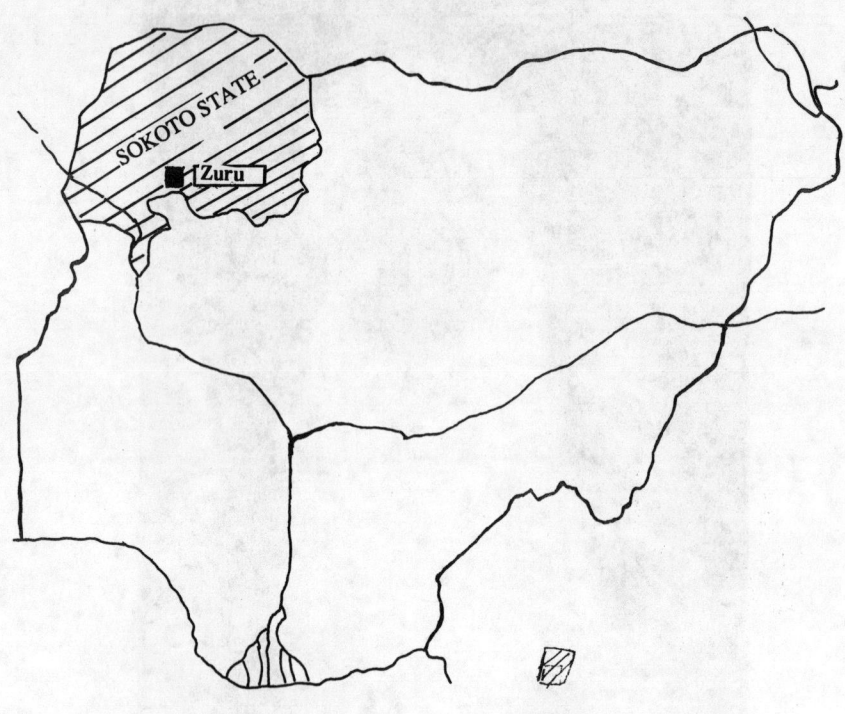

Map of Nigeria showing Zuru Emirate in Sokoto State.

# Studies In
# The History Of The People Of Zuru Emirate

*Edited by*

A. R. Augi
&
S. U. Lawal

Published 1990 by
**Fourth Dimension Publishing Co., Ltd.**
Plot 64A City Layout. P.M.B.01164, New Haven,
Enugu, Nigeria

© 1990 Zuru Emirate

ISBN

978 156 310 9

CONDITIONS OF SALE

All rights reserved. No part of this publication may be reproduced, stored in a retrieval system, or transmitted in any form or by any means, electronic, mechanical, photocopying, recording, or otherwise without the prior permission of the Publisher.

Photoset and printed in Nigeria by
**Fourth Dimension Publishing Co. Ltd.**

**Dedicated**

To the Unity and Progress of the People of
Zuru Emirate

# Foreword

Writing a foreword like this has been likened to finding a dancing partner as the music is about being over. But I think in my own case the situation is different. This is so because I have been in the thick of the Zuru History Project since its conception and commissioning in 1984 right to its delivery now. So that I consider writing this foreword a sort of saying some 'prayers' in a naming ceremony.

The Zuru Emirate Development Society (ZEDS) has since its inception been involved in various projects aimed at not only enhancing the development of our people, but also in creating an atmosphere of understanding for unity through raising the consciousness of our people. We realised that little has been studied and written about our people and society excepting the few colonial summations which was informed greatly by colonial racism, arrogance and the expediency of the day.

Our purpose in commissioning the Zuru History Project therefore rests on a tripod desire. First was the need for an historical inspection of our past for a proper understanding of ourselves and our present. Here, I will say, like I have said during the workshops held in the course of the execution of this project, that we want all aspects of our history good or bad, gleaned and synthesised for us. Thus we are not averred in coming to terms with our past, glorious or not, but we want to be informed by our historical past. And as I expected, most of the derogatory remarks about our people have been proved in these studies to be either colonial misunderstanding and misrepresentation, or are recent phenomena that have developed out of e thnocentricism, lack of knowledge and the inability of other Nigerians to appreciate our people and their culture from our own history, condition and viewpoint.

Our second object in the project was to make our society and people more aware of itself - its past and present and therefore be adequately prepared for the big task of the development and upliftment of the lives of our peoples and Nigerians. Here again, my thoughts on our people have been vindicated by this project. As has been shown, with all our present cultural plurality, people not only had some common origins and similar beginnings, but had developed in the past through mutual interaction with one another. Our people had homogeneity of purpose and within their own time, constraints and resources strove for the betterment of their society.

Our other intent in this exercise was to arouse and develop interests in research and scholarly works on the Zuru people and society. We therefore wanted to make the outcome of this project a sort of precursory one, not only to interest other academics and scholars to pursue their scholarship on Zuru people and society, but also to open up the terrain for them. This work as it is cannot be a finality, but has opened up other areas and visits that could benefit from further researches. My wish here is that scholars will follow these leads and consolidate what has been started in this volume.

My last words in this foreword are pleas - to the people of Zuru Emirate and to Nigerians. That we have more things that unite than divide us. This is probably clear by the contents of this book and I believe by the history of other peoples in Nigeria as well. And what is more, the great task ahead of us, of improving the lots of our people is another great unifying factor that should know no divide. We must then come together and vindicate ourselves and our living by improving it and leaving behind a worthy legacy for our children.

Like the historians will say, 'those who know not their past are wont to repeat its mistakes'. To avoid the errors of the past, we must be students of our past. And it is my belief that this book, the delay in its coming out notwithstanding, can provide us with the humble beginning of knowing our past, learning from it, and using our informed position for the benefit of our land and its people. I, therefore, hasten to recommend this book to all people of Zuru Emirate and to all Nigerians.

**Nathaniel Zome,**
*(National President)*
Zuru Emirate Development Society.

March 1990

# Preface

This book is the outcome of a research project conducted at the instance of the Zuru Emirate Development Society. The Project took off in 1984 under the coordination of Dr. I.L. Bashir, the then Acting Head of History Department of the Usmanu Danfodiyo University Sokoto. The research team then was composed of Drs. Bashir, Swai, Augi, Lawal & Alubo, Messrs Bitiyong, Ilu and Mallam Ahamed Bako. In 1986 the co-ordination of the project fell on Dr. Augi when Dr. Bashir left for the University of Jos. And following the third Zuru History Workshop in December, 1988 it was agreed to enlarge the multi- disciplinary focus of the project with the incorporation of a linguist (Ahmed Amfani) and another sociologist (B.B. Muhammad). In 1986 when Dr. Augi left the University, the co-ordination moved to Dr. Lawal who did the editing.

To prepare the ground for the researchers, Dr. Sullivan compiled a list of the extant literature and sources on Zuru history. In particular, her compilation of a catalogue of Zuru materials in the National Archives, Kaduna, Arewa House, Kaduna and the libraries in A.B.U. and Sokoto eased the identification and follow-up of the Zuru materials, And on her return to the U.S.A. in 1986 she sent a further list of Zuru materials in American Libraries. Obviously, the research team owes a lot of their successes to her efforts and we are quite grateful.

To facilitate the research project and to cross-check information, three workshops were held in the course of the project. Two were in Zuru town all in the month of December 1986 and 1987. The participants were local resource persons who contributed immensely with their wealth of information and knowledge of Zuru society and history. To them our appreciation knows no bound.

The third and final workshop was a purely academic one where the researchers had the benefit of their papers enriched from the lively discussions of a scholarly kind. This took place in the Usmanu Danfodiyo University, Sokoto, in December, 1988. We are most grateful to all those who attended and contributed in that workshop. In particular, we wish to single two persons that deserve mention for their untiring commitment. These are Mr. Michael Gujiya and Mr. Clement Tuko.

As for those who made the research and the publication of this work possible, i.e. the Zuru Emirate Development Society, our gratitude to them is beyond words. Not only have they allowed us explore a 'near virgin' terrain of scholarship of Zuru, but they persevered with us all through, knowing that the exercise of research and writing is not one that can be rushed but allowed to reach its natural fruition.

Finally, we are grateful to Mallam Muhammad Bashar Kalgo for his untiring efforts in the typing and retyping of the manuscripts. He sacrificed all his weekends for the first three months of this year to this work. While the commendable efforts of the typing is his, the errors are ours. Needless to say, all ideas expressed in this book are the authors to whom the credit or lack of it should go.

A. R. Augi<br>
S.U. Lawal<br>
March 1990.

# Notes On Contributors

*A.R. Augi*, B.A. PhD. (A.B.U), was at various times a lecturer in History at A.B.U.; Director of the Sokoto State History Bureau; Lecturer and acting Head of History and Deputy Dean, Faculty of Arts and Islamic Studies, Usmanu Danfodiyo University, Sokoto; Member and Secretary of the Political Bureau; Sokoto State Commissioner for Education; and currently Director of Higher Education, Federal Ministry of Education, Lagos. Dr. Augi has published articles in a number of reputable Journals and has together with Y.B. Usman published the *Cities of the Savanna*.

*S.U. Lawal*, B.A. (A.B.U.), M.A. (London), PhD. (UDUS) has been a lecturer in History and is currently the acting Head of History Department, Usmanu Danfodiyo University Sokoto. Dr. Lawal has articles published in a number of Journals.

*B. Swai*, B.A. (Dar es-Salam), D.Phil (Sussex) has lectured in History at various times in Dar es-Salam and A.B.U. before moving to the Usmanu Danfodiyo University Sokoto in 1983 where he was at various times Acting Head of the Dept. of History and Acting Dean of the Faculty of Arts and Islamic Studies. Dr. Swai has published widely on African Historiography, Tanzanian and Indian History. He has over 50 published articles in reputable Journals. Together with Prof. Temu, he came out in 1981 with the most decisive critique and vent for the progression of African Historiography in *Africa and Africanist History: A critique*. His other book is *Recovery of Local initiative in African History: A critique* published in Dar es-Salam in 1979.

*I.L. Bashir*, B.A. (B.U.K.), M.A. (Birmingham), PhD. (Boston) was a lecturer in History (1976-85) and Acting Head of the Department of History (1982-85) of the Usmanu Danfodiyo University Sokoto. In 1985 he moved to the University of Jos where he has been lecturing History and currently doubles as the University's Acting Director of the Centre for Development Studies. Dr. Bashir is a prolific writer and has got a number of published articles to his credit.

*Ahmed Bako*, B.A. (B.U.K.), M.A. (UCSC) has been a lecturer in History at the Usmanu Danfodiyo University Sokoto since 1981 and is now a Doctoral Candidate in History at the Bayero University Kano.

*Y. I. Bitiyong*, B.A. (A.B.U.), M.A. (Birmingham) was until recently a Research Fellow in Archaeology at the Centre for Nigerian Cultural Studies, A.B.U. Zaria before moving in 1989 to the National Commission for Museum and Monuments where he works at its Jos Museum. Mr. Bitiyong has participated in various archaeological excavations and analysis and has published a number of articles.

*A.H. Amfani*, B.A. (A.B.U.), M.A. (London) has been lecturing Linguistics in the Department of Nigerian Languages of the Usmanu Danfodiyo University Sokoto Since 1981. He is currently a Doctoral Student in the University of Ibadan.

*B.B. Muhammad*, B.Sc. (B.U.K.), M.Sc (Jos) was until this year a lecturer in sociology at the Usmanu Danfodiyo University Sokoto from where he has moved to the Centre from Social and Economic Research, A.B.U. Zaria.

# Table Of Contents

|  | Page |
|---|---|
| Dedication | v |
| Foreword | vii |
| Preface | ix |
| Notes on Contributors | xi |
| Introduction | xiv |

**Chapter One**    1

Towards An Explanation Of The Underdevelopment Of Zuru History. — B. Swai    1

**Chapter Two**    22

A Survey In The Zuru Emirate Region, Sokoto State. — Y. I. Bitiyong    22

**Chapter Three**    47

A Glottochronology Of Four Benue-Congo Languages In Zuru Land. — A. H. Amfani    47

**Chapter Four**    56

The Evolution And Development Of The Economies Of Kasar Zuru Before C.1900 A.D. — S. U. Lawal    56

**Chapter Five**    82

A Survey Of Social And Political History Of Zuru Emirate Before 1900 A.D. — A. R. Augi    82

**Chapter Six**    111

Transition And Changes In Religions And Belief Systems In Zuru Emirate. — Ahmed Bako    111

**Chapter Seven**    132

Some Aspects Of Traditional Marriage Systems In Wasagu And Fakai Districts Of Zuru Emirate. — B. B. Muhammad    132

**Chapter Eight**    147

Socio-Economic Transformation in Colonial Zuru Land 1901-50: A Preliminary Investigation. — I.L. Bashir    147

Select Bibliography    173

# Introduction

It is a truism that the society of Zuru people is one that has had very little compliment of researchers. Thus the whole exercise in this project was to start the process of not filling gaps (as there was virtually little on the ground), but to chart a course that will bring in its trail, further researches on the various aspects of the life and society of the Zuru people in a multi-disciplinary manner.

Our first task, we felt, was to come to terms with the reasons for the paucity of scholarly works on the Zuru Emirate area. That engaged the attention of Dr. B. Swai, who explicated this within the context of the national/nationality question and the problems of Liberal/empirilist historiography that has held away over our scholarship. That minority societies in Nigeria have been caught, like their scholarship, in the throes of the nationality problem in a neo-colony. That just like it can be established of the marginalisation of such peoples in the schemes of the nation, so have their histories become appendaged to that of the 'big three'.

Obviously then, the issue is a political one, hoisted on us by the nature and type of the bourgeoisie democracy dominant in the country. As politicians fall back on their tribal/ethnic cleavages to acquire power, the majority/minority divide also carries with it the categorisation of powerful/powerlessness groups. No wonder then, Swai feels that the situation can only change if we alter drastically the present categorisation of power and leadership in the Nigerian Society. That majority/minority equation has got to be moved from the present tribal/ethnic/regional/state form to one based on socio- economic approximations. With greater class distinction and consciousness, you will have brought to the fore not only a new level of predicating society and its politics, but a new conception and methodology in scholarship.

When we started we had a grand desire of the project being complemented by a number of archaeological excavation of various sites in the Zuru Emirate. This ambition had to be scaled down on the realisation of the dearth of both material and technical imperatives of archaeological works. Mr. Bitiyong then had to do an archaeological mapping of the area and bring out the various features of the material culture of the people and the sites for future excavations. His work has thus opened up the possible areas that could benefit form archaeological works and we hope institutions and the National Commission for Museums and Monuments will follow these up.

But even from his preliminary work he has established a pattern out of the tapestry of the development of the cultures and institutions of the people of the area. It is upon these that the chapters by Lawal, Augi and Bako were anchored. In chapter four, Lawal has followed the trail in the analysis of the economic development of the Zuru people before colonial rule. It was established there how the production of use values was transcended by the production of surplus value and the symbiosis of this with the emergence of cultural and political institutions.

We feel that if our efforts have established beyond doubt, it is the lie that Zuru land was a no-man's land before this century. Augi weaved the various migrations in and out of this area to establish the development of political institution in the various polities of myriad sizes that dotted the Zuru landscape since the 16th century.

Much more, Ahmed Bako situated the various cultural aspects of the Zuru people within the context of the economy and society. It was shown in both Chapter four, six and seven that the people were not ones consigned to 'pristine orgies of drinking' as portrayed in the colonial literature. The rich culture and tradition of the people must be seen from their own point of view, developing from their interaction with themselves and their environment over-time, giving them their identity and a meaning to their lives.

And the dynamism and congruence in the cultures and institutions of the people becomes more apparent from this non-ethnocentric perception. This element of bringing out the areas of continuity and change is infused in all the chapters. In the case of marital institutions, Mallam Muhammad in the last but one chapter brings these out more clearly and also establishes further, like the other chapters, the relative semblance in the cultures of the people of the area.

Certainly, cultural fluidity is a general trait amongst people the world over, but in this case it becomes better appreciated from the import of the chapter on Zuru languages by Amfani. We now know that the languages of the C'lela, Dukkanci, Fakkanci, Banganci had very close affinity with congent genetic relationship. That split between these languages took place from as recent as the 3rd and 5th century A.D.

The affinity of cultures of the Zuru people as was shown by Ahmed Bako in the sixth chapter became enhanced with the taking of roots and flowering of the universal religions of Islam from about the

15th century A.D and Christainity from the colonial times. Of course, earlier belief systems were not wiped out completely but had to come to terms with the intuition of new ones, and this makes the area an interesting one with a multiplicity of religious systems competing and thriving with one another.

Indeed, colonialism brought more than Christianity. It imposed new imperatives on society altogether. These have been treated by Bashir in chapter eight by bringing in lucid outline all the instances of the colonial political economy in Zuruland. In fact one could argue as Bashir did, that the present face of Zuru society has its roots from the colonial period. That the aggregation of the various peoples and cultures into a political unit, the various divisive policies of divide and rule, and the problem of the disarticulation of the economy and society in Zuru land were imposed by the expediency of colonialism and were further cemented and given new colouring and posture by the politics of neo-colonialism.

Chapter One

# Towards An Explanation Of The Underdeveloped State Of Zuru History.

*by*

### Dr. B. Swai

For the most past, Nigerian history continues to be written with a bias. Contemporary historical scholarship tends to see history from the perspective of Emirs, Sultans, Obas, leading politicians, colonial governors, military leaders - that is from the point of view of the hegemonic class. By studying history from this perspective, we implicitly posit the relative irrelevance of the masses whose energy daily creates and recreates civilization. Needless to say, historical scholarship will yield very little, if any, understanding of society in so far as it confines its interest to a small part of society and forgets the rest.[1]

## Statement Of Intent

While the writing of Nigerian history appears to have experienced 'a slightly earlier development' relative to the historiography of the rest of Sub-Saharan Africa, it is now becoming the more disturbing because it still remains 'remarkably self-satisfied within the Africanist paradigm'. Much as it was 'clearly the most developed historiography in the early 1960s, today it must be noted as the most backward.'[2] Nigerian historiography remains highly under- theorized, taking notions aimed to guide the endeavour to apprehend historical reality autonomously rather than as objects of investigation to be problematized and understood historically and concretely. Not even the notions of 'state' and 'statelessness' which have been deployed in the undertaking to study the history of various Nigerian nationalities, have been contextualised with the view to understanding why emphasis has been placed upon either of these concepts, and particularly that of state.

---

[1] C. Ake, "History is the future of social science", Mimeo, Univ. of Port. Harcourt, 1982.

[2] B. Freund, *The Making of Modern African History*, Bloomington 1984, P.9. See also his *Capital and Labour in the Nigerian Tin Mines*, London 1982; For a clearer statement on this issue see S.U. Lawal, "Imperial Policy, Capital Accumulation and Gold Mining in Colonial North-Western Nigeria, 1951 - 55", Unpublished PhD. Thesis, Usmanu Danfodiyo, University Sokoto, 1989.

Rather, with the decolonization of Nigerian history, particularly in the Northern region, there has been a wanton scramble, by historians, to stake claims on state formations and their ideological apparatuses with the aim to recover their histories without at the same time offering a clear explanation of why this enterprise has been given such priority at the expense of other aspects of the past of the country.

Historical research has been 'overwhelmingly oriented to the study of administration, pre-colonial and colonial' as well as the class antecedents of the emerging state bourgeoisie.[3] Nigeria's written history has shown 'an extreme bias towards the point of view of the administrator, whether pre-colonial oba and emir, colonial governor and D.O. or post-colonial military officer and bureaucrat.[4] Thus, then it has been argued: 'Nigerian historical scholarship clearly saw, to its credit, the ways in which the interests and ideology of the colonizer limited historical knowledge and struggled against it, but it did not appear to have seen how in the wake of the nationalist revolution to which it contributed in no small measure, the interests of the indigenous bourgeoisie are limiting the chances of further scientific progress'. In this way then, Nigerian historical scholarship has attempted to grasp the national question but 'missed the all-important class question.'[5]

Yet even at the level of resolving the national question, Nigerian historical scholarship has not fared well either. Indeed, one of the most prominent exponents of the efficacy of 'history elaboration and advocacy in the endeavour to resolve this issue, Professor J.F. Ade Ajayi, who is also the most renowned Nigerian professional historian, has at the end of it all been forced to admit about his own profession that of all fields of African studies, African history is the most useless.[6] For side by side with attempts to resolve the national question, the nationality question which has been compounded by the compromise forged between imperialist forces, nationalist predilections and primordial interests in the course of the struggle for the realization of independence in Nigeria. In this regard, it has at last been discovered that the country is not a melting-pot of nationalities which can be fused into a monolithic nation. Regional interests have continued to be a threat to the centre. The boundaries of the country are

---

[3] Freund, *The Making of Modern African History*, ibid.

[4] Ake, *Loc. cit.*

[5] *ibid.*

[6] 'Canada offers food for thought', *West Africa*, London, 26 May 1980.

also continually threatened by such interests. Nigerian realities continue to defy all that people know about statist developmentalism.[7]

The nationality question has evoked the need to write histories of the various regions to buttress the claims being put forward by the respective intellectual worker aristocraties. But, as with the question of creating more states, this has not necessarily entailed an extension of the democratic rights of the peoples of Nigeria in their quest for the 'simultaneous transformation of existing circumstances and selves' and thus be better able to control the movement of their social processes as well as to satisfy their radical as opposed to ordinary needs for self-determination and social self-determination and social self-emancipation.[8]

In the quest to create new states which are supposedly aimed to give power to the masses at the grass-root level, dominated nationalities have always emerged the loser. Indeed, the aim to create more states has been considered a ploy by dominant nationalities to ensure that their elites are always in control of the affairs of the respective regions. This is the more so because the creation of additional states has not brought about the political splintering of these majority groups as can be seen from the fact that, during the Second Republic, 'the two Igbo states were captured by the same political party.' Likewise with the former Western Region and to a large degree, the Northern Region.[9] As for dominated nationalities in these regions, since their elites are not all that firmly involved in the affairs of distributing the so-called scarce resources, theirs, has been a situation of suffering underdevelopment and even involution, something which has turned their areas into labour reservoirs to supply unskilled and migrant labour to the police, the army, economic enterprises in growth areas under the control of dominant nationalities, and so forth.[10]

If this has been the case with the control of power in Nigeria, a similar observation can be made with regard to the elaboration and advocacy of history in the country. In many cases, only the history of state formations has been written, and to a large degree-particularly in Northern Nigeria, this has necessitated writing the history of the dominant nationalities since these are regarded as the chief agents of

---

[7] M.M. Tukur, 'State-creation, the Economy and the Distribution of Constitutional power in Nigeria', Zaria 1983. See also my 'Intellectualizing upon the national/nationality question: some African pitfalls and Indian examples', Zaria 1987.

[8] E. Wamba, 'History of Neo-colonialism or Neo-colonialist History? Self-determination and History in Africa', Trenton, N.J., 1984, p.2.

[9] Tukur, *op. cit*,p.5

[10] *ibid*, p.2

this kind of history.[11] As for the dominated nationalities, many of which constituted segmentary social formations, however, the writing of their histories still remains underdeveloped. Their past is treated as an appendage of that of the dominant nationalities[12] or still remains scattered in the form of unsystematic oral historical wisdoms and ideas, among the people and has as yet to be recovered, systematized, concentrated and elaborated with the view to extending and deepening the democratic rights of such nationalities within the large body politic of Nigeria.

The problem with Nigerian history is, therefore, not just that it has attempted to grasp 'the national question and missed the all-important class question', an important observation in its own right though it may be, but that it has compounded the national question by pushing to the fore the nationality question in a rather unprogressive manner, and upheld the nationality question of the dominant ethnic groups to the detriment of that of the dominated ones. Thus then, roughly, a generation after Nigeria attained independence, the scattered and unsystematic historical wisdom of some dominated nationalities has yet to be written notwithstanding all the condemnation that was poured on colonial officials and the colonial era for having denied Africans their history so as to be the better able to control them mentally and in that way make it easier for the working peoples of the continent to be oppressed and exploited in the interests of metropolitan and local capital.

It is no wonder then that a young Lélna historian Mallam Ismail Muhammad Hamis, commenting on the state of history- doing and advocacy in Zuruland has observed that the field is, for all practical purposes, still a wasteland. He, therefore, argues that the history of this area has until now been left in the hands of administrators, missionaries and anthropologists or, in other words, amateur historians. Says Mallam Hamis in an attempt to elaborate this assertion: 'P.G. Harris in his work entitled *The Sokoto Provincial Gazetteer* ... claimed to have written the history of the Zuru area, but he only succeeded in discussing the customs, culture, religion and colonial administration of the area'. Nothing about the political, economic and social history of *Aléla* mentioned in Harris' gazetteer. Likewise with a study by Boyd and Hamilton entitled *Notes on the*

---

[11] For the latest on this score see A.M. Kani, *The Intellectual Origin of Sokoto Jihad*, Ibadan 1985. But for a balanced and an admirable piece of this terrain see A.R. Augi, 'Beyond the shadow of the substance: the legacy of Gobir in the Sokoto Caliphate', Sokoto 1985 and also in Odu: *Journal of West African Studies*, Forthcoming.

[12] A. Mahadi.

*Tribes of Northern Nigeria*; it is more of a geographical treatise than a work of history.[13]

In a similar vein, Mallam Hamis argues that recent studies of Northern Nigeria which have attempted to incorporate aspects of Zuru life into their analysis seem to be more informed by prejudice and ignorance than concrete historical and contemporary realities of the area. In point of fact, many of the scholarly projects which have been undertaken with regard to the state of affairs in the Zuru Local Emirate Area, contends Mallam Hamis, have mainly concentrated upon the coming of European education and the implantation of Christianity in the area. While executing his own project on women's role in agricultural production among the Dakarkari, therefore, he found the whole enterprise extremely frustrating for want of even the very general benchmarks in the form of secondary sources upon which to base his own study. Thus he laments:

> On the whole, I could hardly find any document on women's role in agriculture in the area. Not only that, I could not even obtain proper information on the people's agricultural activities in the area from the Agriculture Department of the Local Government Secretariat. As a result of this, I had mostly to base my research on oral information.[14]

Doing historical research in Zuruland, as indeed is the case with many other dominated nationalities in Nigeria, is a daunting pursuit. A good deal of effort has to be spent on gathering the scattered and unsystematic historical wisdom of the people with all the faults that this undertaking involves. But why is it that about a generation after Nigeria attained independence, the history of many dominated nationalities are yet to be written? Why is it that with all Departments of History which have been established in Nigerian Universities, nay with all trained historians of which Nigeria boasts, the initiative to write the history of Zuruland had to wait the efforts of an organisation of concerned citizens in the name of the Zuru Emirate Development Society (ZEDS) to provide the funds for such an undertaking as well as the required stimulus to make this social project a reality?

Questions of this kind cannot be answered merely in terms of scarcity of funds, manpower or documents. On the contrary, the material basis upon which the elaboration and advocacy of Nigerian, and in particular Northern Nigerian history has thus far been done, the power relations which have determined what aspects of the past are to be revealed and which ones are to be concealed, to a large degree

---

[13] I.M. Hamis, 'Women's Role in Agricultural production: A Case Study of Dakarkari People in Zuru Area 1900-1960, B.A., Sokoto, 1986, pp. 5-6.
[14] *ibid.*, p.7

account for the underdeveloped and even undeveloped state of the history of dominated nationalities like the Zuru.

It is the contention of this work that much of the history which has been produced about Northern Nigerian remains responsive to the parameters put forward in colonial historiography, and that such responsiveness is nothing more than a silicon chip of the old block. In this way, not only has the materiality of colonial historiography been exposed but also that many of the inarticulate premises embedded in the historiography under siege have been reproduced in the Africanist alternative which has been brought to the fore. In view of this, therefore, the history of dominated nationalities, for reasons that we shall have occasion to see subsequently, has shamelessly been neglected. Thus, then, colonial chauvinism has been replaced with other forms of misinformed arrogance to the detriment of the democratic rights and social self-determination of dominated nationalities.

## Settling Scores With Colonial Mystagogy The Wrong Way

The Africanist paradigm dominant in the elaboration and advocacy of Nigerian history emerged with the rise of African nationalism which, among other things, sought to establish its legitimacy in the 'African soil' and its antiquity. In this regard, such debates as whether colonialism comprised an important stage in the development of African history or a mere interlude, indeed a period which diverted the development process of the continent from a legitimate trajectory, loomed large among amateur historians and even more so, professional ones. Colonial historiography emphasized the former perspective. The nationalist arm of Africanist historiography, in particular, emphasized the air that postcolonial African development was in reality starting from where 'pre-colonial national-builders and modernizers' like Shaka the Zulu and Jaja of Opobo had been forced by circumstances to put a stop.[15]

This, we have been reminded lately, constituted the 'revolutionary movement in the teaching and writing of African history from the African perspective, that is with Africans at the centre of their own history.'[16] The sources considered necessary for the elaboration and advocacy of a history that was designed to show the 'wonder that was Africa' were debated vigorously. Thus oral traditions, travellers'

---

[15] See J.F.A. Ajayi in T.O. Ranger, ed., *Emerging Themes of African History* Nairobi 1969.
[16] R. Adeleye, 'Tribute by the Head of Department of History, University of Ibadan'; in M.A. Mohammed, ed., *A Giant of a Man: Tributes to Professor Abdulahi Smith, 1920-1984*, Kaduna 1986, pp. 30-31.

accounts and particularly for Northern Nigeria, Arabic manuscripts were accorded their rightful place in the writing of Africanist history.[17] Institutions charged with the duty to collect, collate and transcribe Arabic manuscripts were set up in Nigeria; initially at Ibadan and subsequently in Ahmadu Bello University, Zaria. Such efforts were discussed recently on the occasion of a series of lectures which were given in honour of the late Professor Abdullahi Smith, founder of the Department of History, Ahmadu Bello University, Zaria, the Northern History Research Scheme, and the Arewa House in Kaduna.[18]

Professor Smith was for most of his adult life a strong advocate of writing Northern Nigerian history from an African perspective. Among those who have tried their hand in this territory, opinion is still strongly in his favour and for this reason it has been alleged, he remains a giant. Small wonder then it has been observed that 'no doubt .... in his learned publications and inspiring lectures' Professor Smith 'gives much time and attention to source material in the diverse regions relevant to the study of our history and covering such important areas as Borno-Kanem, among others'. Even so, it is in the study of the Sokoto Caliphate that he devoted much of his energy. Here, it has been alleged, he 'enriched the general level of appreciation of the social and cultural perspective of the period', and clearly demonstrated the 'enviable standard of development attained prior to the dismantling of the heritage by the colonial experience and administrative system it established, and which has remained with us today virtually unchanged in all its essential elements.'[19]

Professor Smith, it is said, is a scholar who could have written more than he did but for his being a perfectionist.[20] What he could not accomplish in the form of publications, however, has been fulfilled by the many theses he supervised, some of which have been published in one form or another. Many of the articles he wrote on the history of Northern Nigeria are on one form of pre-colonial administration or another.[21] So, too, are the theses which he helped to supervise.[22]

---

[17] *ibid.*, p. 32.
[18] L. Ciroma, 'Tribute by the Chairman of the Memorial Meeting', in Mohammed, *Op.cit*, pp. 12-13.
[19] *ibid*, p. 11.
[20] T. Falola, 'Presenting the Evidence: a review of *A Little New Light: Selected Writings of Abdullahi Smith*', Vol.1, Kaduna 1987, in *West Africa*, London, 7 September 1987, pp. 1743-44.
[21] 'A select list of papers and publications of the late Professor Abdullahi Smith', in Mohammed, *op.cit*, pp.84-85.
[22] 'List of thesis supervised by professor Abdullahi Smith', in Mohammed, *Ibid.*, pp.81-83.

In this constellation of theses and articles, little is mentioned about societies which happened to be small in scale, other than as appendages of the larger ones, or as entities which would eventually be absorbed into larger political clusters.[23] Nor are there any attempts in these works to try and come to grips with the nagging question why political formations which were extensive in scale obtained in some regions and not others. At most, the ideological apparatuses which were eventually to act as binding bonds of the larger clusters came to be used as an explanatory factor in line with the binary couplet-civilized/uncivilized, not knowing that 'primitive cultures are neither ridiculous nor undignified till debased by contact with vicious by-products of the feudal or bourgeois mode', and that much as cultures of acephalous societies in Northern Nigeria may be considered 'pagan' and' superstitious', it is this very phenomenon which helped reduce the need for violence and brutality as a means of control, something which was very much pronounced in the so-called civilized cultures.[24]

The so-called 'revolutionary movement' in the elaboration and advocacy of the history of Northern Nigeria indulged in a kind of mythification, embellishment and exculpation because its practitioners wished to free this history from colonial prejudices and stereotypes and so that it is a source of pride and inspiration in the face of the challenge of nation-building.[25] Indeed, for the late Professor Smith, this was a major challenge because much as 'the most important set of political problems facing the African continent today is that relating to the formation of states', political scientists 'seldom appear to draw on the historical experience of African peoples in their attempts at elucidation' of the 'many studies of state-formation in Africa in recent times.'[26]

But in the course of challenging colonial stereotypes, new ones were produced. In place of the hamitic myth as an explanatory factor in the formation of states, for example, appeared the Fulani, Hausa and even religious myths.[27] For how else, following the idealist

---

[23] Mahadi, *loc.cit.*

[24] For the Indian context see D.D. Kosambi, *The Culture and Civilization of Ancient India in Historical Outline.* Delhi 1981, p.23.

[25] Ajayi in Ranger, *Passim.*

[26] A. Smith, 'Some considerations relating to the formation of states in Hausaland', *Journal of the Historical society of Nigeria*, V., 1970.

[27] For a comparative context see M. Mamdani, *Politics and Class Formation in Uganda*, London 1976, Chapter I. But see also Kani, *Passim.*, and well as I.U.A. Musa's 'The rise of Muslim Suddnic historiography in Bilad as-Sudan: a tentative analysis', Zaria n.d., and 'On the nature of Islamization and Islamic, reform in Bilad as-Sudan up to Sokoto Jihad', *Dirasat*, VI, 1979.

problematic, could it be explained that the Hausa or Hausa-Fulani contributed to the formation of states in Northern Nigeria while the Zuru and other 'idol Worshippers of Hausaland' did not?[28] Was it not that some tribes were more intelligent than others? In this manner, the notion of tribe replaced that for race as an explanatory factor in the making of history. Naturally, too, in conformity to the mystification which is produced by reinforcing the division between manual and mental labour, such notions were perceived autonomously rather than as objects of investigation that needed to be problematicized with the intent to establishing their historicity.[29]

In this context, the colonial stance of Northern Nigerian historiography which had posited the histories of social formations of this region as undeveloped was dubbed jaundiced and misinformed. But much as it was considered mythical and some kind of an imperialist mystagogy, little effort was given to locating its materiality. The Africanist response to colonial assertions, therefore, tended to be rather responsive and its results extremely tangential. Instead of a past of 'tribal gyrations' was posited a glorious past of empires and heroes. But as is becoming clearer, the more the African crisis bites deeper and the Africanist euphoria recedes further into the penumbra of reality, 'How does the empty stomach of a *talakawa,* caught between sky and water with eyes staring naked, suddenly become full by merely evoking the glorious past that was Africa? How does the chanting of names of past heroes ensure a balanced diet for the *almajiri* scouring the length and breadth of Hausaland not merely in search of spiritual knowledge but more so to ensure his own survival which is under the constant threat of hunger and disease?[30] To be sure, as the wisdom of the sages goes, man does not live by bread alone. But it also needs pointing out that a species of mankind which does not consume bread has yet to appear on our planet.[31]

That said, to answer all these questions constitutes an historiographical enterprise beyond the scope of this project. What will be attempted here is a far more modest task aimed to show why the Africanist paradigm, given the manner in which it approached the elaboration and advocacy of history as well as its own material base,

---

[28] "The idol worshippers of Hausland", *Today Sunday Magazine*, Kaduna, 20 July 1986, pp. I-IV.

[29] A. Sohn-Rethel, *Intellectual and Manual Labour*, London 1978 is useful for an otherwise rather demanding discourse.

[30] I have argued these points within the context of African historiography on a number of occasions. See for example, *Recovery of Local Initiative in African History: A Critique*, Dar es Salaam 1979. But see also F. Fanon, *The wretched of the Earth*, Harmondsworth 1967.

[31] Kosambi, *Op.cit.*, p. 23.

had to be caught up in the ideological career of colonial mystagogy and so give more time to the writing of histories of empire formations of dominant nationalities and little, if any thing, to those of dominated ones.[32]

## On The Nationality Of Colonial Mystagogy

A good deal of ethnocentric Eurocentricism concerning Africa has come to the light of day, and there is no need, as the saying goes, to continue flogging a dead horse by going through the whole issue again here.[33] But unlike what conventional wisdom would have us believe, this Eurocentrism was not based on ignorance or lack of information. It has been said that Europe grew up with Africa, but in a dialectical manner.[34] This dialectical relationship should not be restricted to the economic or political plane. Rather, it also applies to the ideological level.

In discussions of development, industrialization and the emergence of the nation-state, there has been some tacit understanding that such phenomena emerged in Europe autonomously. But it is just as well to point out that countries like England, France, Holland, etc., emerged as integral nation-states not by chance, but because they were colonizing nations.' In the course of emerging as integral nation-states, they exported their national problem to the colonial empires. It is in this regard then that it has been argued: 'to understand England one must understand Ireland, India and so on.'[35] By the same token, statements made by European adventurers, missionaries and administrators cannot be comprehended properly if viewed through the prism of positivist interpretation. On the contrary, they have to be understood within the contextualist method of interpretation, as Eurocentrism was not motivated by the desire to postulate an understanding of pre-capitalist societies, but rather by the logic of analysis of European capitalist formations.[36] In other words, Eurocentrism tended to extend the logic of defining a form by contrasting it to that which it is not, that 'the other', and in so doing

---

[32] H. Bernstein, "Marxism and African history: Endre Sik and his critics", *Kenya Historical Review*. 4 1974

[33] Ajayi in Ranger, *Passim*.

[34] W. Rodney, *How Europe Underdeveloped Africa*. London 1972.

[35] J. Blaut, "Are Puerto Ricans a national minority"?, *Monthly Review*, 29, 1977, p. 45.

[36] V. Meera and others, Karl Marx and the analysis of Indian Society', *Social Scientist*, 126, pp.10-11.

illuminated, in African societies, the elements by way of which capitalism could itself be defined as the 'other of its other.'[37]

The procedure was dictated by the desire to simultaneously outlaw and control Africa.[38] Small wonder then that Eurocentrism in the form of racism, for example, has been regarded as a typical trait of European/bourgeois culture,[39] and that it was 'not simply a rationale to justify conquest and domination, but for more a means of conquest, domination and rule'; 'a means to unite the conquerors and demoralize the resisters; to enslave by inducing the slave-mentality that ensures docility', and so on.[40]

Eurocentricism reduced empires and nationalities to tribes not because that is what was dictated positivistically but rather by contextualist demands. Similarly, the term tribe began to acquire a bad connotation and those enamoured of the 'Africanist paradigm' came eventually to substitute it with the word 'ethnicity' by virtue of its alleged decency.[41] Materialists, though have thought it proper to stick to the notion of tribe but only after disabusing it of its ideological content and in that way restoring its scientificity. Thus, it has been re-emphasized that the term tribe denotes the earliest and simplest level of human development in which the situation of classlessness and statelessness prevailed. Argues the Ugandan political scientist, Mahmood Mamdani: 'The tribal stage was humanity in its infancy. Population was sparse and implements crude. Without co-operation there was little chance for survival. And without equality, little possibility of co-operation. This single fact marked tribal society with the distinguishing features of communalism/ classlessness, and kinship/statelessness.'[42]

But much as it can continue to be argued that the notion of tribe has been deployed in the study of Africa rather unscientifically, it has been used, nevertheless, and this demands an explanation. Moreover, it has now become part of commonsense language when discussing politics of whatever brand in Africa. It is for this reason that I have attempted to show the materiality of this notion together with the allied mystagogy in the form of Eurocentricism. Europe want to change

---

[37] *ibid*, pp.708. See also S. Kaviraj, "On the status of Marx's writings on India, *social scientist*, 124, 1983.

[38] S.Bhattacharya, "History from Below", *Social Scientist*, 11, 1983.

[39] H. Jaffe, *A History of Africa*, London 1985, p. 86.

[40] *ibid*.

[41] D.J.M. Muffet, "Editorial Foreword", in C. Prazan, *The Dukkawa of Northern Nigeria*, Pittsburgh 1977, Pp.XV-XVII.

[42] M. Mamdani, 'The Nationality question in a Neo-colony: An Historical Perspective', *Mawazo*, 5, 1983, Pp. 36-37.

Africa into its other' so as to confirm its own existence and to be the better able to simultaneously outlaw and control Africa.[43] But this is exactly what was overlooked by the Africanist paradigm in the course of establishing the historicity of the African past. And this, it needs to be underlined, as not accidental or coincidental. Conditions obtaining in Africa in the course of establishing a situation conducive to a neo-colonial takeover of power by a would-be state bourgeoisie from imperial proconsuls seems to me a more plausible explanation.[44]

## The Great Betrayal Or Compromise And The Emergence Of Neo-Colonial History.

The attainment of African independences which, inter alia, facilitated the emergence of the Africanist paradigm in African history under close guidance of the empiricist problematic, constituted a great betrayal to the aspirations of the working peoples of Africa. But it also comprised a compromise between the curse of Africa in the form of the ruthless upstarts normally called the African middle class on the one hand, and the imperialist forces in conjunction with feudal/traditional powers on the other. This compromise was to witness the consolidation of the writing of neo-colonialist history which is itself a portrayal of the story of neo- colonialism in Africa.[45] The situation, moreover, could hardly have been otherwise for African history, as a field of study, was given professional respectability during the Cold War when the ideology of value-freeism and neutrality was re-orchestrated against studies utilizing the problematics of class oppression and exploitation and in favour of the fundamental tenets of the so-called liberal scholarship.[46]

The history of Africa was cast in a manner which posited the rise of neo-colonialism as a happy ending. The Pre- colonial past was also portrayed as a prefiguration of this outcome. And the working peoples of Africa were said to have participated fully and willingly to bring about the present predicament in which they are mired. In a similar manner, members of the state bourgeiosisie were regarded as heroes of the whole drama and more so, nation-building. In its attempt to solve the national question, though, the nationality question was pushed to the background of African affairs or championed by certain elements

---

[43] Swai, 'Intellectualizing upon the National/Nationality question', Part.I.

[44] B. Swai, "In Honour, Remembrance and Vindication of Frantz Fanon or on the apparitions, spectres and whimsies of critical criticism in African History", Sokoto 1987.

[45] *ibid.*, see also 'Fanon, contemporary Africa and relevance of the theory of historical expediency', Sokoto 1986.

[46] See among other texts R. Samuel, 'prefaces', in R. Samuel, ed.,

of the state bourgeoisie, as dictated by the circumstances hatched by the politics of compromise and opportunism. Thus then interests of the oppressed whether as dominated nationalities or classes were also jettisoned in the name of unity, nation-building or whatever it was that was at stake and possibilities of the crisis now prevailing in Africa made even more likely.[47]

The writing of history, too, had its fair share of this confusion. Victorian wisdom which played no small measure in guiding the development of imperialist historiography had viewed the achievements of mankind in terms of the triumph of individual initiative with Anglo-Saxons at the top of the ladder and the 'Negro races' at the bottom.[48] The main ambition of schools subscribing to the Africanist paradigm, it has already been suggested time and again, was to challenge this position but not, necessarily, its materiality. As with colonial historiography, this was not an oversight. Rather, it is an outcome which was socially and historically determined.

History research in Northern Nigeria was seriously undertaken with the establishment of Ahmadu Bello University in 1962. The ideology of academia would have us believe that much as this was a 'social practice', it was undertaken by selfless individuals who cared little about material gains 'much as ours is a society which worships the Naira' and thus pays little attention to academic work. In this regard then, although historians, like Professor Smith married into the Northern Hausa-Fulani oligarchy, this was a private affair, and that in the enterprise of 'history-doing', they 'simply went on doing' what they 'thought was the right thing to do' much as it might have been regarded as marginal in the scheme of things as were then constituted.[49]

But in 1966 the Federal Government felt that there was a need to write a general history of contemporary Nigeria, something which made 'the then Military Governors of the six Northern States, via the Interim Committee Services Agency - I.C.S.A., to think of better ways of making this project more meaningful to their region. In view of this, the Governors 'felt that a better perspective and understanding of Nigeria's recent history would require a much wider time-span cover than the 1966 datum line. For this reason, I.C.S.A. set up its own body, a Committee of about a dozen people, to undertake the

---

[47] Swai, "Fanon, Contemporary Africa and Relevance of the theory of Historical Expediency", *Passim.*

[48] R. Robinson and J. Gallagher, *Africa and the Victorians.* New York 1962.

[49] J.E. Inikori, 'Opening remarks by the Head of the Department of History Ahmadu Bello University', in Mohammed, *oP.cit.*, pp.5-6.

collection and collation of material to supplement the efforts in the compilation of that history.'[50]

The History of Northern Nigeria Committee was therefore, set up to execute the ideal which was put forward by the Governors of Northern Nigeria with members such as Alhaji Ali Akilu, CRF, MBE, Professor Abdullahi Smith, Yusuf Amuda Gobir, OFR., etc. Under the guidance of Professor Smith, a good deal of historical documents were collected. Most of these are now preserved at the Arewa House, Kaduna, the cornerstone of anyone who wants to undertake serious historical research of mainstream Northern Nigerian history.[51]

But there is little of value concerning the history of dominated nationalities, including the Zuru people.[52] What was collected for preservation involved some kind of selection which was tacitly sanctioned by those in power at the time, through I.C.S.A. and the History of Northern Nigeria Committee. Similarly, those so-called selfless academics who sacrificed their time doing what they did were not performing to an empty gallery. The Northern oligarchy wanted history of a particular kind to be written, and for this the state gave out money to be used in laying the foundation of such a 'social project'.

It should also not be forgotten that all this was taking place in an atmosphere in which Marxism was vehemently denounced under the direction of Professors from Northwestern University, Cambridge and so forth.[53] There was therefore little chance to question the paradigms brought to bear in the study of the history of Northern Nigeria and if anything, the position which had then been established could only be radicalized by historians who were at heart cultural nationalists and who felt that they still had scores to settle with imperialism over there across the Atlantic or over the Sahara.[54]

In this way the 'obsessive concern with state-building and nation-building', the emergence of administrative systems and commercial-complexes based on local and long distances trade, as well as moralizing about their destruction continued to be the pre-occupation of historians both explicitly or tacitly. Behind all this, laments C.C. Wrigley has been 'the belief that the whole meaning of progress is the transition from tribe to state, from segmentary to centralized political

---

[50] Ciroma, *op.cit.*, p.12.

[51] *ibid.*, P. 13.

[52] Hamis, *op.cit.*, p.7.

[53] M.A. Modibbo and A. Abba, "Roots of Academic Repression in Nigerian Universities: the Role of the Intellectual Wing of the Northern Oligarchy", Zaria, 1982.

[54] Other than the fundamental positions of idealism and positivist materialism, much of what has been happening at the Department of history, Ahmadu Bello University, Zaria in the name of 'Political economy' falls into this category.

system' but that this is 'a crude form of what Karl Popper identified as 'historicism' and which he traced to Germany.'[55] One of the main problems with historicism, Wrigley argues, is that it combines the social scientists' taxonomic procedures with the evolutionist's concept of inevitable progress, so that classificatory types, formulated for their heuristic value, are translated into developmental stages, conceived as having real existence and arranged in a hierarchy which is both chronological and quantitative'. Such evolutionary typologies, Wrigley goes on to contend, are an immense simplification of historical realities. Moreover, 'one other characteristic of historicism that must be emphasized it its ethnocentricity'. It is based on European historical experience which is generalized as applicable to the development of the entire human race.[56]

To be sure, as Wrigley rightly argues, it is proper to 'begin by enquiring what human ends were served by the process of state-formation, or by incorporation of small political systems into larger ones', rather than just praising empire- building, the more so because this is done at the risk of overlooking the violence which this process brought about.[57] But 'social projects which reflect this tendency were not carried out for their own sake. Rather, their leit motif was dictated by the material conditions then prevalent.

Glorification of the past is some kind of revivalism which went on hand in glove with the tenets of negritude, as well as the demand to respect tradition which were considered inherent in African culture. It has been argued that 'the tradition of all the dead generations weighs like a nightmare on the brains of the living' and that 'just when they seem engaged in revolutionizing themselves and things, in creating something that has never yet existed, precisely in such periods of revolutionary crisis they anxiously conjure up the spirits of the past to their service and borrow from their names, battle cries and costumes in order to present the new scene of world history in the time-honoured disguise and this borrowed language.'[58] But in Africa, and Northern Nigeria for that matter, it was not 'simply a question of using the past to seek inspiration for the present'. Far more important, 'the revivalist appeal' was aimed to provide 'a compromise with the anti-democratic forces of tradition and religious orthodoxy.[59] The class which put

---

[55] C.C. Wrigley, 'Historicism in africa', Sussex 1970.
[56] *ibid.*
[57] *ibid.*
[58] K. Marx, *The Eighteenth Brumaire of Louis Bonaperte* as quoted in the Indian School of Social Sciences, *Social Scientist Marc Centenary*, Vol.I, *Social Change in India*, Trivandrum 1984, Pp.8-9.
[59] *ibid.* p.9.

itself at the head of the nationalist movement, which collaborated with it also found itself, objectively, at logger-heads with the working people of Africa. On this score it could not use class issues to mobilize the oppressed, but rather racial, tribal and religious ones. In the same manner, it had to compromise with the guardians of these issues and so turn the national question into some kind of revivalism, something which has been confused with an attempt to bring about an African Renaissance.[60]

The African bourgeoisie did not create capitalism; it was created by the worst aspect of it; imperialism. It was not therefore the representative of the whole nation to combat anachronism and obscuritism, as the French bourgeoisie in the heat of the French Revolution said 'We are the Third Estate', but rather found itself face to face against the working peoples of Africa as it attempted to combat traditionalism.[61] Given these conditions the African middle class, as Fanon called it, could but act as a huckster, ready to strike a bargain with any social force that could guarantee its survival. Hence its struggle for the reform of colonialism, the international order and its fear of any radically different system of organization. Hence, too, the inadequacy which many of its members feel unless they are given traditional titles of one kind or another.[62]

Continuation of religiosity, communalism and all forms of tribalism were embedded in the compromise forged between members of the African state bourgeoisie, traditional forces and imperialist interests. In this, neo-colonialism continued to fatten in the name of law and order and the attempt to keep Africa free from communism.[63] Thus, then, in spite of the many successes that the messiahs and fathers of the nation might have scored in conjunction with agencies of the package of modernization like the International Monetary Fund, the so-called World Bank as well as monetarist economics, Africa is still in shambles and 'tradition of the dead generations; continues to weigh 'like a nightmare on the brain of the living.'[64]

It is no wonder that the late Sekou Toure, the theoretician of 'African Socialism' and Guinean dictator, traced his origins to Samory

---

[60] Black historians in the U.S.A. and the late Chiekh Anta Diop in Africa strived a good deal to bring about the African Renaissance through erudite refutations of Eurocentrism. See M. Abdulhakeem, 'African American historians and the decolonization of African and world history: A brief overview', Sokoto 1983.

[61] Swai, "Fanon, contemporary Africa and Relevance of the Theory of Historical Expediency", *Passim*.

[62] Kosambi, *Op.cit.* Pp. 6-12.

[63] A. 'Agh, *The Recent State of Imperialism and Non-Alignment*, Dar es Salaam 1980.

[64] The Indian School of Social Sciences, *Loc.cit*.

Toure, the nineteenth-century hero who fought to finish against French imperialist adventurism in West Africa. It is little wonder, too, that the Gold Coast arrogated the name Ghana on achieving independent statehood in 1957. Negative images of reality, indeed, these endeavours are, but this is neither an accident nor a coincidence. As Isaac Deutscher once argued with regard to the Russian Revolution whose leaders claimed to be successors to the revolutionary aspirations of Marx and Engels, 'the truth seems more complex and ambiguous than conflicting assertions suggest.'[65] In this context, the appearance might be completely different from reality, but it is the social materiality of the situation which demands that the refraction should be that way.

Similarly with Africa's appeal to the past and the consequent history-elaborating and advocacy, history production. The material conditions precipitated by the compromise brought about by African political independence, the betrayal of aspirations of African working peoples and the politics of the Cold War dictated what aspect of the past has to be investigated and which ones to be concealed, consciously or otherwise. After all, texts have to be judged not merely by what they say, but also 'by the "invisible presence" of what they do not state', and contrary to sequential analysis which tends to accept such texts on their own terms.[66]

History written within the Africanist paradigm has been exhibitionist. This has tended to satisfy the revolutionary psycho-dramas of the state bourgeoisie, reinforced the mirage of tradition under the custody of the so-called traditional rulers, and allayed the dread of imperialist forces fearful that wide spectrum of nationalism does not only possess the reactionary shade but also the fierce radical pole which is against colonialism and capital. In this exhibitionism there is little room for the histories of acephalous societies. Here, benign historiography which also claims to be universalist regards spontaneous history and its philosophy as non-existent or at worst primitive.[67] Thus, then Africanist historians of the nationalist tinge agree with the metropolitan scholars who claim to be more scientific and less biased, and therefore more creditable,[68] that if 'European had Kings and Queens and their Prime Ministers, so too has Africa, that if Europe had her Gipsies, Africa had stateless societies and that if

---

[65] I. Deutscher, *The Unfinished Revolution*, Oxford 1967, P.5.
[66] S. Singh and others, 'Subaltern Studies II: a review article', *Social Scientist*, 137, p.8.
[67] Wamba, *Op.cit*, p.7.
[68] J.H. Plumb, *The Death of the Past*. Harmondsworth 1970.

Europe could have written 'drum and trumpet history' to the exclusion of the 'faceless rabble' so can Africa.[69]

In this compromise turned into a conspiracy against oppressed classes and dominated nationalities, there was no room for histories like that of the Zuru. Theirs was seen as a story worth neglecting or which could easily be absorbed into the history of the 'civilized' societies. This was what was implied in the inarticulate premises of the Africanist paradigm.[70] But as the African dilemma which has caused a crisis of conceptualization in the Africanist paradigm deepens[71] and as the African state bourgeoisie attempts, in vain, to extend the national question, by other means,[72] the nationality question, together with its attendant demands, is coming to the fore and the question is now being posed whether dominated nationalities have been at the receiving end of history since man started with nature and with himself for the sake of his own livelihood and so, too, began to make history for posterity.

## Conclusion: The Crisis Of Conceptualization And The Issue Of Initiative.

It has been attempted to show in the previous section that 'historians produce not just in response to subjective and professional imperatives', but also, and more so, 'in response to demand'. It is the more necessary to emphasize this because 'society wants the historians product because it seeks an affirmation of the cherished conception of itself and a rendering of the past for transmission to the young.'[73] But history produced under the paradigm of Africanism is besotted in a deep crisis of conceptualization. The knowledge produced about Africa, it is now becoming the more obvious, is purely contemplative. It is not equipped to answer the question: 'How have the African masses of people (workers, peasants, etc) been self-transforming while transforming colonial and neo- colonial circumstances; and how in that process have they acted and live their African past?' Indeed rather than arm the working peoples of Africa with the capacity to control the initiative of making their own history by acquiring a grip of the movement of their own social processes so as to be the better able to simultaneously transform the circumstances facing them as well as

---

[69] G.S. Jones, "History: the poverty of empiricism", in R, Blackburn ed. *Ideology in Social Science*, London 1972.

[70] Mamdani, *Politics and Class Formation in Uganda*, lo. cit.

[71] *Wamba, Op.cit.* p.6.

[72] Swai, "Conceptualizing upon the national/nationality question", *Passim*.

[73] Daniel Fields as quoted by P.Dukes, *October and the World*, New York 1979.

their own selves, the Africanist paradigm has actively contributed to the process of demobilizing them; 'This has been done by directing their attention to the secondary rather than fundamental contradictions facing the African political economy.'[74]

This issue, of development for example, has been approached as some kind of a scientific-technological process in which human society is reduced to a naturalistic complexification of matter and is assumed to progress according to iron laws rather than as a result of people's struggles against nature and in society.[75] In this way, then, the tenets of social engineering take precedence over concrete analysis of concrete realities, according to Weberian ideal types of society and people, in consonance with technocratic culture, are reduced to social amnesia.[76]

It is small wonder then African socialist theoreticians have been arguing that all that Africans need is food, clothing and shelter and that the greatest enemies facing Africa are hunger, disease and ignorance. Following this kind of pedestrian logic, it has also been argued that given the right leadership and the appropriate dosage of capital, the malaise can easily be eradicated; the more so because Africa is well endowed with natural resources and so on. But what is the cause of the hunger? Where does leadership come from? Certainly not from a hole in the ground! And what is capital? Is it hoarded money? These may be obvious questions, but we over-look the obvious only to our own detriment.

In any case, in the course of reducing society to some naturalistic complexification of matter amenable to scientific-technological iron laws of development, we have also fallen victim to a conception of history based upon social forces seeking to maintain their own hegemonic domination. These are the very forces which will 'not entertain any conception of history in which the common people - workers, poor peasants, illiterates, "uncivilized" ... masses, etc., would be allowed/recognized/encouraged to take care of themselves and circumstances under which they live'. It is the more strange that this attitude should be maintained against the working peoples of Africa because 'when stages fail - as is now the case in many neo-colonies - vibrant appeals to act are forcefully addressed to those common, illiterate people, whose capacity to make history is systematically denied.'[77]

---

[74] *Wamba, Op.cit.* p.7.
[75] *ibid.*
[76] This issue has been discussed extensively by H.A. Giroux in *Ideology, Culture and the Process of Schooling*, London, 1981.
[77] *Wamba, Op.cit*, p.7.

Nationalism was aimed to extend the democratic rights of the hitherto colonized peoples of the imperialized world so that they could translate their political emancipation into social self-determination and in that way lay the foundations for the struggle for economic freedom necessary for realizing a self-reliant socio-economic development.[78] Rather than bring this capacity that would make Africans the better able to fulfill their radical needs, though, the process of national liberation has been defeated by neo-colonialism which is counter-attacking whatever achievements have been gleaned by the imperialized world to such an extent that some countries have even lost their political/formal independence and consider neo-colonialism as a legitimate package of the ideological package of authenticity.[79] The petty bourgeois interregnum brought about by the compromise of flag independence stands out as the main guarantor of this state of affairs, turned it into a responsive affair to colonial mystagogy and imperial history. However, those who were left out are now demanding their place in the annals of history. For outsiders with a mere nodding acquaintance of the historiography of Northern Nigeria and who subscribe to the idea of statist developmentalism,[80] such an idea may appear fissiparous. But in the age of imperialism, of global monopoly capitalism where there are more of dominated nationalities rather than sheer national minorities,[81] and where nationalism constitutes a simple category found in modes of production other than capitalism, such an indulgence can constitute a liberatory undertaking aimed to bring in its train the fulfillment of 'the struggles of the African masses of people for self-determination/social self-emancipation, i.e., socialist construction/revolution.'[82]

This is the more necessary because the national/nationality question and the kind of 'history-doing/elaborating' which it engenders is part of the broader question of democracy, as opposed to domination. 'The national/nationality question is a species of democracy in a double sense;' on the one hand, the struggle with a oppressor nation [Nationality] to remove national oppression ... [is] a democratic one. On the other, it ... [is] a condition of full democracy in the oppressed nation [nationality] that the oppression be broken.'[83]

---

[78] *ibid.*, p.4.
[79] *ibid.*
[80] Swai, "Conceptualizing upon the National/Nationality Question", *Op.cit.*, Part I.
[81] Blaut, *Op.cit.* pp. 47-54.
[82] *Wamba, Op.cit*, p. 2.
[83] P. Gibbon, "Imperialism and the National Question: some errors and some thesis", *Utafiti*, IV, 1979, p. 236.

But this will only be so if the writing history of Zuruland does, not turn out to be 'a silicon chip of the old block,[84] and that the struggle of which historical writing is a constituent part of establishing its legitimacy concentrates on attacking' the dominant national groups on egalitarian grounds', counterposing the 'international culture of democracy' 'to the reactionary cultures of dominant groups', and creating the 'condition for peaceful relations between national groups.'[85] Social emancipation is inconceivable without democracy. Indeed, democracy creates the best conditions for realizing social emancipation[86] the struggles of dominated nationalities whether at the ideological plane, or the economic plane, or the economic and political one should help to realize the attainment of such aspirations.

---

[84] Bathacharye, *Passim.*
[85] Gibbon, *loc.cit.*
[86] V.I. Lenin, 'The Rights of Nations to Self-determination', in V. I. Lenin, *Collected Works*, Vol.20, Moscow 1974, P. 405.

## Chapter Two

## A Survey In The Zuru Emirate Region, Sokoto State.

*by*

### Y.I. Bitiyong

When the archaeology aspect of the Zuru Emirate History project was conceived of in 1985, the idea was to pay a short visit to the Zuru Local Government Area for brief observation, especially of few hills, to see the nature of settlement and of any walling system that might be located on the hills. This approach was soon abandoned as it became clear that in as complex a cultural area as one we were dealing with, such an approach would be unfair especially as it would ignore ethnographic data needed to expose the archaeological potentials of the region. It was obvious that the data needed included traditions relating to formation and development of various cultural groups, the site selection, establishment, development of settlements and of polities, the types and dynamics of industries such as pottery, and iron working. Burial practices and religious beliefs also needed to be investigated especially in relation to the material culture these have helped to build up.

### Earlier Works

Several researches have been conducted in our region and its immediate surroundings. These include those of P.G. Harris in the early years of this century, R. Soper in the 1960s, M.Adamu, A. Obayemi, S. Sakaba and J.E.G. Sutton in the 1970s. A number of Bachelors degree projects mainly in the History Department of the University of Sokoto in the 1980s are among the latest in this endeavour. Harris[1] pays specific attention to our region, making some generalizations as well as giving some details on ethnic composition and customs, history of relations between various people of the region and between them and their neighbours. Mahdi Adamu[2] shows similar concern, and needs be specifically commented upon.

---

[1] P.G. Harris, *Sokoto Provincial Gazetteer*, Mimeo, 1939

[2] Mahdi Adamu, "The Hausa Factors in West African History", *Unpublished PhD, Thesis*, University of Birmingham, 1974.

His concern, relates to the extent to which the Hausa have influenced or even have been part of the historical experience of the region. Both of Harris and Mahdi come to definite conclusion that the present composition of cultural groups in the area is largely a result of influx of population from Hausaland which may be traced to the 16th century A.D. and after. Although Adamu warns on some danger in this proposition, he does not appear to oblige, claiming that he has no contradictory data.[3]

This position has given rise to a number of observations bordering on objection, especially in the recent degree dissertation works on the area, which have attempted detailed recording of traditions of specific groups and settlements. These observations are to the effect that the story could not simply have been one of recent immigration of people from Hausaland to populate and give rise to the recognised autochthonous ethnic and linguistic compositions of the Zuru region. The work of J.A. Ballard (1971) which might have been available to Adamu, is relied upon as part of the substance of argument by some of the authors. The 16th century time limit to Mahdi and others before him is understandable in view of what P.G. Harris says:

> It is with these people and the rise of the Kebbi Empire under Muhammadu Kanta that the history of Sokoto as we now know it must begin for there is little record or verbal traditions of events prior to this period.[4]

The Archaeological investigations carried out in the neighbourhood of Zuru region include the work reported by R. Soper[5] on Northern Nigeria stone sites; the works of the Universities of Colorado and Ibadan teams on the salvage archaeology of the Kainji Lake area (now flooded) in the 1960s;[6] the activities of A. Obayemi[7] and J.E.C. Sutton[8] in the Gulbin Kebbi during the early and mid 1970s, which have been followed by Nzewunwa who continues work

---

[3] *ibid*, P.62-4.

[4] P.G. Harris, *Op.cit* p.22

[5] R. Soper, "The Stone Age in Northern Nigeria", *Journal of the Historical Society of Nigeria*, III, 2, 1965.

[6] D.D Hartle, "Preliminary Report of the University of Ibadan's Kainji Rescue Archaeology Project 1968", *West African Archaeological Newsletter*, 12, 1970, P.7-19

[7] A.Obayemi, "Aspects of Field Archaeology in Hausaland", *Zaria Archaeology papers*, vol.I, 1976, P1-14; and "A note on Test excavations at Maleh and Toro, Sokoto Province", *Zaria Archaeology papers*, vol.2, 1976, P.1-4

[8] J.E.G.Sutton, "Kebbi valley preliminary survey, 1975", *Zaria Archaeology papers* Vol.5, 1976, P.1-17.

in the Yawuri are of the middle Niger.[9] Thus, the Zuru region has received no specific attention in archaeological investigation.

## Study Method

At the start of this survey in August 1985, therefore it was decided that the region be approached as unstudied. Consequently, there was need for a few weeks of oral data collection relating to the community composition, a preliminary knowledge of the history of these communities and of specific settlements. Traditions of origin, basket weaving, cloth weaving and dyeing, potting, use of pots, trade in pots, burials and language distribution were sought. The work proceeded through informal oral interview of individuals and of groups as the opportunity arose. Hausa dominated as the language of communication. Tape recording was done of several of those interviews. When sites were mentioned, informants were usually asked if they could locate such sites and, where possible, the researcher was led to see them. Generally, elders were rather reluctant to give information on what was considered traditional religion and even more so to lead on to sites related to the religion.

This combined oral collection and field visits approach paid off a lot as compared to random search in terms of site identification and the collection of information on function of sites, especially pertaining to who constructed and or used them. This was aided by the fact that in this almost completely rural agrarian society the generality of the population knows the field well, being mainly both farmers and hunters who go into the bush a lot.

## Area

Zuru Local Government Area is the same territory as the Zuru Emirate, which is divided into five administrative districts; Dabai, Donko, Fakai, Sakaba and Wasagu in alphabetic order, each headed by a District Head who is also member of the Zuru Emirate Council. The administrative centre is Zuru town in Dabai district, where the emirate headquarters also is located.

This area is what we may also refer to as the Zuru region. It is located in the south-central portion of Sokoto State, Nigeria, occupying an area of about 9,000 sq km. It is bordered by Gummi Local Government Area in the North. This border is shared with Anka Local Government Area. It is an arbitrary line on land. To the South is Niger State. This borderline extends also arbitrarily on land to the

---

[9] N. Nzewunwa, "Recent Archaeological works in the middle Niger valley", *Paper presented at the 9th Pan African Congress of Prehistory and related Studies*, Jos, 1983 P. 1-3.

Southwest to a point where it ends a few kilometres west of a large tributary of the Dan Zaki River. Here, a Northwestward protrusion of Yauri Local Government Area, also of Sokoto State, shows up for a few kilometres in the West and gives way to another Local Government Area, Bagudo, also of Sokoto State, for a few kilometres only. This Western border is then completed in the Northwest by a short Southwestern curve of the (Northern) border with Gummi Local Government Area. This region falls within the area of the 4° E - 6° E. longitudes and the 11° N-12° N latitudes, in what is generally referred to as the Nigerian Middle Belt, that is, the area of Nigeria that extends immediately South of Hausaland Southward to the Niger-Benue valley.[10]

## Environment

The physical appearance of the region is one of generally undulating topography interrupted mainly by a folded ridge which enters the region from the North in a Southward run through old Donko. It passes on to Dabai and Senchi in the central area, from where it extends further South until it leaves Zuru Local Government Area and ends at Rijau in Magama Local Government Area of Niger State. Here, the end is marked by a number of inselbergs. Numerous inselbergs of various sizes are scattered well over the region. They show up as isolated steep sided hills which occur regularly in some sections. Such areas of relatively more frequent occurrence include Bena, Fakai, Kandu and Wasagu. The area of Karishen, Makuku and Sakaba in the South East and of Maikende, Sifawa and Tungan Suya in the Northwest appear to have an even higher density. Accompanying, and partly a result of, this topogrpahy is a drainage system composed of numerous rivers, streams, their tributaries, and springs. The Donko - Rijau ridge serves as a major water divide between West and East flowing channels, all of which, however, end up in the Niger, mostly through the three major channels of the Dan Zaki, Ka and Malendo rivers.

Extensive flood plains exist along the courses of streams and rivers, which are generally of fertile alluvial material. The steep sides of the hills and the Donko-Rijau ridge are of thin even though rich soils.

Rainfall up to a few years ago had attained a high annual average falling mainly in April - September. A dry season lasting November - March is marked by absence of rain and harmattan winds. And

---

[10] Mahdi Adamu, *Op.cit*. P.42.

although temperatures are high throughout the year, December/January temperatures might usually fall to a relatively very low point at night.

The vegetation is of derived guinea savanna type, which is typical of the Nigerian Middle Belt. Human influence is easily observed in the selective preservation of economically viable species which now have become most familiar. Thus, *Parkia clappertonia Butyrosperum parkii* (Shea) (Kadai in Hausa) are not only preserved but may even be planted on farmlands that are either in active use or fallowed. The character of stream and river banks tends to be of richer tree cover in terms of both number and variety especially where disturbance is little. Here other trees like *Canarium Scheinfurthii* (African Elemi tree called Atilli in Hausa), *Eriodendron Orientale* (white silk cotton tree called Rimi in Hausa), *Khaya senegalensis* (a Mahogany called Madaci in Hausa), *Pardaniella oliveri* (Maje in Hausa) may be found. this suggests generally heavier tree coverage prior to intensive clearance by man.

## Population

The present human population of this region is multinational. For purposes of study it can be grouped into two broad categories. First, those that claim long term settlement and or autochthony, the second category is of the much more recent settlers who infact regard themselves and are also regarded by the others as recent immigrants or even (temporary) strangers. In the first category are the Achifawa, Bangawa, Dukawa, Fakawa, Kambari, Katsinawa and Lélna (Dakarkari). It is characteristic to find that some of these lay some claim to origin from Hausa. This is most prominent among the Katsinawa who infact see themselves as immigrants from old state of Katsina which had made political inroads into Zuru region, especially from the 16th A.D. onward, and enable them to settle and to become an integral part of the area's indigenous population. This community is concentrated most in the area of Bena and Wasagu of Wasagu District in the West, which borders kwiambana, a former tributary state of Katsina. Fakawa have claims of immigration from Zamfara through Kebbe. The Bangawa also lay claims to be a product of migration process that brought their ancestors from the Borno Empire in the North-East of Nigeria, having left Borno as a result of political crises.[11] The existence of these claims has informed the position of Harris and Mahdi Adamu already noted.

In the second category which includes those who consider themselves strangers and lay no claims to having traditional rights of

---

[11] District Head of Donko, Verbal discussion January 1988.

descent in the Zuru Local Government Area except for property they recently acquired, are Fulani, Hausa, Igbo, Yoruba and several others from various parts of Nigeria. These are settled mainly in the relatively large settlements of Bena, Dirindaji, Donko, Maga, Mahuta, Ribah, Sakaba, Wasagu and Zuru. The Hausa appear to have migrated into this region in large numbers in the 16th century A.D. as a result of upheavals resulting from events such as Kanta's break away from Songhai control. The Fulani is not a particularly large population but appears to have related closely with the local peasants population to provide cow dung manure to revitalise their farms in return for temporary settlement rights, cultivated food items and other useful materials such as calabash (*Lagenaria vulgaris*). Even though its beginning may not yet have been clearly worked out and dated, it must be of pre-16th century A.D. origin. This is in view of the fact of closer linguistic affinity between these two groups (than say with the Hausa), being together members of the Benue-Congo language family as already closely integrated and interdependent, economically, the 16th century A.D. as discussed below.

Inferences on the emergence and establishment of the human population and formation of groups in this region may be made from the little information that avails. Six ground stone axes which typologically belong to the late stone age have been collected during reconnaisance. Two were donated by the owner at Munsune. Three were collected at Semchilelli. The last was found at Dombo, less than one Kilometre West of Semchilelli in the suburbs of Zuru town. Going by general West African chronology, these tools may have been made not earlier than 3,000 B.C.[12] Similar material has been recovered from sites on the Gangare river, near Dutsi and in the Waleli river valley in Gummi district. Both sites are within short distance of Zuru area. In the Kebbi valley several other such finds have been made.

Ground stone axes have been reported from many places in Northern Nigeria where they generally are considered to be thunderbolts. The Late Stone Age in West Africa is dated to as far back as 12,000 B.C. Pottery and ground stone axes were added to this material culture complex about 3,000 B.C. as has been revealed in data collected from sites such as Mejiro Cave, Iwo Eleru and Rop rockshelter. The Zuru region is geographically located in the central area between all these sites, and may therefore have shared similar experience as these areas.

Direct evidence on language and ethnicity of the populations of this area is not yet available. Deduction may, however, be made from

---

[12] T. Shaw, "Preliminary Report on Archeological work in the Wushishi Area, early 1976', *Zaria Archaeology papers*, Vol.9, 1976, P.1-4.

historical linguistic data of the region, which could be of significant implications. In proffering a solution to a similar situation for the Edo, Gbaghyi, Igala, Nupe, Yoruba and others of the Niger-Benue confluence area, Professor Ade Obayemi has presented a very helpful guide. As Obayemi might put it, the available data shows that considerable populations have occupied our region for several thousands of years, and there has been physical and cultural continuation of these populations to the present.[13] The linguistic classification which places the several autochthonous languages of our region in the Plateau group of the Benue Congo Sub-family of the Niger-Congo family of African languages supports this view.[14] This Kwa language group belongs to this family. Its experience has shown that even languages with specific groups in the Nigerian area have needed several thousand years to develop. Such a specific group would in turn have furthermore required much earlier periods to develop from specific sub-families. A specific family, in view of this must then be considered to be even much older in starting and development than a few thousand years. Thus the development of tens of units of the Plateau group languages in the Nigerian Middle Belt between 8°N - 11°N and 5°E - 13°E must similarly have taken a time span of thousands of years.

This must have involved a process of steady population build up and expansion and the steady development of various culture traits within the similar context of a general assemblage. Obayemi has seen this kind of development in the available data on the Nigerian Middle Belt, and even more particularly concerning the Niger-Benue confluence and areas further South.

If indeed the glotochronological estimates of 2,000 years necessary for development of and separation of a dialect from another is acceptable, and used as basis of calculation, we may safely regard Lélna and other such languages of our region as having been spoken here prior to the Christian era by populations with which the Late Stone Age may be associated. More specifically, it would appear that by the early stages of the Late Stone Age, about 14,000 or so years ago, a general language pattern had emerged which has given rise to the present one and was similar to it except in details. Alterations would have taken place later which shifted the Northern border of this language region Southward in favour of the southward spread of the Hausa language, especially during and following the 3rd millenium

---

[13] A. Obayemi, "The Yoruba and Edo Speaking peoples and their Neighbours before 1600 A.D.", in J.F.A. Ajayi and M. Crowder (eds), *History of West Africa*, Vol.I (2nd ed.), Longmans; London 1976, P 200-01.

[14] See J.A. Ballard, 1971: 294-305; and J. Hansford, et.at., 1976: 1-204.

B.C. (C2, 999 B.C. 2,000 B.C.) when a major phase of dessication of the Sahara forced southern Sahara populations to migrate southward into the region. Pre-existing populations here were generally pressurised to shift south. Continuation of this process into more recent times would have given rise to the waves of migration into our region which have resulted in the establishment of specific Hausa population pockets such as in the area of Bena and Wasagu. These recent migrants are among the most persistent in maintaining their identity as immigrants from other areas, and tend to blur the lengthy historical process that has been involved, thus giving rise to traditions of origin which give the impression of recent occupation of this region. Those traditions may be understood within this framework, and it must be pointed out that while they may relate to various sections or even families among the various people in the region, it would be stretching them beyond their usefulness to expect that any of them is the history of a present day community as a whole.

## Settlement

The study of location of human communities in time and in space is today well established in archaeological investigation. This relates to the understanding of man's exploitation of the environment in the light of possibilities and constraints. During the survey, therefore, areas of human settlement were observed. These can be grouped into two broad categories irrespective of size and location:

(i) *Existing settlements* refer to sites inhabited by human during the time of survey. Such sites had houses deliberately constructed for the purpose of habitation, in which people reside on a regular basis.

(ii) *Abandoned settlements* are all sites formally used as residential units but from which the inhabitants have migrated for some reasons.

The varied relief of this region provided a variety of microenvironments within both areas of undulating plains and of hilly topography, from which man may choose specific settlement sites, depending on factors such as security, food resources and availability of fresh water and hunting grounds. Water could have been taken for granted here because added to the various rivers, streams and springs, ground water was available at shallow levels and rainfall is both high (at least 600 mm) and of good duration (not less than 3 months in the year).

In terms of settlement history Zuru region could be considered suitable environment for early human settlement. However, no specific evidence has emerged that is of considerably early settlement material.

Studies by Soper in the 1960s and especially by J.E.G. Sutton, D.D. Harttle, A. Obayemi and others in the 1970s in the Kebbi Valley and other nearby regions of the Niger River basin and those by Nzewunwa in the 1980s suggest that the Zuru region has high potential in this direction. The present fieldwork has revealed that there is a large number of both existing and abandoned settlements fairly distributed over the region, with few areas of high concentration. Partly responsible for this is the similarly fair distribution of water channels, shallow ground water level, and fertile and well drained soils. This is to be contrasted with the more northern regions of Sokoto State where for several centuries now population distribution is in a pattern of concentration along fertile and river-water-fed valleys which have given rise to the high densities of the regions of Birnin Kebbi, Sokoto, Rabah and Argungu, or other specialized microenvironments such as of Kwatarkwoshi, Chafe and Kwiambana, which added to the advantage of good soil and water supply, provided attractive religious and defence sites in the inselbergs that have standout prominently in their vicinities.[15] This has become general knowledge in relation to the Nigeria Savannah.

In the absence of specific dating, it is difficult to know the chronology of these settlements. For the present, it may only be suggested that the present settlement pattern appears to have stabilised for several millenia. As already stated, the units are small and scattered in virtually all sections of the region. More specifically they may be described as villages and wards, made up of households whose predominant economic orientation is towards subsistence agriculture, hunting and relating professions. This economic activity may infact largely explain the settlement pattern, as the practice of land fallowing would have required relatively large land area per person.

## Abandoned Settlements

The abundance of sites whose inhabitant populations have migrated, all over the Zuru region, is reminiscent of this phenomenon in the Nigerian savannah, which has been recorded specifically for regions not far from here.[16] The present survey was not intensive and therefore looked for only most prominent features such as enclosing walls, foundation stones, potsherds, baobab trees, which are definite evidence of settlement in the region. Among the most prominent completely abandoned settlements are the old Donko which was

---

[15] See A.R. Augi, "The Significance of Hills and inselbergs in the History and culture of people of Hausaland", in *ZARUMA*, A culture Magazine of Sokoto State, February, 1982.
[16] J.E.G. Sutton, Op.cit, and T.Shaw, *Op.cit*.

abandoned about 80 year ago in favour of a new settlement of the same name. The inhabitants, according to tradition, were forced to leave this site, which was considered inaccessible, by British colonialists. The centre of this settlement is located on a hill top in the vicinity of which there are several other hill tops. Numerous large baobab trees and a complex of ruins of stone walls of houses and fences mark the site. Sections of these walls still stood at 1.70m high during the survey. Claims by informants that this central area served as a King's Palace appear justifiable. It is a site of dense concentration of interconnected wall structures apparently related to fortification. The surface scatter is mainly of potsherds and numerous stone bounders. In a specific location at the foot of one of the largest baobab trees, inpalace informants point at a spot they claim was the King's shrine. Several low earth mounds located in this palace site are said to be burials. Located a few metres south west of the palace, is a section of this abandoned settlement complex which is identified as wangarawa. It is also well fortified and said to have housed traders.

In the time available, the full extent and nature of this settlement could not be worked out. Yet one got the impression that this is a very large settlement enclosed by several walls in its various sections. Indeed informants some of whom claim personal knowledge of the last stages of the period of occupation of the complex, claim that the site is very extensive and is enclosed by a set of not less than four

Other prominent abandoned settlements in the region include Azuguru, Birnin Tudu, Debche, Dirin Gari, Kangon Wasagu, Kanya and Uhun Tudu. These and less prominent other abandoned settlement sites abound in the several districts of the region.

## Existing Settlements.

It has already been noted that human settlement in our region is widespread. Bena, Dirin Daji, Donko, Isgogo, Mahuta, Dabai, Ribah, Sakaba, Tadurga, Wasagu and Zuru are among the largest of them even though only the last may qualify as urban, in view of the varied population, concentration of professions in this administrative and commercial centre of the region. The typical settlement is of nucleated rural compounds which make up villages of various sizes.

Distances between compounds and between villages range from a few metres to several kilometres, such that it gives rise to a settlement pattern that is generally sparse in density. From this general character, however, it is observable that hills are more intensely settled than the plains.This pattern reveals careful consideration of certain factors in site selection decisions. Fresh water supply appears to have been very important as all settlements (both the abandoned and the extant) are located in sites that have a steady fresh water supply natural or artificial or both. The artificial source is in the form of wells sunk in related sites, usually meant to augment supply from rivers, springs and streams. Wells appear to have taken on additional significance as supplier of fresh water during the colonial period when populations were forced to migrate from their traditionally preferred sites which usually had natural water sources, for sites near seasonal roads that made them more easily accessible to colonial officials. Reference already has been made to Donko in this regard. Thus the new Donko depends on wells sunk by the colonial government and by individuals, whereas inhabitants of the old Donko had depended on streams for fresh water.

Rivers, springs and streams, as already stated, are numerous and fairly widespread in the region. They appear to have been supported by a high water level which may in turn be related in part, to a high rainfall amount up until the middle 1970s.

Apart from providing fresh water, some of these water courses provided sites for religious and other functions. Dombo Gomo, Germace and Tarubaba in the central area, for instance , are among most renown (religious, medicinal and magical) sites and are associated with natural phenomena such as forest remnants which appear to have been deliberately spared in order to maintain the required image for those sites.

Relief also appears to have played part in site choice. While many types of sites were settled, both in hills and plains, most of the population is located in the plains. Also the largest settlements in the region today are located in the plains, even though this may not always have been the case, in view of the fact that Dirin Daji, New Donko, Mahuta, Ribah, Wasagu and Zuru are relatively new, while Dabai, old Azuguru, old Bena, Dirin Daji, Dabai, Donko, Birnin Tudu and Isgogo were located in hilly environments. In addition, numerous smaller settlements are sited on most of the many residual hills in the region and on substantial sections of the old Donko Rijau ridge, especially the region from Umu through Rikoto, Dabai, Semchileli and Senchi. Debche, Penin Amana and Penin Gaba are located on a western extension of the ridge, a few kilometres west of Zuru town while Birnin Tudu (abandoned) and Fakai (Northwest of Zuru town) are sited on isolated hills. Dago, Gwanki, Kandu, Sindi and Yelmo are few among the many settlements on residual hills east of Zuru, which, here and there, interrupt the generally undulating topography of this territory. The area of Karishen and Sakaba in the southeast has a higher concentration of such hills, which also are intensely settled, and is similar to what exists in the northwest beyond the open plain country of Mahuta. The mainly lateritic residual hills are settled by subsistent agricultural communities of varying sizes at Bangu, Gulbin

Kuka, Marafa, Runfan Maje, Sabon Kengi, and Yanbanga among many.

Even a casual observation reveals an interesting character of the settlement of this region, which is worth noting. The plains are settled by people who claim to be migrants from hill settlements within the region in search of farmland. They constantly refer to the hills as their real home and tend to pay at least short annual visits to the hill settlements for traditional ceremonies. This is especially true of the Lélna speaking people who appear to be in the majority and are found in every district of the region and claim a specific settlement or village area in the central district area of Dabai, Senchi and Ribah, Azuguru and Penni as their home.

## Settlement Walls

The phenomenon of settlement walling in the Nigerian area has attracted some attention, resulting in our knowing that it is particularly recurrent in the Savannah area. Thus in the states of Kano, Kastina, Old Oyo and Zazzau it is an important characteristic of human settlement.[17] The general consensus among historians and other students of this phenomenon is that the practice of constructing walls to enclose settlements is a defence mechanism. This position is reiterated in the oral traditions everywhere in the Zuru Emirate. Here, settlement walling was common in the past, irrespective of relief. Both plain and hill settlements were walled. And whereas in Hausaland, as has been observed in the area of Zaria, most walls are simply single circular constructions, surrounding relatively small, areas, ground observation reveals that in Zuru region most walls form extensive complexes of connected walls enclosing large areas. This is most true of hill settlement which may involve enclosures of specific hill tops which are either further surrounded by walls of wider circumference or walls extending from individual hills to connect with those of other peaks in the same vicinity such that several hectares of land may thus be enclosed. This is similar to the Amina wall in Zaria which encloses smaller walls. The complexity of these wall systems made it impossible to trace them extensively enough for mapping within the time available. The material of which the walls are made is mainly stone which is locally available on the ground surface in the hills. Plain settlement areas like Kanya, Kangon Wasagu, Tadurga and the unnamed abandoned settlement a few kilometres east of Kangon Wasagu, however, are enclosed by laterite walls. The walls of Isgogo

---

[17] K. Effah - Gyamfi, "Ancient Urban Sites in Hausaland; A Preliminary Report", *West African Journal of Archaeology*, Vol. 16, 1986, P.117-34; and Y.B. Usman, *The Transformation of Katsina, C.1400-1883*, A.B.U. Press, 1980, P.1.

are of mixed laterite and stone materials, probably reflecting its location at a point on the west side of the Donko Rijau ridge which is such that most of the settlement is sited in the rich alluvial valley adjacent to a stream in the vicinity.

All these walls, without exception, have been abandoned to disrepair and have collapsed, except for some remains that show where the walls stood. Some of these remains are quite visible and infact sufficient to give a good picture of what the walls could have been like. At the sites of Birin Tudu, old Donko, Semchileli and Yelmo, for instance, sections of these old walls still stand at a height of not less than 1.50m. Informants claim that the walls had been much higher. As those of Yelmo show, they had various gates which led into the direction of field/plain settlements.

Considering the sites as a whole shows that whether on hill or plains, fresh water supply was a prominent factor in site selection. Most settlements were located near Rivers, streams or Springs, some of which as already observed, became important in the mythology of the people.

During the colonial era a new factor was introduced. Need to bring people close to accessible areas as identified by the requirements of colonial administration arose. Consequently resettlement of population was embarked upon. People were either forced or persuaded to move near motor roads newly constructed, even though the implementation of this policy was only partially successful, as many communities, like Kandu and Yelmo, successfully resisted.

This policy introduced need for the government to construct deep wells in the new settlements located far from traditional fresh water sources. The result is that it has been possible to give a new character to settlement pattern in new Kangon Wasagu, Mahuta, Zuru and extensions of old settlements. This gives rise to a generally lineal layout, as compounds are constructed by the sides of the road, partly to take advantage of whatever motor transportation facilities exist. This notwithstanding, the dominant pattern remains one of low density farm house units in the plains interrupted at various intervals by densely settled units like Tadurga, Wasagu, Dirin Daji and Mahuta.

The architecture has been characterised mainly by various sizes of lateritic houses. Most of these are huts of about 2.5m diameter with thatched roofs. An architectural novelty has been developing recently, such that rectangular houses are gradually replacing circular ones, and cement concrete is also being preferred to laterite as construction material, where it is affordable. This is especially true in the relatively new settlements and in new extensions of the older settlements. Thus it is noticed that Bena, new Donko, Mahuta and Zuru are ahead of Dabai and both Penni Amana and Penni Gaba in the adoption of this style. It would appear that this development also relates to reception of immigrant elements and or ideas from outside. Thus the rectangular construction is found most in stranger's quarters and in areas where indigenes already exposed to outside ideas now construct houses in the traditions they now have learnt.

## Economy

Peasant agriculture, the mainstay of the economy of the communities in our region is pivoted on cultivation of many crops. These include hungry rice (*Digitaria exilis*), guinea corn (*sorghum*) millet (*pennisetum*), "Tamba" (*Eleusene corocana*) and maize (*Zea mays*) cereals. Their root crops include Cocoyam (*Colosia antiguorum*), Bambara nuts (*Voandzeia subterranea*) Cassava (*Manihot palmata*), groundnuts (*Arachis Hypogea*), sweet potatoes (*Ipomoes batatas*), "Risga" (*Pleastranthus Spp.*), "Tumuku" (*Colens dysentericus*). Other crops include benniseed (*Sessamum indicum*), pepper (*Capsium frutescens*), "Yakuwa" (*Hibiscus sabdariffa*), garden egg (*Solanum spp.*) Jute (*Hibiscus cannabunus*), Pumpkin (*Cucurbita pepo.*), Cotton (*Gossypium*), gourd (*Lagenaria vulgaris*), Tobacco (*Nicotiana tabacum*), varieties of beans (*Vigna sinensis*) such as Caravalia ensiformis called "sword beans" which is a large climbing bean, Dolichos lablab and so on, and Amaranthus viridis, a spinage- like thorny vegetable, were all cultivated. Pawpaw (*Carica papaya*) was planted in small numbers near compounds and has been a casual pleasantry rather than a significant aspect of diet.

The nature of cultivation can be classified into at least two types. One would be terracing of hillsides and, the other, simple cultivation of open plain and alluvial areas, as already observed while discussing settlement sites. Terracing, which involved serrating of the available space on the hillside in successive stages from top to bottom, is common site in hills all over the region. Among the most accessible for observation are those portions of the Donko-Rijau road on which Dabai, Isgogo, Rikoto, Senchi and Zuru stand today. Bena, Dirin Gari, Kandu, Fakai, Tsohon Birin Sakaba and others including the Penni, Kele and Yelmo all attest to intensive cultivation of hillsides, which may be seen as careful application of effort by man to subject a difficult environment to his desire, which "usually occurs with a highly developed agriculture that can profit from such a major investment of time and energy. Widespread use of terracing suggests at once a special adaptation to their habitat and raises questions about the mobilization of labour and the social organisation of production reflected in this cultural landscape."[18]

This is a system of agriculture that has been reported in other areas of Nigeria in the Adamawa and Sardauna regions, and among the Ika Ibo. It also has been reported in the Cameroon Republic and in eastern, central and southern Africa, indicating that intensive hill agriculture is much widespread.[19]

Substantial density of population could be maintained by this system given a favourable combination of climate, good soils and effective techniques. And our region was not lacking in these, at least until recently. Rainfall and sunshine have been sufficient if not abundant, the soils on the hills not only derive from mineral rich parent material, the manure from homesteads and pastoral cattle provided adequate remanuring to maintain and indeed improve on its crop-bearing qualities, thus making fallowing needless on hillside.

Fallowing was left to the second system, plain cultivation, in which large expanses of land was involved. And it is of interest that the population involved generally claims descent from one or other hill community, sees itself as settling in the plains only "temporarily" for the purpose of farming, having migrated here only due to need for such farmland in view of insufficiency of land at the home hill settlement. Here population density and pressure on land is low. So too is manuring. These combine to make fallowing a requirement. The availability of land and the resultant social organisation recognises this and makes it possible.

The land (whether in use or held fallow) on which one may cultivate is obtained through inheritance along the patrilineage. More land may be secured in an unclaimed field by clearing the bush, and is immediately recognised as belonging to the clearer and their descendants. This system partly explains and has made possible the widespread existence of Lélna settlements in almost all parts of the region and beyond.

The organisation of labour for production involves all able bodied members of the community. At the family level the family head, usually the oldest male, is incharge. He gives general guidance. Real active labour on which the family depends is supplied by the youth. The significance of the young population is emphasized in the organisation of young males into age groups whose farm labour is chanelled through the practice of *Golmo* among the Lelna people. *Golmo* is a complex bridal wealth tradition which every Lélna male

---

[18] R. Mcc. Netting, *Hill Farmers of Nigeria: A cultural ecology of the Kofyar of the Jos Plateau*, University of Washington Press, London, 1968, P.3.
[19] ibid P.4.

engaged in, both inorder to earn his wife and to earn him respect as a hard working and disciplined adult in Lélna society, without which one could not look forward to any advancement in the status strata in society.

Having been accepted through *Golmo*, one was now prepared to make further progress in a wider society which has organised a reward system aimed at encouraging active crop production. The Lélna example still is illustrative, the Lelna being the single largest and most widespread group. Various honouring titles existed, with which one could be bestowed, depending on if one had produced sufficient grain, particularly sorghum, which were distributed in specified quantities to chiefs and to all those who already had attained such honour in one's community at the village level. These titles included *Ch'ganga, ch'gongo, ch'tage* and *ch'im chima*. They were symbolised by playing specific drums in honour of the achiever, to the admiration of the rest of society. This honour was shared by members of one's family especially one's wife and children. Each of the drums is identified in name by the title it represents. Thus the *diganga* drum is played only when *ch'ganga* title is involved, and so on.

The centrality of agriculture in these communities was further stressed in the high esteem in which rainmaking was held. Thus there was a *Gom-vu-menke* (King of rain) to whom was attributed powers of rainmaking. He was revered. The blacksmith/ironsmelter *Zoge* also was highly respected, being the manufacture of the basic tools of production.

With developments in time, these societal practices, mythology and production were incorporated into a system that ensures both surplus production and the extraction of that surplus by the ruling circles. It was therefore, the practice that peasants and craftsmen (e.g. smelters) presented regular taxes and gifts to the dominant group in return for honours as already noted. *Golmo* also assured elders of labour from the organised active young men, so long as these elders had young daughters to offer for marriage. The young men were so much engaged in this that they made little contribution on their parents' farm.

From a general knowledge of crop and agriculture history, the Zuru Emirate, being in the Nigerian Middle Belt, falls in the West African Zone in which yam was subjected to cultivation.[20] This is also the region in which domestication of *Sorghum, Pennisetum, Digitaria Exilis, Eleusine corocana, colosia antiguorum, colens dysentericus,*

---

[20] T. Shaw "Prehistory", in Ikime, O (ed), *Groundwork of Nigerian History*, Ibadan, Historical Society of Nigeria, 1980. P.32.

*Ipomoca batatas, Vigna spp., Voandzeia subtrranea, Solanum spp., Hibiscus sobdariffa, Zingiber,* among others was achieved. The beginning of domestication of crops and animals in this region would not have been less than four thousand years ago and appears to have been associated with the beginning of ceramic technology here.[21]

Rearing of chicken, dogs, goats and guinea fowl appears a long established and integral part of the agricultural economy, even though, like in other parts of the Nigerian Middle Belt region it has so far failed to achieve a high regular meat content of the daily diet.

## Iron Technology

It has been suggested that abundance of iron ore in easily workable form in Africa may have led to a direct transition from stone to iron technology without an intermediate bronze period.[22] Consequently the search for beginnings of the knowledge of iron as a metal and the process of converting the ore into metal in various parts of the continent may not have to be one of seeking to establish a complicated network of roots or migration and influx of ideas and/or traits. This may hold true for the West African sub-region in which the Zuru area falls, and its significance to us not only exists in the satisfaction derivable from knowledge that evidence of iron working is of great antiquity in this region, but even moreso the fact that scholars are growing in the realisation that iron age studies may hold an important position in our knowledge of the late prehistory of such African Societies. The technology of iron, especially in the area of smelting, must not have experienced much regular drastic change from its inception up to the colonial period. And further innovation would have been slowed or hindered by the colonial experience.

During survey, iron-capped hills, ore mining pits, smelting furnaces, slag and turyere remains were identified at several locations. Five mining pits were located within less than ten kilometre radius of Zuru town. Four of them were on iron-capped residual hills. The largest of these pits is on the Doga hill, less than 500m east of Zuru Club. It measured 290m long on the north-south axis about 10m wide at several portions, and up to 10m deep in the middle section.

A second mine in the vicinity of Zuru town is located about 1km northeast of Zuru Club. No measurements have been taken of this mine which is smaller than the one already discussed. And at Dabai, which is 4 km north of Zuru, there is a mine pit that is located about 600m southeast of the Marafan Dabai's Palace. About 6 km southeast

---

[21] *ibid* P.31.
[22] J.D. Clark, *World Prehistory*, London 1969.

of Dabai is new Debche, presently a small settlement of few compounds east of Pennin Gaba. Here, on a residual lateritic hill of the same name, is located a shallow iron ore mining pit which measures about 45m long and is of irregular width. Much of it appears to have collapsed and of not more than 1m depth in any of its portions. Here, like in the first mine is Zuru, pot vessels and potsherds were observed, which are objects of worship, as inhabitants of the area have turned these disused mine shafts into altars, believing that they are mouths of large tunnels in which their ancestors used to take refuge from war and slave raids as well as worshipped. There are however informants who know these places to have been mines, and say that the sacrifice of tobacco was offered regularly in the mines to appease the spirits that were believed to live in the ore deposits, so that they would not harm the miners. This practice is what apparently has developed into turning the sites into religious sites. At Munsune, about 10km south of Zuru at a site which is about 1km astride the Zuru - Rijau road (to the east) is located another iron ore mine.

In view of the fact that mines were located during preliminary search, it may not be far fetched to expect more in the vicinity of Zuru. Indeed, informants in places as far away as Dirindaji, Kanya and Kangon Wasagu refer to the vicinity of Zuru as the main source of iron ore in the region by the beginning of British colonial rule in the area.

Not far from these mines, furnaces were usually located. Brief examination of surface remains shows that on the basis of size alone, two general types of iron smelting furnaces were located which we may now identify simply as large and small furnaces. The large furnaces measure more than 2m diametre, while the small furnaces measure less than 2m diameter. The large type appears to be better preserved than the small type, and a few informants claimed that either their parents or themselves witnessed the use of the large type whereas no such claims were made concerning the small furnace.

At Debche, less than 1km east of Pennin Gaba, the two types were found together on a smelting site a few metres north of the residual hill on which the iron ore mine, already referred to, is situated. Wall thickness of the small furnace is about 10cm, while the walls of the large furnaces at this site measure about 22cm.

Slag, tuyere and furnace remains also have been found in large quantities within Zuru town where a fresh cutting during unsurfaced laterite road repair works have revealed one small type furnace in the middle of Forces Avenue directly in front of the Sammi Gomo House. Earlier, a fresh cutting within the same vicinity had exposed small furnaces in the middle of the Zuru - Ribah road at a point a few metres from its "T" Junction with Mohammadu Magoro Road. This cut revealed that disused tuyeres were incorporated in the construction of these furnaces, which is corroborated by the furnaces at Debche. It was not possible in the situation of transport difficulties and time shortage to verify informant claims to existence of similar evidence in many places in the region.

At Bena the site visited appeared to have only a surface scattered of slag which is insufficient evidence. There is no existing tradition of iron ore mining and/or smelting. All informants point to the colonial period as the era of collapse and end of these. They add that European-imported iron and steel replaced the local forms because they provided an easy and cheap source of material for tool manufacture. The iron mining and smelting was an extremely energy - taxing process which was easily abandoned in the face of competition from an easier source. Moreover the imported alternative was available either free or at very minimal charge, whereas relatively high charges were paid to obtain the local material. This is in spite of the fact that the local material was known to be more suited and would normally have been preferred. Thus the people here believe that market forces were used by the British to destroy the mining and smelting base of local iron industry.

As research progresses it may be revealed that iron technology has been known in this region for many centuries too ancient for specific human memory of its beginnings and pattern of development. This appears most likely, as the region lies adjacent to the region now known to have materials related to the Nok tradition whose iron technology has been dated to between about 1000 B.C. and 600 A.D.[23] Indeed these regions belong together in the Nigerian Middle Belt which already has been suggested as the home of domestication of several crops and which appears to belong to one cultural region as illuminated by linguistic similarity of the ethnic groups spread immediately south of the Hausa culture region. The cultural distinctiveness of this Middle Belt area has been recognised in the Hausa terms, *Bauchi*, which differentiates the people and cultures of the region from those of the people of both the more northern and more southern latitudes.[24]

No specific material evidence of blacksmiting in the old tradition has been located. Yet informants have pointed to a ward of an abandoned settlement (Azuguru) about 500m south-east of Debche hill, which they claim housed blacksmiths. In the Lélna language this ward was called *Zogne*, like the smiths. Here, smelted iron was taken

---

[23] D. Calvocoress, & B.N. David, "A New Survey of Radiocarbon Thermoluminescence dates for West Africa", *Journal of African History*, xx,I, 1979, P. 1-29; and J. F. Jemkur, "Recent Results of Thermoluminescence (Th) Tests on Nok Terracottas and Sherds", West African Journal of archaeology, XXI, 1986, P.165-68.

[24] M. Adamu, *The Hausa Factor in West African History*, Op.cit P.42.

to the smiths to fashion out work tools. In return for their labour and skills, they were paid in grain and smelted iron. They could also ask for farm labour instead or in addition or even as a mark of good neighbourliness.

## Pottery

In spite of the onslaught of metal pots and of metal and plastic containers, clay pot-making continues in this region even though at a scale not as high as informants remember of periods in the past. Vessels vary in size from large beer brewing pots, one of which, in use at Tadurga, measured 72cm high, 89cm external diametre at the middle, to tiny shrine pots located at Debche hill.

*M'bimo* (singular - *Ibimo* )

Apart from the ordinary domestic pots which may be put to various other uses such as offertory containers in shrines and water containers on graves, special vessels may be made specifically for restricted usage. These include the *Ibimo* which is a rather cylindrical vessel constructed in the form of a gourd without a mouth. The only opening in it is the few tiny holes pierced at the bottom, (one) and the top (one or two); the *Igadu,* another gourd-like vessel which differs in having a narrow mouth opening at the top with inverted lips. The base is wider than the top and is rather flat. Both types are placed on the grave for the use of the dead in the hereafter. Pottery figurines are also made and placed on graves to signify achievement of high status during the lifetime of persons buried. The presentations may show human (male and female) as well as animals. The animals would be of the type that one might have hunted down during one's lifetime or simply great animals like elephant and buffalo commensurate with one's status as a great farmer or hunter or both.

At present, hardly are there women capable of making figurines like *Ibimo* and *Igadu,* because of present day unwillingness to go through the rituals required and lack of sponsor, as it involves expenditure that people do not appear ready to or are not capable of incurring at ease. In addition it is generally doubted if there are potters who have the required skill. Consequently the old *Ibimo, Igadu* and figurines already placed on graves are closely guarded to ensure they remain on site. The new dead may be entered into the same graves as their forefathers, if they are deemed to have attained similar degree of success. This is an established long standing tradition and prior to the Christian and Islamic single grave burial tradition, it was the aspiration of every male to succeed enough in lifetime in order to qualify to be entered into the family's multiple burial grave. The practice continues in a low degree, and annually the grave is cleared of any grass or shrub growth and treated to a new libation of either *digitaria* or *sorghum* paste as required by custom, to please the ancestors entered there, who were expected to protect their living descendants from harm, in return.

This usage of terracotta figurines and vessels on graves in this region may be instructive in attempt to interpret the functions of the Nok terracotta figurines. This is not only because the two areas are adjacent and because of other cultural affinities, but also in view of the fact that both societies (as we may say for now) appear to have been at an equivalent level of technological development, at least in terms of iron, by the eve of British colonialist conquest. Consequently, it is not surprising that there was similarity in choice spring, stream and riverside sites in vicinities of lateritic or other residual hills for settlement in the region that stretches from the Zuru area, including the Kainji region to the Nok valley and beyond, which may be associated with iron working societies.

## Dye Pits

A cloth weaving and dyeing industry is said to have been thriving in this region by the time that British colonialists arrived. It is represented by a large number of dye pits in settlements that have a history of a large Hausa immigrant population. Bena is the most outstanding representative of these. Here, there are not less than 15 locations in each of which tens of pits are concentrated.[25] Only few of these sites were visited. At one of them in the southwest section of the settlement, a few metres east of the southernmost protrusion of the Bena rock, 50 such were counted, and this may not be all there are on that site. While some of these pits have been refilled to the brim, others are at various levels of being refilled, some being up to 1.6m deep. Bawa Bena explains that the numerous pits reflect the high degree of weaving and dyeing activity in the town, some of which he saw as a youth. This now, in his opinion, has died out as a result of influx of cheap European textile material.

Both cotton and indigo, the main raw materials were produced in the vicinity of Bena. However the cloth produced could not be consumed here much. There was an influx of traders from Katsina and other towns who carried the cloth to distant markets. Bawa's understanding of this role of Bena is supported in the position of economic importance in the state of Katsina ascribed to the Katsinan Laka region of which Bena and Wasagu are part.[26]

## Stone Tools

Given the stony nature of much of this hilly region, one's first impression is that the stone tool evidence of man's activity is abundant and readily available. This has not proved to be the case, especially if the expectation is of stone axes, adzes, cleavers and the like. Only six tools of this category were recovered: two from Munsune, which were donated by the owner who had used them as sorghum beer heaters, one was taken from inside a small pot at the foot of a pawpaw (*Carica papaya*) tree at Manga, where it was kept to scare off people who were not invited to pluck the pawpaw fruit. Another was collected from the front wall of the entrance hut of a compound at Semchileli, where a special mud protrusion had been made on the wall to accommodate it. Two more came from inside a *Gwom-vun-menke* compound where several others were left intact. These are artifacts of various sizes and apparently different material. Whereas the two from Munsune are of material not immediately identifiable, the remaining four appear to be basically quartz.

Apart from these tools a large number of both upper and lower grinding stones were located especially in hill settlements such as Bena, Debche, old Donko, Isgogo, Manga, Umu, and Semchileli, though none of them was collected. The possibility of uncovering more of the already sighted and other stone tool types exists. In the

---

[25] Bawa Bena, C. 105 years and Dauda Iro, 35 years, interview, Bena, 20/1/88

[26] Y.B, Usman, *Op.cit.*

compound of Idi Manga, the village Head of Manga, for instance, there is a pile of many stone balls which appear to have been used for pounding, of quartz material. Close examination of these has not been allowed yet as they are considered family ritual property.

## Burials

Burials are a striking feature of the settlements in this region. In the dominant non-Christian and non-Muslim tradition, these are located either at the back of the compound or in the open frontal space near the entrance to the compound. Respect and attention are paid to these graves because a mutual reciprocal relationship is maintained between those buried there and their living (descendant) relations. Thus special care is ensured to keep the graves from mutilation or disturbance in some other unwarranted manner. This is with reference only to graves of those who had died in old age, having attained high status through farming and hunting as earlier described. Thus those who had earned *Ch'ganga, Ch'gongo, Ch'hwerke* and *Ch'tage* were entitled to this special honour. The grave was marked by construction of circular monument of daub and lithic material to diametre of about 2m. and up to 1m high, after internment. This was followed by placing water pots and calabashes for the use of the deceased in the hereafter. Terracotta figurines depicting the dead (though not statutes) and animals such as lion, elephant and leopard, which they may have hunted down in their lifetime or which simply show that the dead were great among men, just like these animals were considered great among animals, were placed on the constructed mound.

**Logom built on the grave of a dead leader.**

There was one family burial for such great men of each family such that whenever one died, the earlier mound was pulled down, the grave opened and the new dead entered. The grave was covered again and the mound reconstructed and the old pots and figurines placed in position. New items could be added if considered necessary especially where the old ones got broken. Into the burial chamber would also be entered one's wives and daughters when they died. They were considered as having contributed to such one's success that it was also their achievement. But not one's male children. They were supposed to be struggling on their own to make their individual mark similar to or, better still, higher than their father's, to earn them such honour with their wife and daughter. This struggle, they started at a tender age of seven years or so when they enlisted in *Golmo* which kept them away from their family farm most of the time for the following seven, eight or even ten years.

The not so successful in this society are not so honoured. They are buried in unmarked single graves some distance from the compound. This simple burial system of the muslim communities in the region in which burial is done in secluded areas outside the settlement. The earth is returned after internment and pots secured for the purpose are split into two somewhat equal pieces each and placed on the grave, spanning its full length.

A word for the graves of Kings. Kings are buried in the same manner as other high status members of society already described. But their graves are even more elaborately marked and protected. A hut is constructed similar to normal living huts to both further mark and to protect the grave from factors of weather and human and animal disturbance. And at the appropriate period every year the mound inside the hut and the rest of the hut is cleaned. New thatching is done if necessary. Libation of *Digitaria exilis* porridge is poured, chicken is slaughtered to the honour and appeasance of the ancestors buried there. This is in both expectation that they continue to protect their descendant and in appreciation of such protection already advanced in the preceding year.

## Conclusion

This survey leaves one with the definite impression that this is a culturally complex region in which very active cultural interaction has been going on within and between various groups for several millenia now. The northern fringes have been a buffer one of interaction between two distinct cultural zones of the Afro-Asiatic group Hausa in the north and the Niger-Congo group in the south. The evidence for all this (and more) is imbedded in the language, settlement pattern, burial traditions, pottery and oral traditions among others, even though this cannot be clearly brought out in a brief survey report. Urgent, well defined and systematic research has gone into this project to record these as they avail today for the purpose of good management of our cultural resources. Areas like religion, farming, crop history, language history and geography, burial systems, rainmaking, pottery are indeed easily attractive in this region and have received good attention in the subsequent chapters.

## Chapter Three

## A Glottochronology Of Four Benue-Congo Languages In Zuruland.
*by*

### A. H. Amfani

## Introduction

Historians in their search for insight into the pre- histories of societies, and especially ethnic communities, have always found solace in the methods of glottochronology, which results have always provided valuable information about the speakers of related languages. In the southern part of Sokoto sta e in the northwest Nigeria, between latitude 11º & 11º 45' N and longitude 4º 31' & 6º E, lies an area known as Zuruland, comprising of small independent ethnic communities. A glottochronological study of related languages in the area would certainly provide some insight into their prehistories. This paper is on the glottochronology of Banganci, C'léla, Dukkanci and Fakkanci, the four genetically related languages of Zuruland.

Glottochronology was first proposed in the fourties by Morris Swadesh and the method claimed "to permit the dating of language splits in terms of real time on purely internal basis."[1] Swadesh had always been fascinated by the method of Carbon-14, a technique of absolute dating used in the field of prehistory for determining the relative age of organic matters. In the first half of this century, Swadesh successfully deviced a statistical method parallel to the method of dendchronology and Carbon-14 for determining the relative time-depth of divergence between related languages. His method, known as glottochronology (also referred to as lexicostatistics), is based on the assumption that languages tend to lose their inherited basic vocabulary[2] at a relatively constant rate, and that a carefully designed statistical method (glottochronology) can be used to calculate

---

[1] T. Bynon, Historical Linguistics, Cambridge University Press, 1977 p. 207.

[2] The basic vocabulary of a language for Lexico statistical purposes is a list of some 100 words which bear universal meanings in every human language. They are words 'referring to such fundemental biological activities (such as eating, drinking, sleeping), divisions of the body (as the eye, the ear, the head), natural physical phenomena (like fire, water, the moon, the sun), general rational concepts as are represented by the personal pronouns, the demostratives, size), etc. See ibid.

this time- depth of divergence. His first tentative statement on glottochronology appeared in 1950 and was followed by other works.[3] Lehmann[4] was of the opinion that probably the best statement describing the use of glottochronology is an article by Sarah C. Gudschinsky.[5]

Glottochronology is not without criticism. Criticisms of glottochronology are numerous and have been adequately cited in a number of works such as Lehman[6] Bynon,[7] Hoijer.[8] But despite the criticisms, glottochronology is still in use and of recent, Troike[9] has used it on some six Turkic languages, and his conclusion is really a booster to glottochronology: "This group of six Turkic languages adds another test case to the slowly accumulating body of data confirming the validity of the glottochronological method, and attesting to the significance of Morris Swadesh's contribution to the field of historical ligguistics.[10]

## The Languages Of Zuruland

The entire thesis of glottochronology lies on the basic assumption that related or supposedly related languages separate from their common ancestor to note that in this assumption, the notion of 'relationess of languages' is of vital importance and that no glottochronological investigation ever began without first ascertaining the genetic relationship of the languages under consideration. The present study therefore is on some four genetically related languages found in an area commonly referred to as Zuruland. The languages are Banganci (Bg), C'léla (Cl), Dukkanci (Dk) and Fakkanci (Fk). The genetic relationship of these languages had been adequately established by

---

[3] M. Swadesh, "Salish International Relationships" *International Journal of American Linguistics*, XVI, 1950, p 157-67; "Lexicostatistics dating of Pre-historic , *Proceedings of the American Philosophical Society*, Vol. 96, 1952, p 425-63; and "Towards greater accuracy in lexicostatistic dating", *International Journal of American Linguistics*, XXI, 1955, p 122-37.

[4] W.P. Lehmann, *Historical Linguistics, - An Introduction*, Holt. Rinchart and Winston, 1962.

[5] S.C. Gudschinsky, "The ABC of Lexicostatistics (Glottochronology)", *Word*, XII, 1956, p.175-210.

[6] W.P. Lehmann, *Op.cit*. p. 106.

[7] T. Bynon, *Op.cit*. P. 269-72.

[8] Hi Hoijer, "Lexiscostatistics, A Critique", *Language*, XXXII, 1956, p.49-60.

[9] R.C. Troike, "The glottochronology of Six Turkic Languages", *International Journal of Americal Liguistics*, XXXV, 1969. p. 183-91.

[10] ibid, p.191.

such authoritative sources as Greeberg[11] and Voegeling.[12] According to Greenberg's classification of African languages, the four languages belong to Benue-Congo a subgroup of the Niger-Congo family. However, a recent classification recognises the genetic relationship that exists between the languages, hence their grouping into a more restricted subgroup of a larger family.

## The Word List

The basic word list used in the present study, as contained in Table 1,[13] is Swadesh's standard list consisting of 100 non-complex lexical items. The forms of the selected lexical items were compared on pairwise basis to determine cognates. Ideally, these pairs which, on the grounds of phonetic similarity or phonological correspondence appear or are known to be cognates are counted as "retentions from the common ancestor". Likewise, those pairs which do not exhibit phonetic similarity or regular sound correspondence are considered to own their dissimilarity to the lose of the reflex of the proto-item in one or both of the cognates."[14]

In counting cognates in the Zuru material, I adopted the procedures used by Bright and Troike. Bright[15] had suggested "an objective criteria for judging similarities." two such criteria adopted for the purpose of Zuru material are:"(i) vowels are disregarded in all comparisons, and (ii) two words are considered similar if they contain two identical consonants separated by not more than one consonant and one vowel."[16] Troike on the other hand, suggested that in order to

---

[11] J.R. Greenberg, *Languages of Africa*, Bloomington, 1963.

[12] C.F. Voegolin & F.M. Yoegolin, *Classification and index of the World's languages*, Elsevier, 1977.

[13] The compilation of this list was made in the Summer of 1988 and involved extensive travels into nooks and corners of Zuruland. My principal research assitant was Magaji Sakaba Isgogo, a final year language student at the Usmanu Danfodiyo University, Sokoto. Together we visited many centres with concentration of either Bangawa, Dukkawa, Lelna or Fakkawa. These centres includes Dabai, Danko, Dirin Daji, Fakkai, Isgogo, Maga, Mahuta, Makuku, Ribah, Sakaba and Zuru. At each centre we asked for volunteers who would want to respond to our questions. For each respondent, Magaji would fill in a separate questionaire and I will make a tape recording of the proceeding. In addition to this individual interview, we also conducted group interviews in which one person is the principal respondent and other members of the group were at liberty to comment on and response they deemed improper. These responses were later compared and Table I represents the most popular responses to the basic vocabularies.

[14] T. Bynon, *Op.cit*.

[15] W. Bright, "Glottochronological counts of Hokaltecan material", *Language*, XXXII, 1956, P.42-48.

[16] It must be pointed out that the adoption of this criteria for the Zuru material is necessary in view of the fact that the languages under construction are yet to be meaningfully reduced

"avoid ad hoc or arbitrary choices which may unrealistically skew results" and also to get "a better picture of the range of time-depth", it is necessary that computations for each pairwise comparison be made on the basis of "(a) the choice which gave the greatest degree of divergence, and (b) the choice which gave the least degree of divergence."[17]

## Table 1

|     | Banganci | C'lela | Dukkanci | Fakkanci |
| --- | --- | --- | --- | --- |
| 1.  | I | me | mi | me | me |
| 2.  | you | be | vo | bo | bo |
| 3.  | we | inai | cinna | te | itine |
| 4.  | this | woya | tøyø | wuka | uo'o |
| 5.  | that | osi | ohinlo | wore | uneji |
| 6.  | who | wahanne | we | wa | wane |
| 7.  | what | yaha'o | ye | ya | yana |
| 8.  | not | dalø | ada | babu | dalda |
| 9.  | all | pyaddø | kwe | Kwe? | bet |
| 10. | many | nkyau | hwedi | de | utat |
| 11. | one | øbdø | cin/dø/øvdø | gaa | øvdø |
| 12. | two | yølø | ilø | yor | yør |
| 13. | big | wayatinne | damra | gos's | uyat |
| 14. | long | ødwøle | izisi | mseb | mwar |
| 15. | small | øbleke | cammi | rekwu | møsi |
| 16. | woman | nidda | neta | ne'a | neta |
| 17. | man | wabgubu | ørmø | kyampo? | campa |
| 18. | person | nette | noco | net | not |
| 19. | fish | gyanu | géné | gyan | øbgyan |
| 20. | bird | øbnu | nema | uno? | øbno |
| 21. | dog | øb'o | omo | ubø? | øb'o |
| 22. | louse | kwarkwata | korkoto | kurkuta | korkota |
| 23. | tree | ebte | ce | ute? | øbte |
| 24. | seed | gwø | go | go? | øbgwø |
| 25. | leaf | ødba | køva | uwa? | uwan |
| 26. | root | øsgølø | øvgøru | uger | øbgør |
| 27. | bark | øtkwu | k'kwøkwø | ukeg | uko |
| 28. | skin | ubangø | u'wede | ubar | uba |

to writing. C'lela may claim to have been reduced to writing but the claim cannot be substantiated as no systematic writing system exists. What actually obtains are individual transcriptions which are neither offically recognised nor even collectively harmonized. It is therefore pertinent in this situation to stick to this criteria if only to allow for greater objectivity in determining cognates.

[17] R.C. Troike, Op.cit.

| | | | | | |
|---|---|---|---|---|---|
| 29. | flesh | ucømø | nømø | m'ap | m'ap |
| 30. | blood | mhye | mhibø | mhyø | mhyø |
| 31. | | | | | |
| 32. | grass | ødgwa | c'gwe | øsgø | øtgwa |
| 33. | egg | ødge | ødgyan | ørge? | ørge |
| 34. | horn | øbkalo | kkare | ukar | øbkar |
| 35. | tail | øbturu | twere | utør | øbtor |
| 36. | feather | øbkaho | k'kéné | ukyar | øbcan |
| 37. | hair | is'hi | øvhi | is'hi | is'hi |
| 38. | head | ødhi | ødhi | ørhi | ørhi |
| 39. | ear | | ucøn | | øtøn |
| 40. | eye | isi | ødisø | øryis | ør'is |
| 41. | nose | ørsømø | ødwen | urho? | ørsa |
| 42. | mouth | unu | knwø | unu | unu |
| 43. | tooth | ninu | ninø | øni | nun |
| 44. | tongue | øreme | ødreme | ødreme | ørrerem |
| 45. | claw | kujebø | kukbu | kanku | karanku |
| 46. | foot | kane | una | una? | una? |
| 47. | knee | ørzwønø | ødrwin | rwøn | ørjon |
| 48. | hand | ukumu | akoma | ukom | ukom |
| 49. | belly | ødmene | ødbøtø | ørmen | ørmen |
| 50. | neck | gegse | toro | ucor | gekes |
| 51. | breast | øre | øddøn | ørde | ødde |
| 52. | heart | øbromø | øvdumu | ørhu? | ørhur |
| 53. | liver | øjabø | ød'debe | ørjab | jab |
| 54. | drink | øswa | ømso | swo? | uswo? |
| 55. | eat | ølle | krya | re? | ure |
| 56. | bite | mhahø | s'epe | uhyan | uhyan |
| 57. | see | mhyanø | uheno | uhyan | unhay |
| 58. | hear | mhogo | unhongo | hone? | hog |
| 59. | know | nnahe | snapa | nap | nap |
| 60. | sleep | mlevø | ømløvø | mreu | mreg |
| 61. | die | mmale | awø | mmar | mmar |
| 62. | kill | ølho | ød'hwe | ho? | uhog |
| 63. | swim | mswab | s'hogo | swag | swab |
| 64. | fly | myønø | s'bugu | mhuks | yonne |
| 65. | walk | mha | s'noka | orheu | mha? |
| 66. | come | hane | noka | han | hane |
| 67. | lie | nliti | ød'løcu | ødloi | øriret |
| 68. | sit | ricamø | ød'soco | ci'it | riset |
| 69. | stand | ese | ød'esbo | ine? | ør'is |
| 70. | give | yal'un | unese | ya'as | niyase |
| 71. | say | ma$^2$ | vataze | Ze$^2$ | mwar |
| 72. | sun | ndho$^2$ | ødhwen | nonoho$^2$ | ørho? |

| 73. | moon | øbjili | pete | uren | pyat |
| --- | --- | --- | --- | --- | --- |
| 74. | star | øbbele | keba | rakrend | heger |
| 75. | water | ømbø? | mho | mho? | mbo? |
| 76. | rain | uyø | menke | nkim | uyø |
| 77. | stone | ohale | ødtare | orta'ar | ortar |
| 78. | sand | mhilgi | ch'mama | mhu? | mhyarge |
| 79. | earth | cihi | cihwin/ucopo | øtba | mhog |
| 80. | cloud | øboto | ch'wece | | øtkør |
| 81. | smoke | mhitti | ødhyon | mhui | ørsa |
| 82. | fire | ula | hwela | ura? | ura? |
| 83. | ash | mcua | ømtonh | mcau | mca |
| 84. | burn | u'ndo | sdwah | mdo | udog |
| 85. | path | nøbø | k'leve | cøu | hwøn |
| 86. | mountain | ndalo | seme | uta'ar | uror |
| 87. | red | gyazø | jozo | gyazo | mzan |
| 88. | green | mløgø | ømyoro | otrer | mrab |
| 89. | yellow | øllu | c'gollo | itrø | tøro |
| 90. | white | moko | pusuu | puswo | pus'o |
| 91. | black | limi | irimi | rimwo | rim'o |
| 92. | night | utentete | jopo | mtet | mgyep |
| 93. | hot | mdøngø | ømdøngø | mhog | mdøng |
| 94. | cold | mtulu | k'tudu | uhøu | mtor |
| 95. | full | cusø | uhyøu | custe | sog |
| 96. | new | pu'o | ipoyø | pu'o | po'o |
| 97. | good | ømleve | ikasi | orbo | so'o |
| 98. | round | nare | ødrigimsø | mrig | ryak |
| 99. | dry | mhwa | uhoke | uho'og | gag |
| 100. | name | rigimi | dinø | ørji? | ørdin |

In the analysis of Zuru material, maximum and minimum number of cognates are given for each pair-wise comparisons.

## Results Of Comparison:

Figures in Table 2 below represent the results obtained by comparing pairs of languages. Two languages are compared for cognate words and in each comparison maximum and minimum of cognates are counted. Thus, each square in Table 2 contains two readings representing maximum and minimum number of cognates respectively. Each reading is written as a fraction, with the numerator representing number of cognate words and the denominator the total number of words available for each pair-wise comparison.

## Table 2

|    | Bg | | Cl | | Dk | | Fk | |
|----|----|----|----|----|----|----|----|----|
| Bg |   |   | 62/99 | 1532 | 70/98 | 1135 | 73/99 | 998 |
|    |   |   | 60/99 | 1639 | 67/98 | 1279 | 70/99 | 1135 |
|    | 3½ | 7 | 1-3 | 1-6½ | 2-2½ | 2-6 | 3-2 | 3- 5½ |
| Cl | 62/99 | 1532 |   |   | 62/98 | 1532 | 61/100 | 1639 |
|    | 60/99 | 1539 |   |   | 59/98 | 1639 | 59/100 | 1749 |
| Dk | 70/98 | 1135 | 62/98 | 1532 |   |   | 72/98 | 1043 |
|    | 67/98 | 1279 | 59/98 | 1639 |   |   | 69/98 | 1182 |
| Fk | 73/99 | 998 | 61/100 | 1639 | 72/98 | 1043 |   |   |
|    | 70/99 | 1135 | 59/100 | 1749 | 69/98 | 1182 |   |   |

Also recorded against each of the two readings in each square are the corresponding figures of divergence in terms of years, computed on the basis of the standard formula:

$$t = \frac{\log c}{2 \log r}$$

t represents the time of separation or time-depth, and by this formular is equal to the logarithm of the assumed percentage of cognates, c divided by twice the logerithm of separation, r. r is a constant and is given a high rate of retention value of 86%.

In the third colum of Table 2 fot example, the first square contains results obtained by comparing Banganci and C'léla. The first reading of 62/99 indicates a total of 62 cognate words out of a total of 99 words compared.

To obtain t, the time of separation between Banganci and C'léla, the fraction 62/99 is first converted into percentage. This gives 63%. With constant value of 86% for r,

$$t = \frac{\log 63\%}{2 \log 86\%} = \frac{-0.200659}{-0.131003} = 1.531713$$

To express t in terms of years, the figure 1.531713 is multiplied by 1000. t is therefore equal to 1532 years.

With the second reading of 60/99 (= 61%),

$$t = \frac{\log 61\%}{2 \log 86\%} = \frac{-0.2146701}{-0.131003} = 1.638655.$$

Expressed in terms of years, t = 1639 years.

Table 3 contains actual computations for the value of t for all comparisons shown on Table 2.

## Table 3.

| Cognates per number of words compared | Cognates expressed in % | Log c | 2 Log r | t | Expressed in Millenium |
|---|---|---|---|---|---|
| 62/69 | 63% | -0.2006594 | -0131003 | 1.5317161 | 1532 |
| 60/99 | 61% | -0.1246701 | -0.131003 | 1.6386655 | 1639 |
| 70/98 | 71% | -0.1487416 | -0.131003 | 1.1354061 | 1134 |
| 67/98 | 68% | -0.167491 | -0.131003 | 1.278528 | 1279 |
| 73/99 | 74% | -0.1307682 | -0.131003 | 0.998276 | 998 |
| 70/99 | 71% | -0.1487416 | -0.131003 | 1.1354061 | 1135 |
| 62/98 | 63% | -0.2006594 | -0.131003 | 1.5317161 | 1532 |
| 59/98 | 60% | -0.2218487 | -0.131003 | 1.6934627 | 1693 |
| 61/100 | 61% | -0.2146701 | -0.131003 | 1.6386655 | 1639 |
| 59/100 | 59% | -0.2291479 | -0.131003 | 1.7491806 | 1749 |
| 72/98 | 73% | -0.1366771 | -0.131003 | 1.0433127 | 1043 |
| 69/98 | 70% | -0.1549019 | -0.131003 | 1.1824302 | 1182 |

## Analysis Of Results

Arndt[18] observed that it was a common practice for researchers to put the theory and technique of glottochronology to a searching test within a sizeable system of related languages or dialects where historical, literary and phonological data were available. He demonstrated this in a work of Germanic where evidence obtained from glottochronological investigations were used to attest the claims made by the widely held tripatite theory of quasigenetic decent of Germanic dialects.

Troike[19] in the work on six Turkic languages, also used evidence from glottochronological investigations to show close correspondence of dates obtained from glottochronological counts to known historical developments. In this manner therefore, new evidences are always secured to check the existing position. However, in the event of non-availability of some known facts, as in the present, strict compliance with the basic assumptions of glottochronology, relied upon as effective dates of separation of related languages. The dates in turn provide certain valuable checkpoints for important events of ethnic and lingusitic history.

Table 2 shows figures of divergence in terms of years. In table 4, the years are converted into dates, computed by subtracting the divergence figures from 1980 (chosen as an arbitrary date). Two sets

---

18 W.W Arndt, "The performance of glottochronology in Germanic", Language, XXXV, 1959, P.180-92.
19 R.C. Troike, *Op.cit*

of dates are given: the top most date representing the maximum divergence date, and the bottom date, the minimum.

## Table 4

|    | Bg       | Cl       | Dk       | Fk       |
|----|----------|----------|----------|----------|
| Bg |          | 448 AD   | 845 AD   | 982 AD   |
|    |          | 841 AD   | 701 AD   | 845 AD   |
| Cl | 448 AD   |          | 448 AD   | 841 AD   |
|    | 841 AD   |          | 287 AD   | 231 AD   |
| Dk | 845 AD   | 448 AD   |          | 937 AD   |
|    | 701 AD   | 287 AD   |          | 798 AD   |
| Fk | 982 AD   | 341 AD   | 937 AD   |          |
|    | 845 AD   | 231 AD   | 798 AD   |          |

The four languages in our investigation can be divided into two groups with regard to dates of split. Group one consists of Banganci, Dukkanci and Fakkanci. Split within this group must have taken place between the 8th and 10th century AD. This group is contrasted with group two, whose only member is C'lela. Split between C'léla on one hand, and the languages in group one on the other hand, must have taken place between the 3rd and 5th century AD.

## Conclusion

In this chapter an attempt was made at subjecting some four languages of the Plateau Benue-Congo family of Zuruland to a glottochronological investigation. The languages have shown remarkable degree of relatedness as evidenced by the relatively high percentages of cognates obtained as a result of pair-wise comparison of the languages. We wish to infer from this occurence of high numbers of cognates a very close affinity between the languages, which in all probability suggests cogent genetic relationship. This inference, as it stands, seems to enhance the validity of our results considering the fact that our attempt in the glottochronological analysis of the four languages had been, from the outset, in strict compliance with one of the fundamental requirements of glottochronology, i.e. that the application of its methods shall necessarily be only on 'related languages.'

Chapter Four

## The Evolution And Development Of The Economies Of The People Of Kasar Zuru Before C. 1900 A.D.

*by*
**Dr. S.U. Lawal**

## Introduction

If the study of the history of the people of Kasar Zuru, like that of the societies of the middle Niger, has been a neglected field so far in Nigerian historical studies, this neglect stems as we saw in Chapter One from two erroneous assumptions in Nigerian historiographical traditions.[1] The first of these is the pre-occupation of historians with the so-called centralised societies. In tune with the Nationalist historiography of yore, the vogue has been the historical studies of monarchies, dynasties, commerce and trade routes, such that societies that have been perceived as lacking of these are completely neglected. Rather, they become object and subject of anthropological and ethnographical passion and studies. So that as noted by Freund,

> For Africanists, the economy was a factor in society to be discussed separately from (if it received much attention at all) political or social developments. Analysis consisted of a history of trade at the expense of production, domination, sexual relations and other, more fundamental aspects.[2]

Such that for us who are interested and concerned with aspects of economic history there is a hiatus of analysis and understanding even for those societies that could be said to have got all the perquisites to invoke the curiosity of the scholar. In fact, it is even worst for scholars that are interested in the aspects of the material like of the people of such societies. At least for them, they have nothing to start with, and therefore have to grope about not only in establishing their problematic

---

[1] Kasar Zuru is used in this chapter to refer to the present day Zuru Emirate which is now encapsulated in the Zuru and Sakaba/Wasagu Local Government areas of Sokoto state. It is situated in the south-eastern corner of the state and is bounded in the south and south-east by Magama (Niger State) and Yauri Local Government; by Yabo Local Government to the West; and shares border with Anka Local Government to the east. See P.D. Perera.M.J. Sidhu, and J. Taylor, *Survey of Settlements in Sokoto State*, Ministry of Economic Planning, Sokoto 1981.

[2] B.Freund. *The Making of Contemporary Africa: The Development of African Society Since 1800*, Indiana University Press, 1984, P.6

of study but also in justifying that problematic as worthy of historical scholarship.

The other erroneous assumption also flows out of the old persepective of studying African history. This concerned the fetish with societies that could readily make available to the scholar sources that are considered 'traditional', that is written sources, archaelogical data and oral traditions as supplement. So that societies that were not literate and are yet to evoke the interest of archaelogists are considered an anathema, difficult to study, because they could not easily be punctuated by the spectacle of the scholar.

These assumptions are, however, happily loosing hold on historical tradition in African scholarship. Thus even for 'curiosity sake', historians are taking the gauntlet from anthropologists and ethnographers, at least to explain the unique. Now historians have been asked to answer for the so-called stateless or less centralised societies why they never developed a superstructure commensurate with their economic base. Also the gradual ascendance of marxist tradition in African studies has also greatly helped in puncturing the proclivity in producing political and dynastic histories. At least that will not do in explaining the economic problems of the continent after over two decades of acquiring the 'political kingdom.'[3]

This has also brought to question the fetish with the supposedly 'traditional source! For to explain the materiality of the quagmire the continent is in, Africanists have come to accept the potency of other sources. In particular, scholars have realised the cogency in calling into use other diverse sources like linguistic and glottochronoiogical sources, ethnographic mapping, environmental data, and any other source that could be relevant in unriddling what has come to be seen as the 'African dilemma'.[4] Beside, the potency of theory has also been gradually accepted as an indispensable tool in the analysis and understanding of African societies.[5]

Examples abound of studies of what have refused to be constrained by problems of sources in studying societies that have hitherto been neglected.[6] And if we have to do justice to the Zuru

---

[3] See, A.J. Temu and B. Swai, H*istorians and Africanist History: A Critique*, London, Zed Press, 1981, Chapter 3

[4] On fetishism of facts in African History see A.J. Temu, "Cults of facts and Festishism in Professional African History", *Postgraduate Seminar Papers*, A.B.U. Zaria 1978; and ibid, chapter 4.

[5] *ibid*, chapter 1.

[6] For example, A. Obayemi "The Yoruba and Edo Speaking peoples and their neighbours before 1600", In J.F.A. Ajayi and M. Crowder (eds) *History of West Africa*. Vol.I, second edition 1976; D. Northrup *Trade Without Rulers: Pre-Colonial Trade Among the Ibo*,

History Project and make our analysis of the history of Zuru people transcend the given assumptions about them, we have to go about our study on the right bearing. This involves making use of a wide array of sources that for our purpose will help us see through what may not easily be seeable to others. We have to go right down to the base to see how these people produce and reproduce their lives and society overtime for them to have developed the political and cultural institutions that could have made them knowable or unknowable in the past, which means we have to call into relevance here the cogency of theory in historical scholarship and employ in such an endevour a wide range of sources that are for the time being extant.

This paper therefore, attempts a preliminary analysis of the economic foundation and development of the peoples of Kasar Zuru up to about the period of the advent of the colonialist. This will use essentially not only secondary sources and data derived from the archives, but also archaelogical evidences and inferences where possible and feasible. The paper will also benefit from the fieldwork by the author amongst the people of Kasar Zuru during which oral sources were collected.[7] Ethnographic and environmental data will also be called into use in the study.

But if we take the stumping ground of the historian to be the past, an understanding of which involves an analysis of the interaction of man with man and with his environment overtime, we have to first of all understand the environmental setting, for us to appreciate the parameters within which the Zuru people eked out a living, reproduced themselves and made history worthy of a sponsored research and study by the Zuru Emirate Development Society.

## The Material Environment

It is important, even at the pains of repeating some of the things discussed earlier in chapter two, to bring out here the nature of the material environment of our area so as to appreciate the parameter within which our people developed their economy and society. Our area of study lies in the south-estern part of the Sokoto State. The districts of Kebbi, Gummi and Bukkuyum border it in the north and the emirates of Yauri and Kontagora share borders with it in the south and south-east. Zuru Emirate is bounded in the west by Gwandu and

---

London 1976; and T M. Makar, "A History of political change Among the Tiv in 19th and 20 centuries", *Unpublished Ph.D. Thesis*, A.B.U. Zaria, 1975.

[7] I wish to acknowledge the help of Mallam Bello (S) Magawataa with whom I traversed the length and breadth of Kasar Zuru in the course of the fieldwork.

Yauri Emirate while in the east its border is shared with Kuyambana district.[8]

In topographical terms, the area lies in between the transition zone between the High Plains of Hausaland and the Niger trough.[9] The overall altitude is from 700 ft to over 1,000 ft, increasing to the east and reaching more than 2,000 ft east of Bena.[10] As we shall see, the topography came to have a lot of bearings in the peopling and economy of the people of this area.

This topography has informed two sharply defined divisions of the area. The first is a narrow range of stormy hills along the western boundary generally between two to six miles wide but with a greater depth to the south.[11] The other area is the plain land to the east which consists of a low watershed which runs east and west across the centres of our area, with the drainage to the north being into the *Gulbin ka* and to the south into the *Gulbin Boka* and Molendo river systems. This area is well-watered and attractive for habitation and is dissected by a large number of small streams and *fadama*. Consequently, water can be found almost everywhere at a depth of 15-20 ft.[12] At various points the *fadamu* of the region give rise to fertile alluvial plains important for growing some crops and dry-season farming.

Geologically the area is underlain by ancient crystalline precambraian basement with outcrops of granitic rocks. Soil conditions vary greatly, and support a vegetation which is transitionary, between Northern Guinea Savannah and Sudan/Savannah, characterised, where not modified by cultivation, by fine-leaved acacias together with some of the broader-leaved types of the more Southerly climate.[13] The area is thus covered by a more or less continuous grass cover but in the lower wetter parts, trees grow as to suppress the grass growth. But we should note that these vegetational features have over the years been inundated by human activities, especially due to the nature of settlements and the farming method of the past which was characterised by long-bush fallowing as we shall see.

We said the soil conditions are not uniform in the area. But the basic soil types are the more extensive sandy brown soils (*H.Jigawa*) and the alluvial soils of the rivers and stream beds of the *fadamu*.

---

[8] P.H. Perera et.al, Op. cit.

[9] R.K. Udo, *Geographical Regions of Nigeria*, Ibadan, 1967

[10] See "Some notes on Zuru and its Peoples" *Intelligence Report, Sokoto* State History Bureau, File No, Zuru Emirate History /2.

[11] See "Brief Historical Background of the Division/Districts Zuru", SSHB, 2/32/355, File No. HIST/1.

[12] *ibid.*

[13] Some Notes on Zuru and its People"..., "*Op.cit.*

While the *Jigawa* soils could be less fertile, they are more widespread and support such staples as guineacorn, *acca*, millet, tubers (*gwaza, makara*, etc.) and beans. The *fadamu* on the other hand sustain crops and vegetables like rice, tomatoes, sugar-cane and tobacco.[14]

As for aridity in the area generally, this increases from south to north, and rainfall varies accordingly, ranging from 36 inches per year in the southern and south-eastern parts to 27 inches per year in the north and north-western parts. Most of the rainfall occurs between the months of June and September. And as we should expect, rainfall, the vegetational cover types, and soil have had great influence on the evolution and development of settlements and economies of the people of Kasar Zuru.

## Early Settlements and Evolution of Economy

If anything has evoked the passion of past scholarly endeavours in the study of Kasar Zuru, it is the origin, peopling and formation of communities in the area. Attempts have concentrated in identifying the autochtones and then the origin and sources of migrants. While this could be an important historical exercise, such endeavour in our area of study have come to assume political undertones.[15] Each of the five or so groups habiting our area seem to want to be vindicated as the original inhabitants and therefore see the other groups as latter migrants or even intruders.

This trend, though can be obscurantist to scholarly endeavours should not be suprising to us. This is because politics permeates the nature and process of the production of all knowledge through scholarship. The pretension to science and objectivism notwithstanding, the production of all knowledge is a political issue laden with heavy dosages of value judgements.[16] And therefore, for the scholar, he cannot run away from taking sides, but, to as much as possible see that he is on the side of the people and the progress of the society he has chosen to study. Which means for the historian of Kasar Zuru, his object should not only be in tracing the peopling of the area. Much more, he has to concern himself with the primordal issue of how the people, in interaction with the environment and themselves, produced and reproduced themselves, and how this process of production and reproduction brought about the evolution(s) of the economy and society. As we know, Kasar Zuru has been

---

[14] See "Brief Historical Background of the Division/Districts Zuru,..." *Op. cit.*

[15] J.I. Ganya, "The History of Zuru", Final Year Project, History ept. College of Education, Sokoto; and See also P.G. Harris, *Sokoto Privincial Gazetter*, MS, 1938.

[16] B. Swai, "How the past is Politically Inspected and Historically Produced", *Lecture in Honor of Prof. B.Pachai*, University of Sokoto, March, 1985

habited through history by diverse peoples. Principally these have been the Dakarkari (or *Lélna* as they call themselves) that are found mainly in Dabai District but also very much widespread all over our area; the *Achifawa* or *Dukkawa* dominating in Sakaba District; the *Fakawa* of Fakai District but also found in some numbers in Danko District; the *Bangawa* of Danko District and some trickles of them in Fakai District; the *Katsinawan Laka* that are found mainly in Wasagu and Bena areas of Wasagu District and the *Kambarawa* associated with Sakaba District (see table 1).

Table 1: Tribal Statistics, 1945

| Name | Zuru | Dabai | Danko | Fakai | Sakaba | Wasagu | Total |
|---|---|---|---|---|---|---|---|
| Dakarkari | 5257 | 19238 | 5279 | 2923 | 3307 | 6770 | 42774 |
| Fakai | 73 | 13 | 2001 | 10216 | | | 12303 |
| Dukawa | | 256 | | 241 | 2819 | | 3316 |
| Bangawa | | | 2579 | 73 | | | 2652 |
| Achifawa | | | | | 2158 | | 2158 |
| Katsinawan | | | | | | | |
| Laka | 45 | 42 | | | 48 | 6215 | 6350 |
| Gimbanawa | 101 | 169 | | 5711 | | | 5981 |
| Hausawa | 982 | 335 | 68 | 1723 | 1816 | 171 | 5095 |
| Kambari | 23 | 8 | | 36 | 1007 | | 1074 |
| Fulani | 32 | 62 | 27 | 1052 | | | 1073 |
| Nufawa | 36 | 11 | | 63 | | | 110 |
| Yarbawa | 31 | 12 | | 35 | | | 78 |
| Adarawa | 25 | 36 | 36 | | 462 | | 523 |
| Baribari | 22 | 17 | | 53 | | | 92 |
| Gungawa | | | | 45 | | | 45 |
| Zabarmawa | 15 | 8 | | | | | 23 |
| Gwangawa | 8 | 7 | | | | | 15 |
| Total | 6650 | 20214 | 9954 | 22633 | 11155 | 13156 | 83762 |

Source: *Nak Zurna 81/Vol.2: Annual Reports*

So far, the most important sources (as was seen in Chapter Two) that could help us study the early peopling of this area are for the time being not extant. This is principally due to lack of archaeological excavations in the area, and as we noted earlier, and the nonexploration of linguistic, ethnographic and other sources. And if the Zuru Emirate History Project is to make any break-through in our understanding of the history of people of the area, it should do through the unearthing and incorporation of these types of sources in its historiography. But it is because of the dearth of these sources that some scholars have tended to see the Zuru Emirate in the past as a 'no-Man's land.[17] This could be because readily available sources allow us

---

[17] S.U. Lawal "The Use and Relevance of History" *Public Lecture Delivered to the History Club College of Education, Sokoto*, April 1987.

go only as far back as about 1700 A.D. in mapping out the occupation of these areas.[18] But it seems doubtful if our area was empty before 1700 A.D. The environment we have described must have attracted Stone Age or Neolithic people into the area by the prospect of fertile land and good hunting ground. Also, the characteristic topography of our area is littered with hills and inselbergs, which have been characteristic centers of early settlements, in Northern Nigeria. This is because as Augi noted,

> The plains of the foot of all those hills and inselbergs where ancient settlements were founded, were invariably fertile. Coupled with the security they provided and the traditional attachment the early populations would have felt for them, the hills and inselbergs would be very ideal place to live around. [19]

Such areas were also significant as centres of early religious beliefs and practices associated with the worship of natural spirits (*Iskoki*) that are believed to inhabit major natural phenomena like rocks, huge trees, water and thicket.[20] The hills have also been important centres as source of *tama* (iron ore) and we know that this has also attracted waves of migrations into our area of study.[21] So that our area must have witnessed continuous habitation at least from the Stone Age period. It was during the Stone Age that man not only perfected his techniques of game hunting but also saw the transition from gathering of raw foods for subsistence to farming as an organised and systematic human activity. Evidence of the existence of this period and such transition in the Nigerian area goes back to about half a million years ago.[22] But in Kasar Zuru, due to what we noted earlier as the absence of archaelogical investigations, no direct evidence of the Stone Age period has been furnished as yet. This paucity of direct evidence of Stone Age man in Zuru Emirate should not to taken to imply that, *ipso facto,* the place was empty at that epoch. Evidence of the period in very close proximity to our area especially from the Late Stone Age time seems to indicate that our area must have been associated with that culture also. Thus Late Stone Age tools recovered on the Gagare River near the famous ancient settlement of the state of Zamfara (Dutsi), as

---

[18] "Brief History Background of the Divisions/Districts Zuru.," *Op. cit* P.3.

[19] A.R. Augi, "The Significance of Hills and Inselbergs in the History and Culture of the People of Hausaland", in *Zaruma*, A Culture Magazine of Sokoto State, February, 1982, P.18

[20] *ibid*, P.18-119.

[21] M. Adamu, *"The Hausa Factor in West Africa History*, A.B.U. Press 1981 P.32, and Y.B. Usman, *The Transformation of Katsina, 1400-1883*, A.B.U. Zaria, P.83

[22] See. R.C. Soper, "The Stone Age in Northern Nigeria" in *Journal of the Historical Society of Nigeria*. III, 2, 1065, P. 179-94.

(Dutsi), as well as along the Waleli River in the Gummi area of the ancient State of Zoma, are from areas historically closely associated with Kasar Zuru, especially as regards sources of migrations.[23] For example, Dutsi haas been linked with the tradition of origin of the Lélna while the state of Zoma was believed to have at one time brought parts of Donko and some Lélna under its suzerainty.[24]

Evidences of Late Stone Age culture has also been reported from other areas that had great and close relations with the peopling, and migrations into our area. Y.B. Usman has noted the 'continuous settlement since the Late Stone Age' in the Katsinan Laka region following the discovery of Stone axes and microciths along the banks of the Sokoto River and its tributaries.[25] From Kebbi, too, pieces of evidence of the Stone Age culture have been uncovered.[26] And we all know the supposed claim of the origins of the Lélna, the Bangawa and the Dukkawa from Kebbi, while the area of Katsina Laka is said to provide the origin of the people of Bena and Wasagu (among others), and even of some Lélna.[27]

Consequently, we can infer with some certainty that Stone Age population did obtain in Kasar Zuru as farmers and hunters using Stone tools before they gradually but surely went through the transition to the Iron Age. Again, there is no direct evidence relating to how and the time this epoch making transition took place in our area. But as Bitiyong showed earlier, there is the existence of early iron working sites in several areas of Kasar Zuru. When these are thoroughly studied and the results published, our understanding of this important phenomena and its consequences, will be further enhanced. But evidence from an area bordering Kasar Zuru to the South-West seem to indicate that the place could have gone through the transition from stone tools to iron usage at an early time. Iron working has been dated in Yelwa to the second century BC.[28] In particular, we should

---

[23] *ibid*, P. 16-93; and A.R. Augi, "The Gobir Factor in the Social and political History of the Rima Basin C. 1650-1808 A.D. *"Unpublished Ph.D Thesis*, A.B.U. Zaria 1984.

[24] Some elders of L'elna at Dabai are recorded to have derived their origin from somewhere in Bukkuyum in Gummi area, which was the principal centre of the State of Zoma. That a man from the region went to Dabai to hunt and then settled there with his family, see M.M. Gujiya, "The Dakkarkari people (Lélna)' part 1 in *Zaruma* March 1983, P.10-11; and P.G. Harris, Gazetteer ... *Op.cit* P.255-7.

[25] Y.B. Usman, The Transformation... *Op.cit* P.7; and R.C. Soper, The Stone Age..." *Op.cit* P. 190.

[26] See, A.R. Augi, "The Gobir Factors..." *Op.cit* P. 1-201-202.

[27] P.G. Harris, *Gazetteer,...Op.cit* P.255-7. That Lélna of Kanya, Chinoko and even in Zuru claim that they are of Katsina Origin, see *proceedings of the Zuru Workshop*.

[28] See, A.J. Priddy, "An Iron Age Site Near Yelwa Sokoto Provience: Preliminary Report" in *West African Archaelogical News Letter*, No. 12 1970, P.20-32

should note that Ade Obayemi has linked this iron using culture of Yelwa with the Kambarawa, a people that have been associated with our area as one of the earliest inhabittants of the area around Sakaba District.[29]

Therefore, all said, it seems safe to say that early populations obtained in Zuru land. These people witnessed the transition from Stone to Iron Ages and were the earliest settlements of farmers, hunters, and iron workers here. Their population was expanding with time due to agriculture and migrations which further consolidated their ability to tame their fauna and flora for games and agriculture. It is of significance that we noted that with the exception of the Fakkawa most of the people of our area trace their habitation of the area to hunter-migrants. This was so even for 18th century migrations like that of the Katsinawan-Laka of Wasagu.[30] For these early settlements, agriculture was perfected on the cultivation of guineacorn, millet, *acca, tamba*, rice, beans etc. Hence also we noted that this early agriculture was based on the system of shifting cultivation or long bush fallowing. And the development and use of iron technology we noted must have enhanced not only hunting and agriculture but also other service industries that developed in that area.

These early settlers, in consonance with their agricultural type, lived in nucleated hamlets scattered all over the area. With time it was obvious that ours will be a recipient of more settlers with various population movements that came into our area. These migrations were both from internal and external sources, even though much attention seems to have been paid to the later. While migrations from outside could have originated from many areas, it seems that those that came from the north, north-west and possibly the south of Kasar Zuru were the most significant.[31] One could in fact view the various and sometimes conflicting traditions of migrations from especially Kebbi,

---

[29] A. Obayemi, "The Ulaira Site and The History of the Yauri Area, Some Questions", *Seminar Paper, Dept. of History*, A.B.U. Zaria, 1979.

[30] Besides other examples already cited, Kele, Isgogo and Rambo were all said to be hunters who founded the settlements bearing their names, see P.G. Harris "Notes on the Dakarkari people of Sokoto Provience, Northern Nigeria", *Journal of the Royal Anthropological Institute*. Vol IXVIII, 1938; J.I. Ganya, "The History ..." *Op.cit* P.3; and H.N.D. Ribah, "A History of Rebnah" *Final Year Project*, History Dept., College of Education, Sokoto n.d. P.7

[31] The claims of the Achifawa descent from the east seems unplausable. As the relations of the people of Borgu and Illo, they with other like the Nupe, Igala, Yoruba, Idoma, etc belong to the Kwa lingustic group which Obayemi mapped as developing and spreading from around the Niger-Benue confluence Area. It seems therefore, that the origin of the Achifawa may have a southern and not eastern source, see A. Obayemi' "The Yoruba and ... *Op.cit*.

Zamfara and Katsina as attempts to recall the various waves and patterns of migrations that have emptied here. There is no denying the fact that factors like the rise of the kingdoms of Katsina, the consolidation of the state of Kebbi with the founding of a new capital at Birnin Kebbi in the 18th century, and the cataclysmic upheavals and changes that took place in the central Rima Basin especially between Gobir and Zamfara led to our area being affected in more ways than one.[32]

Migrations further served as a catalyst in economic development of our area. Firstly, these population thereby leading to the expansion of old settlements and the rise of new ones. Population growth stimulated further economic activities through the consolidation of agriculture, hunting and manufacturing. The ability to bring in more land under cultivation, and thereby increase their mastery over their environment through the development of service industries must have increased economic productivity and led to the development of exchange relation both within our area and with other regions. It seems the earliest forms of exchange involved the distribution of items like iron products, Shea-butter (*H.Mankade*), salt (*jan gishiri*), spice (*H.daddawa*) etc.

Migrations also led to the spread of occupational skills, crafts and certain institutions amongst the people. For example, the migration of *Katsinawan-Laka* into Kakihun must have fostered the iron working industry there. And the diversity of our peoples of study notwithstanding, migrations and interactions came to ensure some relative degree of similarity in some of their cultural and political institutions. Thus the *'Mgilø'* cult was common both among the Lélna, the Dukkawa and the Kambari, while *Makoki* (wøh) obtained among the Lélna, Dukkawa and Kambari. The institution, of *Golmo* and such festivals as the *Uhola* and *D'biti* also came to be widespread amongst many of the peoples of Kasar Zuru. [33]

All these developments we have been talking about so far helped to see to the formation and development of political and cultural communities in our area at least by the end of the 17th century. The polities that developed in the area varied and were not of equal status in relations to size, power, social structure and their influence or even economic base and their ability to control and benefit from commerce. Thus while among some Lélna, Dukkawa, the Kambari and the Makuku, most of their polities consisted of no more than single

---

[32] See for example, Y.B. Usman, *The Transformation... Op.cit;* A.R. Augi "The Gobir Factor... *Op.cit*; M.B. Alkali "A Hausa Community in Crisis: Kebbi in the 18th century" *Unpublished M. Thesis*. A.B.U. Zaria 1969; and G. Nadama, 'The Rise and Collapse of a Hausa State: Social & Political History of Zamfara", *Unpublished Ph.D. Thesis* A.B.U. Zaria 1977

autonomous settlements that have been approximated as village units, there obtained relatively large polities that incorporated several other settlements in such places as Danko, Dabai, Karishen, Fakai, Wasagu and Bena.[34]

The settlements and polities became prominent not only politically but also as economic centres. They were not only centers of political power and authority, but also important centres of production and exchange. Therefore, the economy of the people of Kasar Zuru came to be firmly rooted on a tripod of agriculture and hunting, manufacturing, and commerce. We shall now look at each of these, in some greater details beginning with agriculture.

## Relations of Production in Agriculture

That agriculture was basic to the economy and society of all the peoples of our area of study is beyond doubt. And what we have established already include the fact that farming was among the things that first attracted people to the area and has also greatly helped in shaping most of the institutions of the people. In fact, we shall see how the farming cycle became embedded and shaped the various institutions and festivals prevalent in the area.

We did establish that agriculture must have developed here at a very early time. Thus we inferred that the first farmers of Kasar Zuru were people of the Stone Age culture. This is more evident from the agricultural type that prevailed amongst most of our people up to the end of our period of long bush fallowing. This was one of the erliest agricultural systems developed by man due to his inability to ensure and regenerate the fertility of the land without leaving it to lie fallow. The system presisted up to the 19th century in Kasar Zuru because of abundance of land, the level of technological development, relative insecurity due to slave raids and the low level commodization of the economy.[35] All these combined not only to inform the land tenure system, but also the relations of production in agriculture.

The organisation and relations of production in agriculture and other productive activities of the people of Kasar Zuru of our period follows the general pattern of other similar societies in central Nigeria. For all the people in the area, land was shared out among the patrilineages that had some relative degree of usufruct rights over them. Rights over land seem to have been more pronounced in the large settlements like Danko, Kele, Fakai, Birnin-Tudu, Chonoko,

---

[34] M. Adamu, *The Hausa Factor... Op.cit* P.33-35

[35] On the system of agriculture see "Some notes...", op.cit P.1; interview with Mallam Kamso, 90 years, farmer, Tudun wada, Zuru on 26th December 1985 ZHP Tape 1; and also *Proceedings of the Zuru Workshop Tape 2*

Tsohon Birni (Sakaba), Karishen, etc. And for the small communities, rights over land seem less defined.

In all these societies, the elders and chiefs exercised some supervisory role over the distribution of land and agriculture generally. These involved settlement of disputes over land use and ownership and leading in the performance of rites concerning land and agriculture. And for these services, the elders and the various *Sarakuna*, (*Gomo* among the Lélna and the *Womo* or *Ashifa* of Karishen) were entitled to various services and tributes from the people.

The labour process involved in agricultural production involves all members of the lineages or the family working as a unit. Like similar societies, women had the function of reproducing the labour force and taking charge of the domestic chores. In some places, they also had their plots on which they grow crops like *acca,* beniseed and beans.[36] The harvests from these farms belong to the women which they used as they wanted, either for consumption, as gift or for the market.

As for the males, right from the time they were children, the art of farming was inculcated into them. From about the age of six, they learn how to farm using a miniature hoe, working from morning to afternoon. They also tend to pasture the domestic animals, and then learn the important skill of hunting by practising at an early age with miniature bows and arrows.[37] By the time they reach the age of fifteen they are ready to join the various organisations and groups that took over their preparation for the society.

By the time first rain falls, the people of Kasar Zuru would have retired to their farms in the bush to prepare the land for the planting season. They stay there on the farm for most of the farming season, coming into the towns only for certain festivals and after harvests. The labour force on the farms was provided by all members of the family under the leadership of the head of the family, who provided the seedlings from the harvest of the previous years. The output was under the charge of the head who uses it to feed the family, give out as gifts and for various feasts and ceremonies that were held at various times of the year. Some of the output was also entering the market as we shall see.

While the Hausa societies, for example have developed the communal labour system of *gayya* to supplement the agricultural labour needs of the various households, some of the people in our area also developed a similar practice the *dibohe* in addition to the institution

---

[36] H.D. Gunn and F.P. Conant, *People of the Middle Niger REGION, Northern Nigerian* London, 1960, P.23-35, 451 and passim.

[37] See M.M. Gujiya, "The Dakarkari People (Lélna)", Part II in ZARUMA, 6th edition P.11.

of *Golmo*. And as we said, the agricultural cycle of the people involved practices and ceremonies aimed at the propitiation of the various deities and earth spirits, from rains, fertility and good harvests and for thanksgiving services. Such as centred around the cult of *M'gilø*, and the festivals of *Uhola* and *D'biti*.

## Towards a Political Economy of Golmo and some Festivals

We did infer earlier that the various cultural and religious institutions developed by the people of Kasar Zuru have some inklings and were closely tied to agriculture and the economy. In this section, therefore, we wish to establish the materiality of the most important aspects of these cultural and religious practices as an integral part of the political economy of the societies of Kasar Zuru.

We all know that our area of study is a large one that like other African societies provided more of a problem of labour and technology than of the availability of land. And so our people developed very early, systems and institutions to provide for the optimal use and general spread of the available labour for all or most of the agricultural production units in the society. These were effectively ensured among most of our people of study by the institution of *Golmo*, which is a compulsory farm work done by suitors for about seven years on the farms of their prospective fathers-in-law. This was perfected most among the Lélna, the Dukkawa, the Fakawa, and the Bangawa.[38]

We have seen that by the age of twelve a boy would have been prepared enough to join various types of communal groups. These include the *C'rinø* (in Dabai the *D'bugu*). While these groups were mainly concerned with character training, members were forced to do other things. They had to do communal farming for the youngmen's (Lélna; *Yakenpana*) special farms. And while in these groups, members were organised into age sets, with each belonging to the same set as his age mates (Lélna; *Skeme*).

In these groups, the socialisation of the youths that we saw started in the family and continued. Members provided communal labour and learnt further the skills of hunting and wrestling. It is after about seven years in these groups that the members of the eldest age set began their *Golmo*. Among the Lélna, this is ushered in by a special farewell dance to C'*gamba* (adolescence) for the *Yakenpana*.[39]

During their period in *Golmo,* members are in an organisation similar to clubs, each with its officials and members of different ages. Thus while one is at his last year of service others could be in their

---

[38] On golmo see Ibid P.13; P.G. Harris, Gazetteer... *Op.cit* P. 264; and 'Some notes...'' *Op.cit* P.3.

[39] M.M. Gujiya, "The Darkarkari..." Part II *Op.cit* P.13.

first. They work as a unit on the farms of their various prospective fathers-in-law, working on each farm in turn during the farming season.[40] While this was going on, certain festivals and rites were observed at various times. At the end of the service, which is normally seven years for the Lélna, and could be less for the other people like the Fakkawa, Kelawa, Dukawa and Bangawa, the marriage takes place with the bride moving to join her husband.

*Golmo* is considered very vital and important amongst these people. Not only was it considered as the final initiation into life, it was the institution through which the patience, perseverance and manliness of young men are not only tested but exhausted in the attempt to test their readiness to stand life.[41] Those not having done *Golmo* are not considered manly enough and are so derided and even their burial ceremony was different. And for the Lélna, it was only after *Golmo* that a K'léla could be included into the councils of decision makers at either the clan or village level.[42]

The materiality of the institution of Golmo lies in the way and manner agricultural labour of the society was harnessed and distributed to the various farming units. *Golmo* ensures that labour force was optimally employed by making sure that any man with marriageable daughters, provided he himself did his service (golmo) as a youth, is thus assured of many years of free labour in his old age.[43] So that *golmo* could be a cultural or matrimonial affair, but at its core, it was fundamentally an economic phenomenon. As a labour mobilising and labour-utilising affair, one could even argue that *golmo*, plus the relative abundance of land and the low level of commoditization of agriculture, all helped to preclude the development of wage labour in agriculture and the economy generally. This had to wait for the colonial period when new market forces were injected into the economy and society.

Other religious and cultural institutions and festivals that came to be closely embedded to the economy, especially agriculture, were those involved in the propitiation of the earth spirits and thanksgiving for the wherewithal of, and the bounteous harvests. The most important of these in Kasar Zuru were the '*Uhol*a' and *D'biti* which were also closely tied to the *M'gilø* cult. These two ceremonies were normally celebrated at different times and in connection with the harvest of the two most important crops in the land.

---

[40] "Brief Historical... *Op.cit* P.3; See also interviews with Kamso, *Op.cit*.
[41] M.M. Gujiya, "The Dakarkari..." Part II *Op.cit* P.13.
[42] "Brief Historical... "*Op.cit* P.3
[43] P.G. Harris, *Gazetteer... Op. cit* P.3.

*D'biti* is held traditionally on the first day of the new year of the Lélna calendar and falls towards the end of August, that is when the rain is at its peak and the people were about to harvest *'acca'* (hungry rice). The festival entailed the *Sarkin Zaure*, (Gom-vud-købø) who is the chief priest of the *M'gilø* **cult**, going out of the town, accompanied by drummers and young wrestlers to give thanks to the spirit of *M'gilø* for all he did to make possible for the good harvest and also to pray for similar bounty with the other crops not yet harvested.

After that, the people retire to an open place where cooked guinea corn and salt are served and various activities especially wrestling took place up to night fall. The next morning, a special food was prepared to make the young men strong, after eating which they retire back to the bush to start harvesting the hungry rice.[44] The *'Uhola'* is a similar festival but was held on a sunday at a time guinea-corn is ripe for harvest. A watch-night service is held by the elders at the house of the *M'gilø* who is said to come down at mid-night to bless his followers. In the morning, the youth come down to the towns from the bush. Feasting then takes place, where rice, goat and dog meat are brought and served at the house of *M'gilø* to all those present. Beer was also served at this occasion but only to the elders. While feasting and drinking was continuing in the afternoon, people will move out of the town to give thanks to *M'gilø* for the harvests. After, wrestling and dancing took place and the next morning the harvest of guinea corn would start.

It is obvious that these two festivals must have developed simultaneously with agriculture, in close association with the cult of *M'gilø* which came to have wider influence and acceptance in our area. So that while each autonomous unit could have its own rites of ancestor worshipping and each family its 's'cepkor' or worship practices, the *M'gilø* cult seems to have become important and widespread at a time when settlements in our area were enlarging and various activities through which the people were interacting, especially farming and hunting, necessiatated the development of belief systems and practices that could unite them.

Consequently, the *M'gilø* cult became pervasive as representing a cosmology that is believed to be the agency through which men meet the earth spirits of their ancestors.[45] The ancestors and the earth spirits

---

[44] M.M. Gujiya, "The Dakarkari..." Part II P.13.

[45] *ibid*, P.12; and H.D. Gunn and F. Gonant, *Op.cit*, passim. For example among the Dukkawa, the most important deity is als the *M'gilø*. Followed by the *Ilga*. The latter is suppose to reside on a hill, Dukku, and is worshipped for two days every year at a time when guinea corn is about ripening. At that time the *Gom vud-købø* the priest of *Ilga*, will be accompanied by three elders to the Shrine for worship, and on their return, feasts and ceremonies followed and no one was supposed to leave the town that day, see E.C. Duff,

are held with awe and reverence by most of the people of Kasar Zuru as they are believed to be the protectors and providers for the living in terms of rains, fertility, peace and progress.[46]

Beside all these festivals and thanksgiving, the people also honour success in agriculture by the investiture of titles and other special privileges to those that have succeeded in farming. Special drum beatings were done to them and and their funeral rites at death were also differently special.[47] Thus activities during *Makoki/Wøh* (funerals) were fashioned in such a way as to honour those who were successful either as farmers, hunters or blacksmiths.[48]

For example, the main aim and object of a male *Lélna* and *Dukawa* is to have a proper funeral ceremony (wøh) which involves a desire for large attendance and also prolonged drumming.[49] For while each deceased person receives the original drumming on the *'V'Kiru'* separate beats differentiate and signify the achievements of each person. Thus:

> a chief or a village head or skilled blacksmiths and their wives and daughters... receives all grades of drumming. Similar honour is accorded to friends of the deceased chief or village head who may have given him valuable gifts. *Danwere* (chief of farming), less skilled blacksmiths and similar relations.. are saluted with drumming on the 'Ch'ganga'. Noted worriors.. and in the former days slave catchers received the C'gula, *kama*' beaten together, while hunters.. are accorded the 'Ch'chimchima different beats being given for the slayers of elephant, buffalo, hartebe astes and roan antelope. Dakarkari (sic) chiefs and (*gomgomno*) important men receive special beats on a drum called *'Cigongo.'*[50]

The *Kasinawan Laka* of our area also have their method of bestowing honour on success in agriculture in what they call *bukin dubu* (ceremony of a thousand).

Those who aspire to be *Sarkin Noma* made efforts to produce as much as one thousand bundles of grains. After harvest, the ceremony is held and the man with the largest harvest of a thousand bundles or more was turbanned the *Sarkin Noma* amidst feast and fanfare.[51]

---

"Gazetter of Kontagora province, in *Gazetteers of the Northern Kingdoms*, London, Frank Cass 1967 P.63.

[46] P.G. Haris, "Notes on..." *Op.cit*

[47] See *Proceeding of Zuru History Workshop*, Tape N.6

[48] E.C. Duff, *Op.cit* P.58, footnote 11

[49] *ibid*, P.58

[50] See group interview at the palace of Sarkin Wasagu on 23/12/85, Tape No. ZHP 6: *Proceedings of Zuru History Workshop*, Tape no 2. For a similar ceremony in Zamfara see G. Nadama, *Op.cit* P.100.

[51] See NAK-SOKPROF/S. 2524, *Annual Reports Southern Division* 1942.

All said, therefore, the various ceremonies and festivals of the people of Kasar Zuru were not a manifestation of primitive appearance, and certainly not 'primitive ideas' of 'pristine stage of beer' orgies as the colonialist saw them.[52] Rather, as systems of beliefs and practices, they had their cosmic and metaphysical significance, and were an integral part of the culture and religious milieu, and the political economy of the people as we have just seen. Consquently, they not only provided a focus and object in production, but also helped to increase productivity in agriculture, hunting,

## Hunting

Hunting played a similar role to agriculture in the development of the economy and society of our people. As a good hunting ground with abundant game, the area attractive, very early, as we said, people into the area. The hunting origin of some of the people have come to be ingrained in their traditions.[53] And as one of the earliest occupations of man in the area, like agriculture, it came to be embedded and informed greatly the economy and society of the area under study.

Hunting was mostly a dry season activity embarked upon in groups mostly after harvests have been taken in. Such expeditions could last for days and a successful return involved festivities and celebrations. Such meat as was returned with was normally consumed and shared out among the people for the community to know and appreciate how successful a hunter one has become. But it seems that by the end of the 18th century meat could have become one of the items entering trade, especially long-distance to places like Katsina.[54]

We have earlier on noted some of the honours and privileges attendant to be successful hunter. We said these included special drumming at one's funeral. And besides a befitting funeral, renowned hunters were also accorded respect by being given special titles and other privileges and recognitions.[55]

## Industry

Just like agriculture and hunting, manufacturing activities were very important to the society of Kasar Zuru and various industrial activities developed early amongst the people. These include iron smelting and iron working, pottery, mat weaving, leather and wood working, shea

---

[52] See Footnotes 24 and 30.

[53] See Footnotes 68.

[54] Oral interview, Mallam Kamso, *Op.cit*.

[55] It is certain that this table has under estimated the number of practitioners of some industries.

butter (Man kade nevmichrigø) production, processing of *dorawa* or *c'golo* seed to make *daddawa C'landa* (Kalwa seasoning), basket making, etc. Table 2 below is indicative of the relative size of some of the industries in the 1920.[56]

Table 2: List of Industry, Zuru Divsion 1920

| Industry | Number | Remarks |
| --- | --- | --- |
| Brewers (for sale) | 20 | Female only |
| Traders | 65 | Male or Female |
| Weavers | 30 | Male or Female |
| Dyers | 12 | Mostly males |
| Blacksmiths | 35 | Mostly males |
| Butchers | 15 | Mostly males |
| Carpenters | 3 | Mostly males |
| Mat Weavers | 23 | Mostly males |
| Canoe Builders | 2 | Mostly males |
| Potters | 2 | Females only |
| Smelters | 15 | Males only |

Source: *Gazetteer of Kontagora Province*, by E.G. Duff, in *Gazetteers of the Northern Provience of Nigeria Vol. 111. The Central Kingdoms.* Frank Cass London 1967 P. 35

The most important industry and the one that seems to have developed earliest is that of iron smelting and iron smithing. We alluded to this earlier when we talked about the transition from the culture of stone using to that of iron in the region. In fact, as noted by Y.B. Usman, the iron resources of the area was one of the factors that helped in the peopling of the area.[57] By the 18th century a lot of people from Katsina had moved to the area of Kakihun principally to exploit the iron one deposits of the area and for trade. Here, a trading polity was established which incorporated 'disparate clans' of the *Kamuku Achipawa*, *Lélna* and the *Kambari*, living in the area, that was exporting smelted iron to *Hausa* markets.[58] The *Kambari* and the Achifawa could have been the first people here to have developed the technology of iron working, with the technology probably been introduced from Yelwa in the south-west where we said iron technology obtained from about the second century B.C. Willet has

---

[56] Y.B. Usman Op.cit P.83-84; and M.Adamu Op.cit P.33-34.
[57] *ibid*, P.34.
[58] See F. Willet, "Nigeria" in P.L. Shinie (ed), *The African Iron Age*, Oxford, 1971 P. 1112.

recently included the area of Yelwa-Yauri as part of the NOK culture with its long tradition of iron working from about 500 B.C.[59]

All the same, the technology did spread early to other parts of Kasar Zuru. Thus beside the iron smelting and iron working centres of Kakihun, iron ore was also smelted at Morumo near Karishen and around Senchi in the Lélna area.[60] The present town of Zuru is underlain by iron ore deposits which have been mined from the 18th century.

The method and technology of iron smelting may have been similar to what obtained in Kasar Hausa as described by Jagger, Y.B. Usman and Nadama.[61] This involved professional smelters who congregate and travel to the various iron ore sites during the dry-season. The actual mining and smelting was done as an organised affair under a leader and could last for the whole season, after which the smelters could have smelted enough iron ore (*tama*) to go back either to sell or to use themselves.

Therefore, and as we shall see in greater details, trade developed very early between iron smelters and the blacksmiths. These blacksmiths, producing various items ranging from farming and hunting implements to other products concentrated at Kakihun, Karishen, Zuru (Lélna: Azuguru) and Senchi.[62] But one thing which is certain is that by the time the Zuru History is completed more iron working sites would have been discovered and these will make our knowledge of the industry much more comprehensive.

What we can say for now with some degree of certainty is that the industry was well developed during our period. Among the Achifawa they were using single bellows of goats skins, with a wooden nozzle tipped with iron.[63] This could be the general type of bellows used all over Zuru land. But we also know for sure that the occupation was an all male one and was hereditary and a part time affair that occupies their time in the dry season.[64] And we also know that the products of these blacksmiths have been an integral part of the items of exchange both in local and long distance commerce. Other industries that pre-occupied the peoples of our area like mat weaving, and dyeing were

---

[59] "Achifawa - Historical and Anthropological Report" by A.B. Mathews, NAK/MIN/PROF/125/1926.

[60] See P.J. Jaggar, "Kano City Black Smiths:, Pre-Colonial Distributions, Structure and Organisation", in *SAVANNA* Vol. 2, No.1; Y.B. Usman *Op.cit*; and G. Nadama, *Op.cit*.

[61] E.C. Duff, *Op.cit*. P.55; Y.B. Usman, *Op.cit*, P.83-84; and M. Adamu *Op.cit* 33-34

[62] "Achifawa - Historical..." *Op.cit*.

[63] "Brief Historical" *Op.cit* P.3; and Oral interview with Mallam Rikoto Maianguwa, farmer, 65 years. Tudun Wada Zuru, 26/12/85, Tape no. ZHP.2

[64] M.M. Gujya "The Dakarkari...", Part 2, *Op.cit* P.11

also the preserve of men. But others like pottery, beer brewing, calabash making, grinding, stone cutting, shea butter making and the manufacture of *daddawa* (cilanda) were all preserve of women. And according to Gujiya, girls at young age were taught not only to learn domestic household chores but also some 'industrial techniques of making' these things. And the products of these female industries were also entering the market.[65]

## Commerce

The development of exchange relations was also a very crucial factor in the evolution and development of the economics of the people of our area of study. These trades involved both what would be termed local and long-distance trade. The local trade involved exchange between the peoples of our area of study and certainly cut across ethnic and tribal lines. These involved exchange relations between such groups as farmers and hunters and the specialised occupational groups we have just seen like blacksmiths, potters, barbers, medicine men and so on.

By the end of our period, there has already developed specific market centres and market days to service the needs of the people.[66] For example, the Dukawa were obtaining products like iron, hoes and tobacco from the Lélna in exchange for products most especially medicine. The people of Bena and Wasagu could also have been exchanging meat and grains for iron products from the Lelna and the Achifawa. Hence by the end of our period the whole of the people in our area become tied into a closely knit economy through exchange relations.

By that time also long distance trade had become an important and entrenched aspect of the economy. These involved the importation of products like horses, salt (*Gishiri*), dogs, kolanuts, swords and cloth, (especially loin cloth: *Bante*) from areas as far as Kebbi, Zamfara, Gobir, Katsina, Nupe and Zazzau, and the export of *daddawa*, *Man kade*, (Shea Butter), tobacco, grains, honey, slaves, iron ore and iron products, etc. Among imported items also included decorated leather girdles, beads, coweries and brass bangles. These traders in Kasar Zuru centred in towns particularly Bena, Wasagu, Isgogo, Sanchi, Danko, Dabai, Karishen, Kakihun and Tsohon Birni (Sakaba).[67]

In these long-distance trades, the Hausa especially of Katsina played a prominent role. By the 18th century as we have seen, these Hausa traders have not only settled in our area of study but had

---

[65] H.D. Gunn and F.P. Conant, *Op.cit* P.37

[66] E.C.Duff, op.cit P.3; Oral Interview, John Zomi Rikoto; Clergy man, 75 years, Zuru 16/9/85, tape no ZHP 3; and Proceedings of Zuru History Worshop tape No. 2.

[67] M. Adamu Op.cit P.32; aand Y.B. Usuman *Op.cit* P.83

effectively linked the area in important exchange relations with the Kasar Hausa and Nupe. Thus Katsina was supplied with iron ore and iron products and slaves from Kakihun and Karishen by a trade route that passed through Birnin Kogo, Yandoto to Birnin Katsina. In exchange from Katsina was acquired salt, horses and leather products.[68] This trade was quite important for as Y.B. Usman suggested, there were agreements between Katsina and Karishen regarding the supply of slaves to the government of Katsina and also the treatment of Katsina merchants in the area. And Katsina seems to have been interested in the area, and the expedition during the reign of Gozo (C. 1796 - 1801) against Sarkin Karishen may be due to the latter's breach of some agreements.[69]

Another important trade route linked the area to the west and south-west to Yauri, Nupe, Nikki and then to Gonja from where Kasar Zuru acquired such products as kola, beads, brass products and cowries. For the Dukawa, it seems that this trade route had become very important to their economic life to the extent that if a man dies, he is buried with his 'feet towards the west and the head towards the east'. And the reason for this is to show that the Dukkawa 'always travel westwards to Tillo market, etc. and hardly ever eastwards.'[70]

Other trade routes effectively linked the area with Zamfara, Kebbi and Gobir. And besides slaves and iron products, the area was also exporting to its immediate neighbours in Zamfara and Kebbi consumables like *Man kade, Daddawa* and honey.[71]

In terms of organisation, the commerce of Kasar Zuru seemed to have been predicated on a similar line with that of Kasar Hausa.[72] In particular, we should note the role of the Hausa disapora community in Kasar Zuru in the facilitation of long-distance trade. Like other commercial diaspora, they provided that important foundation of 'cross cultural exchange by bringing both the economic and cultural gap between the local societies and that where the traders come

---

[68] *ibid*, P.83.
[69] E.C. Duff, *Op.cit* P.64.
[70] Group Interview at Wasagu, *Op.cit*.
[71] See for example, A.R. Augi "The Gobir..." *Op.cit;* G. Nadama *Op.cit*; Y.B. Usman, *Op.cit;* and I. Anagbogu "Trade in 19th century Sokoto - Zamfara Confluence Area, *Unpublished. M.A. Thesis* Ibadaan, 1980.
[72] See M. Adamu, *op.cit;* P.E. Lovejoy *Caravans of Kola: The Hausa Kola Trade, 1700-1900*, A.B.U. Press 1980; and A. Cohen, *Custom and Polities in Urban Africa: Study of Hausa Migrants in Yoruba Towns.*

from.'[73] These allowed the commercial diaspora advance the course of trade by providing services like brokeage, insurance, agency, accommodation and provisioning passing traders.

And while the local trade may initially have been based on a barter basis, by our period, various currencies have entered to mediate in both the local commerce and the long-distance trade. For the later, the most important currency was cowries which as we say being imported into the region. Other items that were used as currencies in the general trade of the area include cloth, salt, slaves and iron products. And as evident, these items were prestige goods that overtime came to assume values as units of exchange and storage of wealth.

We have seen that slaves served important aspects of the commerce of the area, serving both as merchandise and as one of the units of exchange. This means that the assumption that our area was just one of slave raid and recruiment is erroneous. For while it is true that the area has suffered as a victim of slave raids from places like Kebbi, Zamfara and Kontagora, the area was similarly, an important exporter of slaves on its own right.[74] Various wars between our people were producing captivies that were disposed as slaves. And what was emphatic on the discussion of slavery during the first Workshop has been that *Mazuganci* (slave kidnapping) was a very lucrative business producing large numbers of captives for export generally,[75] most especially to Hausa markets. By the end of our period, it seems Fakai and Karishen had excelled in *Mazuganci* and slave raids. For example, Fakai was notorious for its constant raids and kidnaps especially in Kele, Gele and among the Lélna on the fringes of Dabai. This notoreity also seems to have been an important reason in Fakai allying with Nagwamatse in the 1860's during his foray of raids in Kasar Zuru.

Because most of the slaves generated within the societies in our area were exchanged for other goods, there was little or no investment of slave labour in agriculture.[76] This could be explained by the low

---

[73] "Brief (Historical..." P.2,.Isgogo in particular was noted as one of the largest slave markets this portion of the country possessed, see" Report on the Kontagoraa Province for the quarter ended June 1907" NAK: KONPROF of 2990/07

[74] On Mazuganchi, see P.G. Harris, *Gazetteer... Op.cit* P. 360; Oral interview with Sarkin Sakaba 55 years, Sakaba Town, 24/12/85 tape no ZHP 9: and *Proceedings of Zuru History Workshop* tape no.2.

[75] Karishen may be an exception here as some slave labour was used in agriculture, see interview with the Sarkin Sakaba, Op.cit.

[76] This contrast with the emirates of Sokoto, Kano and Katsina in the 19th century where servicing the needs of settlement and use of large number of slaves on agricultural plantations obtained. See P.F. Lovejoy and S. Baier "The desert side Economy of the

level development of agriculture due to weak market forces in grains.[77] Hence slaves were valued most as a means of exchange to acquire prestige goods by the elders and men of status. And like other lineage societies in Africa, the control over the traffic in slaves and the monopoly in the acquisition of presitge goods by the elders provided them with the wherewithal not only of directing and controlling the economy and society, but *ipso facto*, as the beneficiaries of the surplus generated in the society. Therefore, the economy and society of Kasar Zuru under our period of study could be conceived as being characterised by a lineage mode of production.

## Lineage Mode of Production

The concept of mode of production is derived from Marx and had been subseuently developed by other scholars.[78] According to Lovejoy, mode of production as a tool of analysis 'emphasizes the relationship between the social organisation of society and the productive process, on the one hand and the means by which this relationship is maintained.[79] And Watts has broken down the concept into three 'lower-order' ones in order to make it less abstract. These are 'the purpose of production; the form of the producer's surplus labour; and the mode of exploitation.'[80] And as he has rightly pointeed out, the recent insertion of the mode of production analysis into African studies is the attempt to 'revivify African historiography by identifying the dominant forms of extraction place in the social formation.'[81] This has led to the identification of various modes of production characteristic of different African societies, ranging from lineage, postoral, slave or Asiatic or of overlapping modes of production.[82]

The boldest, and seemingly most successful attempt to analyse African social formations as based on lineage mode of production has

---

central Sudan", in *International Journal of African Historical Studies*, VIII, 4, 1975, P.551-81; "Sokoto Caliphate" in *Journal of African History* XIX, 3 1978, P. 341-68.

[77] See K. Marx, *Pre-Capitalist Economic Formations* (ed by E.J. Hobsbawn and translated by J.Cohen), New York 1965; see also B. Hindess and P.B. Hisrst, *Pre-capitalist Modes of Production*, London, 1975; and J. Taylor, *From Modernisation to Modes of Productions* New York, 1979.

[78] P.E. Lovejoy (ed) *The Ideology of Slavery in Africa* London 1981, P.18.

[79] M. Watts *Silent Violence: Food, Famine and Peasantry in Northern Nigeria*, University of California Press 1983, P.75.

[80] *ibid*, P.74-75.

[81] See D. Crummey and C.C. Stewart (ed) *Modes of Production in Africa: The Pre-Colonial Era*, London, 1980

[82] See C. Meillassoux "From Reproduction to Production" *Economy and Society*, Vol.I February 1972; P.Rey *Les Alliances Declasses*, Paris 1973; and P.Rey "The Lineage Mode of Production" in *Critique of Anthropology* No. 3 Spring 1975.

been by Meillassoux and Rey.[83] The former in his study of the *Gouro* of Cote d'Ivoire has shown that lineage societies, relations of production is characterised by the direct producers (whom he called cadets) being dependent on the societal elders. This dependence is predicated on the elders' control and monopoly of 'social knowledge' (geneologies, history and marital regulations), which is further perpetuated by being cemented with certain rituals of magic and divination. He also argues that elders' monopoly over accesss to women and of the 'elite goods' (like salt and iron) needed for one to be married further strenghten their hold over the cadets. That these relations of production were perpetuated by the solidarity of the elders and also by the desire of the youths (cadets) to be obedient with the hope that one day they would also become elders to enjoy the same rights and privileges. So that elders control over marriage will seem to have given them control over the important 'demographic reproduction of the lineages'. And Rey in his study of the Congo Basin added to the array of powers and control elders enjoy the youths the dimension of slavery. That while linages in the Congo Basin could incorporate slaves, they could also reduce erring cadets into slavery in exchange for elite goods. And the very threat of enslavement further ensured the acquieiscence and obedience of the cadets. This was further made more secure by the fact that offences like adultery, sorcery and theft had to be propitiated by fine in 'elite goods' over which they help the monopoly.

While the societies of Kasar Zuru before c. 1900 A.D., cannot be said to fit perfectly the above description, it seems some of them contained certain similar elements and phenomena as to warrant their being categorised as lineage societies. For example, from what we have said so far, unlike the Gouro of Cote d'Ivoire, marriage amongst most people in the area did not involve much, if any, are material transaction through which the elders could gain undue sway over the youths.

But it is true that in most societies of Kasar Zuru that we have seen, the elders played very great and significant roles and had very important functions through which they could control the labour and production of the youths, and there by appropriate their surplus labour. Thus elders through their acquired monopoly over social knowledge (especially geneologies, history, rituals and beliefs) came to exert great influence on the society and the youths. For example, they were the ones that help initiate the male children into the *M'gilǫ*. They also controlled and super-intended over rituals, rites, and all the ceremonies that we saw. Through these they came to acquire a lot of

---

[83] For these see E.C. Duff *Op.cit* P.60.

aura of respectability and consequent control and domination over the societal relations of production. And like the *Gouro* society, the council of elders (decision makers) that obtained at clan and village levels especially among the Lélna and the Dukkawa served to ensure their solidarity and therefore hegemony over the society and its production relation and processes. Here, too, the desire of the youths and the up-coming to themselves became elders or acquire titles which only the elders could bestow and sanctioned have functioned to perpetuate this gerontocratic control of the society and its surpluses.

Most importantly, these controls allowed them to dominate and direct production processes in their respective households, lineages and clans, through which they came to appropriate the surpluses so produced in the society. Such surpluses they exchanged for other products (elite goods) which further served to enhance their hegemony. In fact, as we have argued, the institution of *golmo* was fashioned and used by elders to ensure their control and access to the labour powers of the most productive segment of the society (the youths).

Also, while unlike the case of the Congo Basin studied by Rey, elders in Kasar Zuru may not have enslaved their youths at whim, the fact that they controlled and determined what could be used to propitiate offences and misdemeanours may have served to further entrench their hold over the youths. For example, among the Lélna, a murderer or his relations had to pay the victim's relations either two girls or a boy, who could either be retained or sold into slavery or ransomed by his relations with a girl or a boy. An adulterer also paid a fine of a girl or a boy to the household of the woman.[84] In all these, it were the elders that determined whether to ransom the victim or allow him to be sold into slavery. Certainly, recalcitrants or disobedient children or youths may not be so ransomed.

At this stage of our knowledge of the history of the people and societies of Kasar Zuru, it is only further research that would help consolidate our grasp of the dynamics of their society and economy. Such researches, especially at the micro level of individual societies will provide us with more data and facts not only in further attesting to the validity and appositeness of theorising them lineage societies, but also help in cementing our knowledge of the basic motor of the dynamics of their society and economy.

## Conclusion: A Natural Economy

---

[84] The early colonial record spoke of enslavement by parents buy owing to either an epidemic, disease or famine, see for example, "Annual Reports of Kontagora Province 1906 KONPROF/1829/1907."

The concept of 'natural economy' has been developed and used to describe economies and societies that have developed a relative balance in the exploitation of their environmental resources and endowments towards the provision of the needs of the people generally.[85] It is not that such economies and societies were not characterised by exploitation. Rather, there was no crude and primitive accumulation of resources and surpluses characteristic of capitalist economies. So that while such societies could also be permeated by inequality and differentiations, there were overt and sincere attempts to ensure that the people are assured of decent living.

What we have seen for the people of Kasar Zuru is a situation where economy and society evolved and and develoiped through the exploitation of the abundant natural resources of the area catering for the needs of all and sundry. And the institutions they developed were tailored towards achieving and consolidating these lofty aims. Thus everybody was assured access to land and hunting grounds. Brazen accumulation of property was also non-existent, instead, surplus were ploughed back into the society and used for the general benefit through ceremonies, festivals and gifts.

It was this economy that was gradually but surely incorporated into the world capitalist system from the end of our period. And with the injection of capitalist relations of production into the society, the 'natural economy ' we have seen was defiled. Colonialism, which ushered in harsh and extortionate taxation in the white man's currency, forced labour monetization and commoditization of the economy gave the society of Kasar Zuru, like that of the country, a new *raison d'etre* and orientation.

Consequently, production now became principally geared towards the market and not first and formost for subsistence and the satisfaction of the basic needs of the society. What came to matter, therefore, was the production of cash crops and/or the supply of labour to the state and its agencies so as to acquire the wherewithal of subsistence and reproduction in a colonial capitalist society. This brought in its wake cataclysmic changes and consequences not only in the ecomomy, but in the society and its institutions generally. But this is beyond the bounds of this chapter and will be addressed in the last chapter.

---

[85] See D. Bradby, *"The Destruction of Natural Economy" Economy and Society*. Vol. IV, No.2 May 1985.

## Chapter Five

# A Survey Of Social And Political History Of Zuru Emirate Before 1900 A.D.

*by*
A. R. Augi

## Introduction

It needs no emphasis to state that the study of the history of the area now designated Zuru Emirate has been a neglected field. This is partly the situation which the Zuru History Project is attempting to correct. This neglect seems to have arisen, at least in part, from earlier perspectives of studying African history which generally equated history with kingdoms and empires. Communities not identified with kingdoms and empires were regarded as having hardly any history worth studying. The neglect of the study of the history of such communities was further justified by the claims or assumptions that sources for studying it were scanty if not totally lacking. Invariably, therefore, the study of societies such as those of Zuru Emirate were left to anthropologists whose main preoccupation was the description of customs and traditions, belief systems and material culture of such societies as they existed at the time the enquiries were being conducted. The changes in these customs and traditions, belief systems, material culture and the life of the people in general, were scarcely given any consideration. Thus, up till today, the main studies available, in published literature, on the societies in Zuru are the ethnographic works of P.G. Harris and H.D. Gunn and F.P. Conant.[1] The old perspectives of studying African history and Nigerian history in particular are, however, being gradually reversed. Today, we are much better informed about the history of many societies which, like those of Zuru, had previously been regarded as stateless societies and, therefore, societies with no significant history to study. One of the best examples in this direction is the rich study of Professor Ade Obayemi of the societies of the Middle Niger-Benue

---

[1] P.G. Harris, "Notes on the Dakarkari of Sokoto Province, Northern Nigeria", *Journal of the Royal Anthropological Institute* Vol. LXVIII, January - June, 1938 pp. 113 - 152; H.D. Gunn and P.P. Conant, *Peoples of the Middle Niger Region, Northern Nigeria*. 1960

confluence.[2] This study has thrown up a whole new perspective for understanding the history of not only the "stateless societies", such as the Gbari (Gwari), Kakanda, Kyede, Igbirra, Ijumu, Yagba and other north-east Yoruba communities, the Etsako, Ishan and the Igbo-speaking people, but even the societies associated with states e.g. Nupe, Oyo, Ile-Ife, Idah and Benin.

Ade Obeyami's study, and others like it, have been made possible because the writers have refused to regard sources for studying history as being only archaeology, written records and oral traditions which have conventionally and even fetishly, been so regarded. Besides these "traditional" sources, they have extensively utilised all available ethnographic data, linguistic studies and any other source or evidence relating to the material culture and belief systems of the societies studied including data derived from the physical environment. In this way, these studies have revealed the enormity and complex nature of the data available for studying the history of those societies rather than scarcity of such data. This situation appears to be equally true of the societies of Zuru even if one is examining only the data in the existing ethnographic and historical studies on the area. One of the major challenges for the student of Zuru history, for example, is to reconcile the numerous and conflicting traditions of origins of the peoples and polities of the area, and produce a meaningful picture out of the situation.

This chapter attempts a general survey of the social and political history of Zuru before the 20th century. The issues discussed are some current assumptions about Zuru history; the geography of the area; peopling of the area and formation of communities; and lastly, the main dimensions of the social and political development of the societies over the period studied.

## Some Assumptions On Zuru History.

Although there has been a neglect of studying the history of present Zuru Emirate, it is, nevertheless, true to say that there have been many attempts at interpreting its history. Such interpretations are evident in the various conserved traditions of the many groups inhabiting the area as well as in the several studies made on the area. From such various interpretations, several stereotype views of this history have developed among which are the following:

---

[2] Ade Obayemi, "The Yoruba and Edo-Speaking peoples and their neighbours before 1600 A.D. "in J.F.A. Ajayi and M. Growder (eds), *History of West Africa*. Vol. II 2nd edition, Longman, 1976.

(a) Tendency to see the history of the area essentially in terms of some fixed, unchanging and mutually exclusive groups viz. the Dakarkari or Dakarawa, Bangawa, Fakawa, Katsinawa, Dukawa, Kambarawa (Kambari) and Achipawa;
(b) Tendency to perceive the history of these groups in terms of their being indigenes or strangers to the area in which claims and counter-claims over such issues as ownership of land, political leadership, etc. are made. In this regard, there is, in particular, a tendency to see the people defined as the Dakarkari as being virtually synonymous with the Zuru Emirate;
(c) Tendency to regard the area as isolated in its historical development in spite of the overwhelming evidence to the contrary;
(d) Tendency to perceive the political and social institutions of the peoples as having been similar in nature with hardly any noticeable differences or changes; and
(e) Tendency to explain the origins of the various groups identified above in terms of lineal ancestral or place of origin.

Let us briefly elaborate on these tendencies. With regard to the first tendency, it is the general assumption in the available literature on Zuru history to see the Dakarkari, Bangawa, Fakawa, Achipawa, Katsinawan Laka, Dukawa and the Kambarawa as fixed and unchanging entities existing in this area from time immemorial.[3] In the various traditions recorded by ethnographers and colonial administrators, impressions have been created that many of these groups migrated into Zuru area more or less in the same form as we conceive them today.[4] This has continued to be the general picture even in the more recent writings on the area.[5] This picture has been built up by colonial historiography which generally perceived African societies to have been made up of tribal or ethnic units, each with distinct origins, culture, language and even biological features.

The picture outlined above however, is far from the truth, indeed, as many studies in other parts of Nigeria have revealed, it is a historical to see the present ethnic groups e.g. the Yoruba, Nupe, Hausa, Barebari, Ibo and Edo as having existed throughout history in

---

[3] Cf.P.G. Harris, *op. cit;* H.D. Gunn and F.P. Conant, op, cit, but various other studies on Zuru reflect this position.

[4] *ibid.*

[5] See, for example, S. Mohammed, *Some Aspects of the Culture and Institutions of the Dakarkari People examined in the light of their contiguity with the Hausa people.* M.A. Thesis, Bayero University Kano, October, 1982; M.M. Gujiya, "The Dakarkari People (Lélna) "*Zaruma* Nos. 5 and 6 1983 and 1985.

the way they are perceived today.[6] The term, Yoruba, for example, was used to refer to the people of old Oyo Kingdom only up till the beginning of the 20th century. Before then, the various Yoruba-speaking groups had different names for themselves or by which others called them, e.g. the Ifes, the Egbas, the Modakekes, Ijeshas, Ijebus, Ijumus and the Igbominas, and even these terms had their specific historical origins, i.e they did not exist from time immemorial. Similarly, there is no evidence that the Hausa people, as we know them today, always saw themselves as Hausa until the more recent times. Rather, various Hausa- speaking groups regarded themselves to be Katsinawa, Zamfarawa, Bangawa, Zagezagi or Zazzagawa, Kanawa or the Gobirawa.

While, therefore, we cannot deny the existence of groups such as the Dakarkari or Lélna, Achipawa and Dukawa in the contemporary history of Zuru Emirate, we must be very wary of projecting these categories to the historical epochs in which they had hardly any meaning. The conflicting traditions associated with the origin of the Dakarakari and Bangawa, for example, clearly reveal the problem and, indeed, the futility of thinking that such groups had always existed in history or that they had a common place of origin or ancestor. As Michael Gujiya has pointed out, for example, in the region inhabited by the Dakarkari today, various groups are still identified with their settlements e.g the people of Gele are called Gelawa and those of Kele are known as Kelawa.[7] Shouldn't such groups as the Gelawa, Kelawa, Mangawa, Dankawa, Benawa, Mutanen Wasagu and Mutanen Karishen be more basic units of reconstructing the history of Zuru than Katsinawa or Bangawa or Dakarkari?

It is the contention of this chapter that for us to have a clear picture of the dimensions of the history of various groups and entities which existed in Zuru, we have to examine carefully the pattern of peopling and community formation in the area. A major feature of this process, as with other Nigerian communities, were the constant movements and intermixing of peoples of diverse origins.[8] It was this process which eventually produced the groups now identified as Bangawa, Katsinawan Laka, Dakarkari, Dukawa, Achipawa and Fakawa.

The second tendency towards perceiving the history of the various contemporary groups in terms of their being indigenes or strangers in

---

[6] For a critique of this view of Nigerian and West African History, See Y.B. Usman, "The problem of ethnic categories in the study of the historical development of the Central Sudan: A critique of M.G. Smith and others", In Y.B. Usman (ed) *Demystifying Nigerian History*, New Horn Books, Ibadan.

[7] M.M. Gujiya, in *Zaruma*, No.5 (1983), op. cit pp.9 - 10.

[8] This is discussed below.

Zuru, especially in relation to such issues as ownership of land and political leadership in the area, is less evident in the available literature. But its manifestations are, nonetheless, perceptive in the everyday politics of Zuru emirate. An aspect of this, for example, is the tendency in virtually all recent studies on Zuru to present such studies essentially in terms of the Dakarkari even when they are purportedly focusing on the whole of the emirate.[9] Another dimension to this tendency is reflected in the latent opposition to the leadership of Zuru by various groups in the emirate.

The third tendency of regarding the area as isolated or exclusive in its history is reflected in such assertions as Zuru being hilly, thickly forested and inaccessible; its people developing little commercial contacts and, therefore, remaining basically self-sufficient; and the absence of large territorial states. This view of Zuru history, like the others examined earlier, is very faulty. Although the area is undoubtedly hilly and forested, and would have been so particularly in the period before this century, it has never been inaccessible or isolated. As we shall see later in this paper, and as the local traditions clearly reveal, there were constant movements of people and ideas into and within the area. Even commerce appeared to have been more significant than has usually been thought to be the case. This is discussed later in this chapter.

The fourth tendency in the study of Zuru history, as mentioned earlier, is the perception of the social and political institutions of its peoples, especially political units, as having been essentially similar in nature before this century. The political units are regarded as having been generally small-social in nature with little or no political differentiation. Among the Dakarkari, for example, it has been asserted that every settlement was politically autonomous of the others.[10] This picture of social and political organisation in Zuru land before the 20th century does not seem to be true. There were varying social and political systems many of which had complex and hierarchised structures as discussed later in this paper.

The last tendency is that of explaining the origins of the various groups noted above in terms of either a common ancestor or an area. This is most evident with regards to the origins of the Dakarkari. Most writings on this group, including the most recent ones, display this tendency, often, with considerable tenacity.[11] The purported ancestor

---

[9] See, fro example, Joshua I. Ganya, "The History of Zuru" College of Education, Sok to. (N.D.)

[10] *ibid*, pp.6 - 11.

[11] . Cf. P.G. Harris, op.cit.; M.S. Sakaba, "Themes in Lélna History in the 19th and 20th centuries". B.A. Thesis, A.B.U. Zaria, 1974; S.Mary, The History of Christian

of the Dakarkari is variously named as Dakka Yanusa, Dakka na Umma or simply as Dakka. Attempts to reconstruct the origin of many groups in Nigeria in terms of descent from a common ancestor are, of course, a very familiar feature in Nigerian historiography. The legends of Kisra, Bayajida (Abu Yazidu), Saif b. Dhi Yazan and Oduduwa are very familiar to us. But the superficiality of these stories as far as origins of people are concerned, has been exposed in many writings and we are today very well aware that these stories do not explain the origins of the people they purportedly sought to explain. In the same vein, it does not seem useful to explain the origins of the Dakarkari around the story of Dakka, especially when we consider the many conflicting traditions around this issue. This is discussed in more details later in this chapter. The tendencies outlined above dominate the current literature and perception of the history of Zuru Emirate. As pointed out, however, all the tendencies give a faulty picture of this history. No serious attempt, therefore, has been made to clearly understand the history of Zuru Emirate. For us to understand the history properly, we have to be clear about the basic fact of all human history. This basic fact is that history is about relations between men and between them and their environment and the changing nature of these relations over time and space. It is a fact of history that people of varying origins are often brought together in an environment. As they come together, they develop various forms of relations with one another and create various institutions through which such relations are regulated. Their customs and traditions, belief systems, language and culture in general, are shaped and modified by long period of such relations in the process of which new communities are formed and re-formed.

In the case of communities in Zuru Emirate, as is true of other Nigerian groups, the process of their formation should be traced as far back in time as historical evidence can allow us. In so doing, we should examine how man began to emerge in the area and then trace processes and forces which changed his life in the course of time. Such attempt should eventually inform us about how the Dakarkari, Katsinawa Laka of Wasagu, Bena and other towns, the Fakawa of Fakai, the Bangawa of Danko and the Achipawa, Dukawa and Kambarawa of Sakaba district came to acquire their distinctive nomenclatures and names and so be in a better position to appreciate their real significance in Zuru history.

---

Churches in Zuru town. College of Education, Sokoto June, 1981; and J.B. Bauta, *A brief historical origin* of Dakarkaris of Zuru and some of their cultural traditions Ms (n.d.)

## Peopling and Formation of Communities.

Chapters three and four of this book have already given the background to the development of communities here as regards geography and natural resources. What remains is for us to build on these to map out the process of the peopling and formation of communities in Zuruland.[12]

It must be admitted that available sources for the study of the very early peopling of Zuru Emirate are very scanty indeed. This is not only because the science of archaeology is just being tried on the area, but also because the potentials of other useful sources for the period such as linguistics, ethnography and even oral traditions are yet to be substantially explored. In spite of this situation, however, it is still possible to begin to reconstruct this process even if only roughly. We can do this using the available sources on both Zuru and its neighbours.

The earliest known epoch in man's history is the stone Age.[13] This period covered well over 90% of the known period of man's history, but it is also the least known era. While in some parts of East Africa, evidence for the existence of Stone Age has been traced to well over one and a half million years ago, in Nigeria, such evidence hardly goes back to half a million years ago, and even then, the evidence has not been properly examined and dated as that in East Africa. With regards to Zuru Emirate, in particular, no substantive evidence of Stone Age has come to light from the area. Evidence of Late Stone Age populations has, however, been recovered from a number of sites in areas surrounding Zuru. The most notable are the Late Stone Age tools discovered along Gagare river, some 40 kilometres from Dutsi, the famous ancient settlement of the kingdom of Zamfara as well as along the Waleli river in Gummi district within the territory of the ancient kingdom of Zoma.[14] Both Dutsi and Zoma are closely associated with the history of Zuru-Dutsi is linked with some traditions of origin of the Dakarkari while the territory of Zoma is believed to have, at some

---

[12] See Chapters three and four.

[13] It is called Stone Age mainly because the commonest evidence for writing the history of man during that period were the Stone tools he made. He had no iron or other metals to use. But, in addition to stone, he also made tools out of bones, wood and other available materials.

[14] R.C. Soper, "The Stone Age in Northern Nigeria", *Journal of the Historical Society of Nigeria*. Vol. III, No.2 December, 1965. pp. 189 - 193

period, incorporated some parts of Danko.[15] Another area from where pieces of evidence of Stone Age have been uncovered is Kebbi, an area from which several groups in Zuru claim to have migrated from.[16] While, therefore, we have no direct evidence of Stone Age in Zuru so far, the existence of such evidence in some area bordering the emirate and with which it shared close history, may be an indication of possible existence of population in the region since the stone Age.

The Stone Age populations which probably existed in Zuru Emirate would have eventually gone through the transition from the Stone Age to the Iron Age.[17] Indeed, while no concrete evidence has come to light of the existence of Stone Age in the area, the presence of local iron working has been reported from several places in the preliminary work of Isa Bitiyong. It is only when this evidence is properly examined and dated that we shall be able to know the antiquity of iron working in the area. In Yelwa area, bordering Zuru to the south-west, however, iron working has been dated to as far back as the second century B.C.[18] What is even more interesting with this Yelwa evidence is that it has been suggested to be associated with the Kambari (Kambarawa) people of the area and we very well know that some of the Kambarawa inhabit parts of Zuru Emirate.[19]

It is possible that the early populations which inhabited Zuru during the Stone Age and early Iron Age formed the nucleus of some of the linguistic and cultural groups that are today found in the area. The Niger-Congo languages which most of these groups speak are similar to many other groups found in central Nigeria. These languages are of distinct family from the Hausa language in particular. These early populations would gradually have expanded especially with the transition from the Stone Age to the Iron Age and the growth of agriculture based on the cultivation of guinea corn, millet and *acca*.

---

[15] See P.G. Harris, op.cit. See also P.G. Harris, *Sokoto Provincial Gazetteer*. MS 1938, pp. 313-320; *Bukkuyum District Notebook*, Sokoto State Government Archives, pp. 129 - 131.

[16] A.R. Augi, *The Gobir Factor in the Social and Political History of the Rima Basin. C.1650-1801 A.D*. Ph.D. Thesis, A.B.U Zaria 1984, pp. 201 - 202.

[17] The Iron Age refers to the period when man began to smelt iron ore and other metals to manufacture his tools. The period superseded the Stone Age. The invention of the use of iron was very important to man as it allowed him to make much more sophisticated tools and improve his life and speed up his historical progress. Mankind is still, technically, within the Iron Age.

[18] A.J. Priddy, "An Iron Age site near Yelwa, Sokoto Province: Preliminary Report". *West African Archaeological Newsletter*. No.12, 1970 pp. 20 - 32.

[19] .On the suggestion of a linkage between the Iron Age evidence of Yelwa and the Kambari people, see Ade Obayemi, "The Ulaira Site and the History of the Yawuri Area: Some Questions" *Seminar paper*, Department of History, A.B.U., Zaria 1979.

Other occupations of these populations seemed to have included hunting and iron working. The people would have lived in hamlets scattered over the region. Over the period, however, movements of populations into the region began to occur, especially from the north and north-west, i.e from the directions of Katsina, Zamfara and Kebbi and possibly, from the south as well. Some of the migrating populations might be linguistically and culturally similar with the population already established in the area. We shall discuss these movements in more details below.

## The Migrations

Available sources on Zuru history are generally very emphatic on the importance of migrations in the peopling and community formation in the region. Almost all the groups presently living in the area are believed to have migrated into the region from somewhere else.[20] This is led to a view, in some writings that the area was, at one time, "a no-man's land",[21] i.e. it was not previously inhabited by any populations. We have, in earlier paragraphs of this section, suggested the possibility of the area being inhabited from a very early period. This early population, as further suggested, would eventually have been augmented by various migrant groups and individuals as recalled in the traditions of the area.

Migration was, therefore, no doubt, an important phenomenon in the history of Zuru Emirate. While, however, its importance is obvious to us, we are not very clear about the exact nature of these movements particularly their patterns and timings. The traditions, for example, tend to suggest that whole groups, as we know them today, i.e. as Dakarawa, Bangawa, Fakawa, Katsinawa and Dukawa moved together into Zuru from areas outside. But this cannot be plausible. What is more correct is that the movements occurred in waves of individuals and groups who came to settle in various parts of the emirate. The conflicting traditions of such movements among some of the groups clearly indicate this. With regards to the times when the movements occurred we can relate many of them with historical development in the surrounding areas from where the migrants are believed to have originated. We discuss below, the movements.

---

[20] P.G. Harris, "Notes on the Dakarkari", op.cit; P.G. Harris, Gazetteer, op.cit pp.310-317; E.C. Duff and W. Hamilton Browne, *Gazatteer of Kontagora Province*, London, 1920 pp. 30-31, and "Zuru Re-organisation, 1938 - 55" op 38-40.

[21] M. Adamu, *The Hausa Factor in West African History*, A.B.U. Press, 1978, p.31.

## (a) *The Achipawa*

Karishen is regarded as the oldest settlement known in the history of Zuru emirate.[22] This settlement which is located in the hills of Sakaba district, is said to have been established by the Achipawa. The Achipawa are said to be an off-shoot of the Borgu or Bariba people, the main sections of whom inhabit the middle Niger in parts of present Kwara and Sokoto States in Nigeria and the Benin Republic. The Bariba traditions generally claim that they descended from a certain ancient hero in the history of the present Middle East called Kisra and that they migrated to their present locations from that area.[23] The Achipawa traditions claim that they were left in Karishen by the bulk of the Bariba during the course of these migrations and their ruler still preserves a sword which is claimed to be that of Kisra.[24]

In terms of the Kisra legend, therefore, the direction of migrations of the Achipawa and other Bariba groups was from the east. There are, however, some traditions which suggest movements of the Bariba from the west, i.e. from present south-eastern Niger Republic (area of the Dallols Mauri,[25] Fogha and Dosso). Besides, linguistic evidence suggests very close relationship between the Bariba language and the languages of some of their neighbours such as the Nupe and the Yoruba.[26] Language is one of the most, if not the most, distinctive feature of a group. Using linguistic and archaeological evidence, in particular, Professor Ade Obayemi has strongly suggested that the Bariba, Yoruba, Nupe and many other groups around them with whom they shared a common language family, the Kwa group of languages, has an ancient origin in the Niger-Benue confluence going back to the Stone Age period.[27]

The suggestion, therefore, is that the Bariba, and so the Achipawa, did not originate in the Middle East as the Kisra legend claims. Rather, their origin should be looked at within the Nigeria region. In his study of the Bariba people, Musa Baba Idris has gone into considerable details to analyse the significance of the Kisra legend in Bariba history

---

[22] Duff and Hamilton -Browne, *op.cit* p.30.

[23] M.B. Idris, *The Political and Economic Relations of the Bariba States*, Ph.D. Thesis, University of Birmingham. (n.d.)

[24] P.G. Harris, *Gazetteer*, op.cit. p.311; Duff and Hamilton Browne, *op.cit*. p.30

[25] J. Perie and M. Sellier, "Historie des populations du cercle de Dosso", *Bulletin de L'Institute Francaise de l'Afrique Noire*. Lome XII, No.4. 1950. pp. 1019-1025.

[26] See J.H. Greenberg, *Studies in African Linguistic Classification*. New Haven. 1955. p.11. See also Ade Obayemi, "The Yoruba and Edo-speaking peoples......" *op.cit*.

[27] Ade Obayemi, *ibid*

in Bariba history which he saw not so much in terms of the origin of the people now called Bariba, but more in terms of its ideological significance in the social and political domination which the various ruling dynasties of Bariba States exercised in the history of the people.[28]

It, therefore, seems most probable that the Achipawa, as an off-shoot of the Bariba, arrived in their present location from the middle Niger region where the majority of the Bariba and their close neighbours, linguistically, live today. The period of their arrival is not clear to us, but it was probably very early as suggested in their traditions, hence the precise nature of the movements have been forgotten. On their arrival, they probably established several settlements of which Karishen became the most important politically. Later, an off-shoot of the Achipawa moved northwards out of present Zuru Emirate and established itself at Kanoma in present Maru district of Sokoto State.[29]

## (b) *The Kambari*

The Kambari appear to be autochtonous to the region they inhabit today-Sakaba district of Zuru, and in Kontagora and Yawuri emirates.[30] Like many Nigerian groups, the Kambari have traditions of origin from the present Middle East. But the significance of these traditions should be analysed in terms of the way this has been done with the Kanuri, Hausa, Yoruba and Bariba traditions. The Kambari have been linked with an old Iron Age culture unearthed at some sites in Yelwa district of Yauri emirate which has been archaeologically dated to the 2nd century before the Christian Era.[31] The nucleus of the origin of the group is not clear to us, but since Sakaba district appears to be on the fringes of their present distribution, it is possible that the group gradually expanded to this area in the course of history, i.e. as its population grew.

---

[28] M.B. Idris, *op.cit*

[29] P.G. Harris, *Gazetteer. op.cit*, p. 161

[30] Especially when the link between them and the old iron age culture in Yawuri is considered.

[31] Ade Obayemi, "The Ulaira site", *op.cit*.

**Alhaji Musa Mohammed Sakaba.**
District Head of Sakaba
*(Installed March 1, 1976)*

### (c) *The Dakarkari (Lélna)*

The people called the Dakarkari or Lélna today are, also it seems, autochtonous to the present Zuru Emirate.[32] Although probably, they were more widespread in the past than they were today. They form the largest group in the emirate. Autochtonous as they seem to be, however, there are strong traditions of migrations among these people which have been used by writers to suggest external origins for the group. The traditions variously suggest that the Dakarkari migrated into Zuru from Kebbi, Zamfara or Katsina. Yet another tradition claims that the Dakarkari originated from the Achipawa.

According to a version of these traditions, the region formed today by the towns of Aliero, Birnin Kebbi and Argungu was formerly occupied by the Dakarkari.[33] They moved out of this region into their present location, it is believed by some writers, following the establishment of the capital of Kebbi at Birnin Kebbi, early in the 18th century.[34] A version of this story claims that it was a section of the Dakarkari, the Kelawa, who moved under the leadership of three hunters named as Kele, Isgogo and Jambo who apparently came to establish the settlements with these names.[35] Another version states that the Dakarkari were originally *dakaru* (foot soldiers) of Kanta, the famous ruler of Kebbi.[36]

The traditions relating to Zamfara claim that the Dakarkari were descendants of Dakka, the purported ancestor of the Zamfarawa.[37] A version of this Zamafara linkage asserts that the Dakarkari originated from Bukkuyum through a Bazamfare named Bogazai who was sent by his brother into Zuru region who was then the Sarkin Bukkuyum.[38] It was he who eventually founded the town or chieftaincy of Dabai.[39] There is also story that a sub-group of the Dakarkari called the Lillawa were descendants of Hausa hunters from Zamfara who migrated in

---

[32] The linguistic affinities of Dakarkari with other groups, particularly the Dukawa, suggests this. See also, "Zuru Re- organisation, 1938 - 55" Sokoto State Government Archive, p. 38, and M. Adamu, *The Hausa Factor* ...... *op.cit* p. 31.

[33] P. G. Harris, "Notes on the Dakarkari", *op. cit.*

[34] M.B. Alkali, *A Hausa Community in Crisis: Kebbi in the Nineteenth Century*. M.A. Thesis, A.B.U Zaria, November 1969. P. 86; P.G. Harris, Gazetteer, *op.cit.* 310.

[35] P.G. Harris, "Notes on the Dakarkari", *op.cit.*

[36] *ibid.*, P.G. Harris, *Gazetteer, ibid,* pp. 313 - 314.

[37] P.G. Harris, *Gazetteer, op. cit* p. 313 - 314.

[38] S. Mohammed, *op.cit*. p.3; M.M. Gujiya, op.cit pp. 10-11. The reference to Bukkuyum is to Sarkin Danko which is the title of the Chief of present Bukkuyum. The town of Bukkuyum was founded late in the 19th century.

[39] *ibid.*

small waves over different periods and established the towns of Dabai, Kyabo, Kandu, Rikoto, Manga, Ribah and Zuru.[40]

The traditions of Katsina origin mention that the Dakarkari were descendants of one Dakka Yanusa who, according to one version went to settle first at Illo (on the river Niger) and then eventually moved into Zuru.[41] There are also several traditions linking various settlements of the Dakarkari such as Peni, Kanya and Ribah with Katsina.[42] More recently, Murray Last has suggested that the Dakarkari, Achipawa and other groups, now south of Katsina and Zamfara, were, in the past, widely spread up to those areas and that a ruler of Katsina called Ibrahim Badankari was probably of Dakarkari origin.[43]

The various traditions outlined above have posed a considerable problem to many students of Zuru history because of the latter's primary concern with discovering the area from where the Dakarkari originated. Consequently, a lot of confusion has been created in such writings which has made it difficult to understand the real significance of these stories. The basic question is: are these traditions trying to explain the origins of the Dakarkari? In some sense, one can say yes. But, this is not in the sense in which most of the existing writings have tended to see it. These writings seem to generally see the issue in two ways:

(i) Those concerned with discovering a common ancestor for the Dakarkari, be he Dakka Yanusa, Dakka na Umma or simply Dakka, have tended to discard those traditions which do not talk about such an ancestor as being not plausible. This appears to be the case with M.S. Sakaba and S. Mary.[44]

(ii) Those who could not properly reconcile the apparently conflicting traditions or understand their full significance either simply regard all of them as being true or, in most cases, they tend to completely ignore interpreting them.[45]

---

[40] P.G. Harris, "Notes on the Dakarkari", *op.cit.*

[41] A.M.D. Ribah, *A History of Ribah.* Final Year Project, College of Education, Sokoto n.d. p.3

[42] *ibid*, p.2, "Zuru Re-organisation, 1938-55", *op.cit.* p.38.

[43] See M. Last, "Beyond Kano, before Katsina: Friend and Foe on the Western Frontier". *Paper presented at the Second International Conference on the History of Kano*, Bayero University Kano, 15-20 September, 1985.

[44] M.S. Sakaba, *op.cit.*; and S. Mary, *op.cit.* See also A.M.D. Ribah, *op.cit.* p.3.

[45] M.M. Gujiya, for example, is of the view that all the traditions he discusses are true because, according to him, each of the sub-group referred to in different versions of the traditions "has got at least a slightly different language, customs and traditions". The latter observation is quite an important one, but Gujiya did not analyse its full implications for the origins of the Dakarkari.

Obviously, both approaches are faulty. They fail both to resolve the issue of the origins of the Dakarkari and understand clearly the historical significance of the diverse traditions. It may be true, as Michael Gujiya asserts, that the various stories are authentic. However, they can be authentic not in terms of explaining the origins of the Dakarkari *per se*, but rather in terms of their explaining the various circumstances which influenced Dakarkari history in particular and that of Zuru emirate in general. The traditions of migrations from Kebbi, Zamfara and Katsina could be essentially talking about various waves of immigrants who settled in present Zuru intermixing with the people already established in the region or certain social and political influences from those areas which set in motion considerable social, economic and political changes, notably the establishment of new settlements and the emergence of chiefdoms such as Dabai. The tradition of Dakarkari origin from Achipawa appears also to be talking about the latter's influences over the former.

Any attempt, therefore, to explain who the Dakarkari are or were, must see the formation of the group not in terms of its origin from any one particular area outside, but rather in terms of how different individuals and groups within and outside present Zuru emirate came together in this region to develop the common language, culture and socio-political institutions which came to be distinctively identified with the Dakarkari. In other words, the Dakarkari appear to have been formed by groups and individuals of diverse origins under varying social, political and economic influences. The origin of the Hausa name of the group may never be clear to us. The suggestion that the name may have originated from Dakka or the Arabic word, "dakakirr" (meaning idolater) or the Hausa word "dakakiri" (meaning slow worker) are mere attempts at rationalisation of some unknown or forgotten historical phenomenon and clearly unsound.[46] Such rationalisation has also been made with regards to several other neighbouring groups.[47]

To conclude this discussion therefore, we wish to restate our contention that the Dakarkari, as a group, were formed in their present habitat over a long period of historical interactions of many diverse groups and individuals. Many of these probably spoke different

---

[46] For such rationalisation, see the following works: C.L. Temple (ed), *Notes on the Tribes, Provinces, Emirates and States of the Northern Provinces of Nigeria*. Frank Cass. London. 1922. p.88; S. Mohammed, *op.cit* pp.3-7; P.G. Harris, "Notes on the Dakarkari", *op.cit.*, etc.

[47] Such as for example, explaining the origin of Hausa from "hau" (climb), and "sa" (ox), i.e. "climb an ox" or the origins of the Zamfara from the story of a princess of Zamfara named Fara and her adventure with some purported Gobirawa hunters.

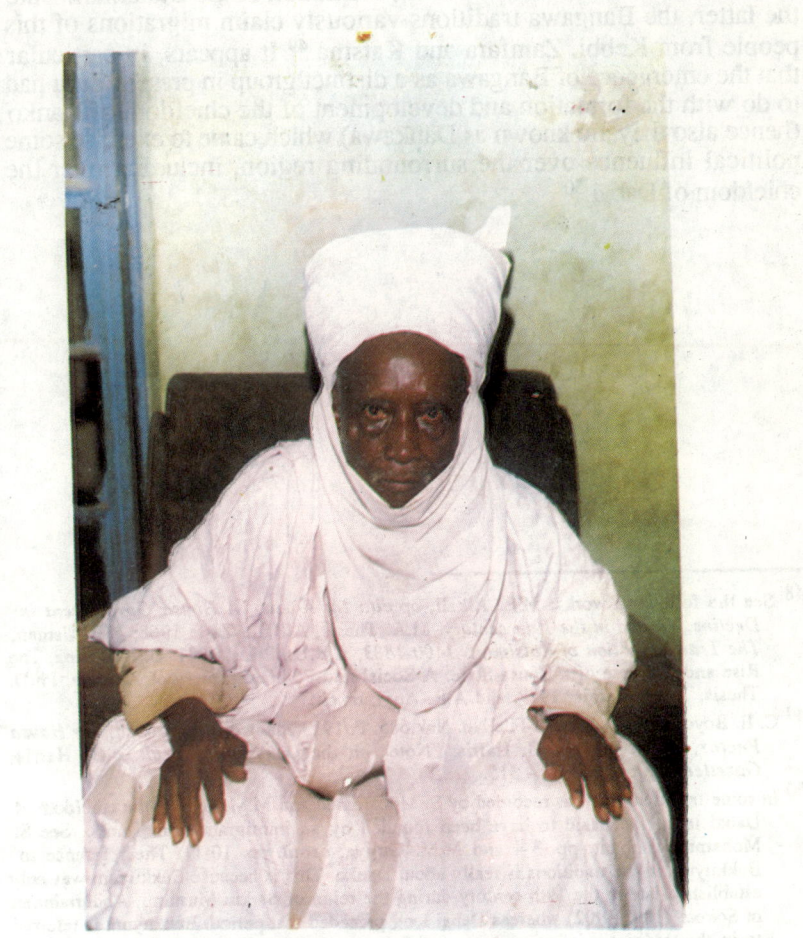

**Alhaji Ibrahim Sakaba**
District Head of Dabai
*(Installed March 18, 1958 )*

languages from the one now spoken in the area but, eventually, they all emerged to speak the C'lela which was indigenous to the region and spoken by the dominant original group in the area. This process is similar with those which, for example, led to the emergence of the Yawurawa, Kabawa, Zamfarawa, Katsinawa and Gobirawa.[48]

### (d) *The Bangawa (Dankawa)*

The process of the formation of the people now called Bangawa is also very similar to that which led to the formation of the Dakarkari. Like the latter, the Bangawa traditions variously claim migrations of this people from Kebbi, Zamfara and Katsina.[49] It appears, in particular that the emergence of Bangawa as a distinct group in present Zuru had to do with the formation and development of the chiefdom of Danko (hence also they are known as Dankawa) which came to exercise some political influence over the surrounding region, including over the chiefdom of Dabai.[50]

---

[48] See the following works: M.B. Alkali, *op.cit.*; M. Adamu, *A Hausa Government in Decline: Yawuri in the 19th century*. M.A. Thesis, A.B.U., Zaria 1968; Y.B. Usman, *The Transformation of Katsina, C.1400-1883*, A.B.U., Press, 1981: G. Na-Dama, The Rise and Collapse of a Hausa State: A Social and Political History of Zamfara. Ph.D. Thesis, A.B.U., Zaria, 1977. and A.R. Augi, op.cit.

[49] C. E. Boyd, "Sakaba District File No. Nak.685. P./1913" quoted in M.Adamu, *The Hausa Factor, op.cit* p.31., P.G. Harris, "Notes on the Dakarkari", *op.cit*. p.G. Harris, *Gazetteer, op.cit.* pp. 314 - 315.

[50] In some traditions such as recorded by S. Mohammed and M.M. Gujiya, the chiefdom of Dabai is, in fact, said to have been founded by an immigrant from Danko. See S. Mohammed, op.cit. pp. 3-4 and M.M. Gujiya, *op.cit.* pp. 10-11. The reference to Bukkuyum in the traditions is really about Danko. This is because Bukkuyum was only established late in the 19th century during the reign of Sarkin Musulmi, Abdurrahman of Sokoto (1891-1902) whereas Dabai long preceded that period. Bukkuyum is referred to in the traditions, it seems, because of the association of its ruler with the title of Sarkin Danko. The chiefdom of Danko is also said to have controlled a number of other Dakarkari settlements particularly Kele. See "Zuru Re-organisation, 1938-55" *op.cit.* p.39.

### (e) *The Katsinawan Laka*

The traditions of migrations of Katsinawan Laka are less complex than those of the Dakarkari and the Bangawa. As their name suggests, the group claims migrations from southern part of Katsina, the Katsinan Laka. The migrants are said to have initially gone to settle among the Achipawa in the surrounding hills of Maburia, Kumbashi and Karishen.[51] Subsequently, other migrants went and settled at Mohero and Tsohon Birni (close to Sakaba) and later, other immigrants went to establish Wasagu, Bena and other surrounding settlements.[52]

The dates for these movements are not clear, but Katsinawan Laka is associated with significant historical developments from early period. Some of the most ancient centres of population of Katsina were established in this area, notably Kwatarkwashi and Kuyambana.[53] There were also significant migrations from Kuyambana to Yawuri and Kebbi which were believed to have led to the foundation of these two kingdoms in the 15th and 16th centuries respectively.[54] According to P.G. Harris, the establishment of Wasagu and Bena by the later Katsinawa immigrants occurred at the beginning of the 19th century which suggests that the earlier migrations took place earlier than that century.[55]

The establishment of katsinawan Laka undoubtedly made the political process in Zuru more complex as new settlements and political units as well as various new cultural, economic and political relations came to be developed in the region.

### (f) *The Dukawa*

Like the Dakarkari and the Bangawa, the Dukawa have traditions of migrations from Kebbi, Zamfara and Katsina although the Kebbi traditions have been most emphasised[56] As Professor Mahdi Adamu asserts, therefore, [57] it is doubtful if Dukawa claim of origin from Hausa is correct because neither their language nor the basic tenets of

---

[51] Duff and Hamilton - Browne, *op.cit.* p.30; P.G. Harris, Gazetteer, *op.cit.* pp. 311-312.

[52] Harris, *ibid*, p. 312; Duff and Hamilton-Browne, *ibid*, p.31.

[53] Y.B. Usman, *The Transformation of Katsina op.cit* p.7-10.

[54] M. Adamu, "A Hausa Government in Decline", *op.cit* P.46 ff; M.B. Alkali, *op.cit* p.43 ff.

[55] P.G. Harris, *Gazetteer, op.cit* p.312. See also, Duff and Hamilton-Browne, *op.cit* p.31

[56] A.B. Matthews, "Historical and Anthropological Report on the Katsinawa". File No. SNP. 17-8/K.2100, National Archives, Kaduna, P.G. Harris, *Gazetteer, op,cit* Pp. 312-313.

[57] C. E. Boyd and J. C. O. Clarke, "The Dukkawa" in C.L. Temple (ed) *op. cit* p. 96.

their society are of real semblance to the Hausa.[58] What appears to be true is that some autochtonous population were infiltrated by many waves of migrants with the latter being absorbed, culturally and linguistically, by the former.[59]

### (g) *The Fakawa*

The Fakawa are believed to have moved into Zuru from Fakka in present Yabo district early in the 19th century.[60] They seem to be the most recent immigrant groups in the region. The Fakawa are connected with the formation of the chiefdom of Fakai which played a prominent role in the political history of Zuru in the 19th century.

## *Internal Migrations*

The migrations discussed above are essentially migrations from outside Zuru Emirate. Sources are generally silent on internal migrations within the region. This, however, should not lead us to believe that there were no such movements. The silence of sources on such movements might simply be because they were not spectacular, i.e. they did not involve large groups and were generally less politically significant. Nonetheless, however, there are some glimpses of such movements such as are associated with the influences which the Achipawa and the chiefdom of Danko are believed to have exercised on Dabai. It is also possible that the spread of Katsinawan Laka in the areas of Karishen, and Kumbashi, Mohero and Tsohon Birni as well as Wasagu and Bena did not simply involve new waves of immigrant groups arriving, each time, from outside the present Zuru Emirate, but also involved movements of some of the already established Katsinawa in the area. Besides these, the practice of shifting cultivation, which has been widespread in Zuru, and hunting must have involved frequent movements of people within the region. However, only more research may help throw further light on this issue.

## *The General Significance of Migrations*

There were four major ways in which migrations played a very important role in the history of Zuru Emirate before the 20th century. Firstly, the phenomenon appeared to have greatly expanded the populations in the region thereby leading to the expansion of

---

[58] M. Adamu, "The Hausa Factor", *op.cit* p.31.
[59] *ibid*, pp.31 - 32.
[60] P.G. Harris, "Gazetteer" *op.cit* p.314. See also Duff and Hamilton - Browne, *op.cit* p.32. (fn.) for a variant of this tradition.

settlements or emergence of new ones such as Karishen, Tsohon Birni, Mohero, Wasagu, Bena, Ribah, Dabai, Isgogo, Sanchi, Manga, Peni, Chonoko, Fakai and Danko. Secondly, the expansion of population seemed to have stimulated economic activities including agriculture, hunting, manufacture or processing of products e.g. iron and shea-butter and commerce. Thirdly, the phenomenon of migrations promoted cultural and political interactions e.g. the spread of *m'gilø cult* among the Dakarkari, Dukawa and Kambari people, inter-marriages and exchange of occupational skills. Lastly, migrations contributed greatly to the emergence of the cultural and political communities in the region i.e. the various groups discussed earlier and the many polities established by them such as Karishen, Danko, Dabai, Fakai Wasagu and Bena. In the rest of this paper, we shall discuss the main social and political developments in the region by 1900 A.D. which were, in many ways, associated with the migrations.

## 5. The Dimensions of Social and Political Evolution of Zuru Society by 1900 A.D.

There are two major dimensions of Zuru society that we shall examine in this section - (a) the political systems, and (b) the structure of the society.

### A. *The Political Systems*

There existed many political systems in Zuru before 1900 A.D. These polities were of much smaller territorial sizes than the major states which surrounded them, i.e. Yawuri, Kebbi, Zamfara and Katsina. But, as said earlier, the polities were not of equal status in terms of territory, power and influence exercised by them as well or in terms of their social structures. Many of the polities among the Dakarkari, Dukawa and Kambari hardly extended beyond autonomous settlements. Many, however, incorporated several settlements thereby covering sizeable areas of territory. Among the latter were Karishen, Wasagu, Dabai, Danko and Fakai. We shall briefly discuss some of these polities and the various kinds of relations among them and their neighbours and the political factors which affected these relations.

### (i) *Karishen*

This state was centred on the town of karishen, but its authority seemed to have extended over the surrounding settlements. Its king, known as the *Womo* or *Ashifa* appeared to have wielded considerable spiritual powers part of which seems to derive from the claims that he was the custodian of the sword of Kisra, the purported ancestor of all the Bariba peoples.[61] As has been mentioned earlier, Karishen's influence extended up to Dabai and Kanoma area in Maru district of present Anka local government area. On the other hand, however, Karishen appeared to have come under the influence of the kingdom of Katsina. For example, late in the 18th century, Sarkin Katsina, Gozo Tsagarana (C.1796 - 1801), was reputed to have sent a military expedition against Sarkin Karishen.[62]

(ii) *The Politics of the Katsinawan Laka*

These polities were established within Zuru and surrounding areas of Kontagora. As stated earlier, the polities included Maburia, Kumbashi, Kakihun, Ukata, Mohero, Tsohon Birni, Wasagu and Bena. Also, the polity of Ribah is said to have been established by Katsinawa. The various polities, as suggested earlier, emerged at different moments in history, the latest being Wasagu and Bena which were probably established early in the 19th century. Among these polities, Wasagu appeared to have been politically more prominent as its territorial control expanded particularly west-wards to incorporate such D'akarkari settlements as Kanya and Chonoko.[63]

The establishment of the polities of Katshinawan Laka, as discussed earlier, came in the wake of a series of waves of migrations from southern Katsina. As some of the traditions of these migrations tend to suggest, these immigrants were attracted to Zuru particularly because of the agricultural and hunting opportunities offered by the area.[64] Other economic attractions to the population were the prospects for iron ore mining and commerce linking the region with Katsina and Zamfara in the north and Nupe, Yawuri and other areas lying to the south. In the 19th century, for example, Bena became an important centre for such commerce.

Like Karishen, these polities seemed to have come under much influence from Katsina. They are said for example, to have borrowed many of their political titles from Katsina, some obtained their regalias for their chiefs from that kingdom while the Sarakunan[65] Katsina occasionally arbitrated in their disputes.

---

[61] P.G. Harris, *ibid*, p.311.

[62] Y.B. Usman, The Transformation of Katsina, *op.cit.* p.84

[63] "Zuru Re-organisation," 1938-55" *op.cit* p. 39.

[64] For such traditions, see P.G. Harris, "Notes on the Dakarkari" *op.cit.*; Joshua I. Ganya, *op.cit* p.3; A.M.D. Rabah, *op.cit* p.7., etc.

[65] Y.B. Usman, *The Transformation of Katsina*, *op.cit.* p. 84 .

(iii) *The Polities Of The Dakarkari*

The polities established among the Dakarkari included Dabai, Kele, Isgogo, Jambo, Kyabo Rikoto, Peni, Manga and Azuguru (Zuru). Many of the polities of the Dakarkari, as indicated earlier, consisted of no more than single autonomous settlements. Some, however, exercised influence over other settlements such as Dabai. The position of Dabai was probably enhanced by its role or control over the religious practices associated with Germache Shrine which many Dakarkari revered as well as the pre-eminent role of its rain-maker. Some of the Dakarkari states including Dabai, as seen earlier, came under the influence of both the Achipawa state of Karishen and Danko. The ruler of Danko was, in fact, said to have, before the 20th century, emerged to be responsible for installing a new Sarkin Dabai. Similarly, as we have seen, Kanya and Chonoko were subordinated to the authority of Wasagu. In the latter part of the 19th Century, Fakai is also said to have subordinated several Dakarkari settlements to its control.

The general structure of the Dakarkari polities was one in which there was an overall ruler known as the *gomo*. The *gomo* exercised the overall political and judicial powers over his state with a number of subordinate officials including clan elders-*Gonvun* Dkøbøh, the Chief Priest of the M'gilø cult and various other title holders.[66] Many of the titles were of Hausa origin e.g. *gadema (galadima)*, *magazi* (magaji), *Obandake* (ubandawaki) and ch'zagi (*zagi*) which is an illustration of the significant influences of the surrounding Hausa-speaking state on Zuru.

(iv) *Danko*

The pre-eminent position of the chiefdom of Danko among the states established in zuru Emirate before colonial role is generally acknowledged. It is not, however, clear when the state was established although P.G. Harris tends to associate it with the emergence of Zoma state in the middle Gulbin Ka region which probably occurred in the 17th century.[67] The state is believed to have controlled all the territory which today forms Danko district and is also said to have brought under its control the Dakarkari settlements around the hill country of Kyabo.[68] It is also said to have exercised some nominal suzerainty over Kele, a factor which is probably connected with the close similarity between Kelanci, the language of the people of Kele and

---

[66] Joshua I. Ganya, op.cit pp. 6-11; A.M.D. Ribah, op.cit. p.8.
[67] P.G. Harris, "Gazetteer" op.cit p. 129.
[68] "Zuru Re-organisation, 1938-55" *op.cit* p.39.

Banganci, the language of the people of Danko. This state also exercised some suzerainty over Dabai as seen earlier.

**Alhaji Ibrahim Allah Aje**
District Head of Danko
*(Installed October 1980 )*

During the mid - 18th century, Danko, along with settlements of Zoma kingdom, were affected by the developments brought about by the conquest of Zoma by a renegade prince of Tunfafi (Mafara) in central Zamfara named Ali Bazamfare. Following an unsuccessful succession dispute with this brother at home, Ali is said to have moved southwards into Zoma where he initiated a military career which led to the establishment of his dynasty over the area.[69]

(v) *Fakai*

Fakai was established in the 19th century by some immigrants from present Yabo district. The settlement, however, gradually expanded and its rulers are said to have built their power over and above that of other settlements around, e.g. Gele, several of which they eventually brought under their control.[70] Fakai also entered into an alliance with the rulers of Kontagora which seemed to have greatly strengthened its position in the inter-state politics of the area. This positions, however, was dealt a severe blow when the Fakawa and their kontagora allies were severely defeated by the Dakarkari at Penin Amana.[71]

As with the evolution of the cultural and linguistic groups of Zuru emirate, the discussion on the polities which sprang up among them clearly reveals the complex nature of these polities not only in terms of their structures, but also in terms of the historical factors which shaped them. Internally as we have seen, the various polities developed many kinds of relations, including alliances among themselves, which influenced their developments. Externally, factors such as the growth of power of the kingdom of Katsina, the establishment of the capital of Kebbi at Birnin Kebbi early in the 18th century and the political crises in the central Rima basin, involving particularly Gobir and Zamfara in the 18th century, all had significant repercussions for many of the polities in Zuru Emirate. The Sokoto Jihad similarly affected the region in various ways, e.g. some of the polities of Zuru came under Sokoto's influence through the establishment of *aman* relationship between the two sides which is said to have included making some annual payments to Sokoto;[72] the area suffered several raids from Kontagora; the alliance between Kontagora and Fakai contributed to

---

[69] P.G. Harris, "Gazetteer" *op.cit* pp.314-320; "Bukkuyum District Notebook", Sokoto State Government Archives.

[70] Duff and Hamilton-Browne, Ibid, pp. 32.fn.7. See also "Zuru Re-organisation, 1938-55", op.cit pp.39-40.

[71] Duff and Hamilton-Browne, *ibid*, pp. 32-33; S.J. Hogben and A.H.M. Kirk-Greene, *The Emirates of Northern Nigeria*. Oxford, 1966, p. 504.

[72] See M.S. Sakaba, *op.cit*. See also P.G. Harris, Gazetteer, op.cit pp. 319-320 especially on the tributes said to have been paid to Sokoto authorities via Tambuwal.

the growth of power of the latter with serious consequence for its neighbours, etc.

## (b) *The Society*

The main dimensions of the society in Zuru Emirate before 1900 A.D. which we need to focus our attention on are the settlements, the economy (production and commerce), religion and culture and the social groups

### (i) *The settlements*

The emirate of Zuru has not been noted for large towns or urban centres. Indeed, as mentioned earlier, even in the present times, the overwhelming population lives in small hamlets scattered over the region. Nevertheless, however, settlements in pre-1900 Zuru could still be classified into two major types: the fairly sizeable settlements which served as centres of administration, commerce or religion or a combination of these such as Wasagu, Bena, Karishen, Tsohon Birni, Dabai, Danko, Fakai, Peni, Kele and Ribah and the small hamlets or homesteads scattered over the region.

There is a view which seems to suggest that the population of Zuru Emirate lived in larger settlements before the 20th century than they do today.[73] This view is mainly based on the assumption that there was an atmosphere of internecine wars especially raids on the populations of the region which forced many people into compact and, in some cases, fortified settlements especially on hill-tops in order to protect themselves[74]. This is of course a popular assertion with regards to the history of many central Nigerian communities, notably those associated with the activities of the emirate of Kontagora. We cannot, however, clearly verify this view without a more detailed research on the subject.

It appears that in pre-1900 era, there were concentrations of settlements around politically and economically prominent towns such as Danko, Dabai, Fakai Wasagu and Bena. In particular, the triangle formed by the towns of Fakai, Danko and Dabai seemed to have been one of the most, if not the most, important areas of such concentration. These three towns were not the only ones located in their region, but others included Gele, Isgogo, Penin Amana, Penin Gaba and Kele.

### (ii) *The Economy*

The economy of Zuru was principally based on agriculture with hunting and manufacturing activities being other important

---

[73] Gunna and Conant, *op.cit* pp. 25,37-38 and 52.
[74] *Ibid.*

occupations. The organization of production among the people of Zuru in pre-1900 followed the general pattern obtained in many Nigerian societies. Land was shared out among patrilineages who held such land more or less on hereditary basis. Although there was widespread practice of shifting cultivation which made it possible for occasional change of plots of land, such practice did not seem to apply to areas of concentration of settlements where land seemed to be more or less permanently held. Over and above the lineages, the chief, in each settlement, exercised overall supervisory role in land matters especially over its distribution, settlement of land disputes and providing leadership in rites involving land and agriculture. For this role, the chief received various services from the people.

Agricultural production involved all members of lineages including women and children. The women did the household chores and performed the natural role of reproducing the labour required on the farms. In various societies, they also held plots of land on which they grew *acca*, benniseed and beans.[75] Agricultural circle involved various religious practices including those relating to propitiation of the earth spirits for bountiful harvests and thanks-giving purposes. Such practices included those around the *M'gilø* cult which was widespread in the region and *Uhola* and *Dbiti* ceremonies among the Dakarkari.

Extended communal labour was also practised such as *golmo* among the Dakarkari. Wealthy farmers were honoured with titles and other special social privileges.[76]

Hunting involved both groups and individuals and was mainly a dry season activity, i.e. outside the main agricultural season. Successful hunters who were able to kill large animals were also given titles and other privileges in the society.[77]

The main manufacturing activities in the society, as noted earlier, were the processing of *dorawa* seeds to produce *Kalwa* or *daddawa* seasoning, the smelting of iron ore and the making of tools and weapons and the production of shea-butter.

Local and long distance trade appeared to have occupied a significant place in Zuru society in spite of the tendency to regard it otherwise. At local level, exchange relations involving farmers, hunters, potters, barbers, blacksmiths, medicine men and other such specialized groups were widespread. Meat, for example, is said to

---

[75] *ibid*, pp.23,35 and 51.

[76] Other privileges included special drum beatings and special funeral rites at death. See P.G. Harris, "Notes on the Dakarkari" op.cit. Duff and Hamilton-Browne, op.cit pp. 58-59.

[77] P.G. Harris, *loc.cit.e*

have been exchanged for hoes and cutlasses.[78] The Dukawa obtained iron hoes and tobacco from the Dakarkari in exchange for other products, possibly including medicine for which Dukawa had great reputation. Neighbouring settlements had alternating market days which promoted exchange relations among their populations.[79] By the end of the 19th century, long distance trade appeared to have involved the importation, into Zuru, of horses, salt, dogs, swords and cloths (e.g. *Bante*:loin cloth) and the export of *Kalwa, man kade* (sheabutter), other foodstuffs, tobacco and slaves.[80] Important centres of trade included Bena, Isgogo, Wasagu, Dabai, Fakai and Danko. The view that trade in Zuru in the past was difficult and restricted because the area was hilly, thickly forested and inaccessible and because it had few natural resources does not, therefore, appear to be quite tenable.[81]

(iii) *Cultural And Religious Dimensions*

The societies of Zuru and the neighbouring areas as we shall see in the next chapter shared many similar cultural and religious institutions and practices as well as relations.[82] Linguistically, as Amfani showed, most of the groups belonged to a common sub-branch of languages within the central branch of the Niger-Congo family. Inter-marriages between the various cultural groups in the region are said to be common. Wrestling and rites of passage were not only common in the region, but were, in many ways, similar in nature. At religious level, the various groups practised many kinds of rites pertaining to ancestors and to the earth spirits and also developed the concept of supreme being which united the various groups at the level of cosmology.[83]

The religious features of Zuru society clearly indicate the changes which its people had gone through in the course of their history. The rites to ancestors such as demonstrated in the *wøh* and *skokkoboh*

---

[78] S. Mohammed, *op.cit*. p.100

[79] Such as among the Dakarkari. See Gunn and Conant, *op.cit* p. 37

[80] Salt, *bante* and dogs are mentioned by M.S. Sakaba as imports into Zuru which were obtained for slaves and cowries from markets of Zamfara and Jega; Horses and swords are mentioned as occupying important role in the history of Zuru especially in the 19th century. Horses in particular, but swords also, could only have come through exchange. *Kalwa, man-kade*, tobacco and grains were produced in surplus in Zuru and exchanged in surrounding area where they were needed e.g. with the Dukawa, Zamfara, Kebbi and Sokoto. *Man Kade*, for example, was reputed to have been used by the Dakarkari in building up the portion of the city of Surame in Kebbi assigned to them by Sarkin Kebbi, Kanta.

[81] This view has been expressed by S. Mohammed, *Op.cit*. p.100.

[82] Gunn and Conant, *op. cit passim*

[83] *Ibid.* pp. 28 - 29, 46 - 84 and 54.

ceremonies of the Dakarkari and the various family worship practices of other groups were clearly the earliest forms of beliefs and practices to emerge out of these societies. They seemed to have developed at the period when families lived in autonomous units before historical circumstances such as the growth of permanent agriculture and sedentary life pulled these families together into settlements. The coming together of many families within the same settlements and the development of various common relations among them, including agriculture and hunting necessitated the development of belief systems and practices to unite them. The development of beliefs and practices around earth spirits such as the *M'gilø* cult, *Dbiti* and *Uhola* among the Dakarkari for example, seemed to have emerged in such circumstances. *M'gilø* was widely practised in Zuru Emirate and surrounding region. The last stage in the development of local religious beliefs and practices in Zuru was the development of the concept of the supreme being known variously as *kashilu, Usulu* or *Kashile* among the Kambari, *Assilø* among the Dakarkari and *Isbili* among the Dukawa.[84] Among the Achipawa, the chief was regarded as the supreme being, his epithet being "*daidai da Allah*" (i.e. he was equal to God.)[85]

Islam no doubt had significant influences on the society of Zuru Emirate even before the 20th century. Many of the groups which migrated into the area came from areas where Islam had made some inroads in some cases, as far back as the 15th century, notably Katsina and Kebbi. Many of the individuals and groups among the Katsinawan Laka and the Fakawa would have been muslims, even if only nominally, by the time of their movements into the region. The area was also affected by the Sokoto Jihad movement in the 19th century as a result of which it must have received further Islamic influences.

(iv) *The Social Groups*

In spite of the absence of large territorial states in Zuru Emirate before the 20th century, yet the society was hierarchised and was made up of unequal social classes. At the top of the social ladder were the chiefs - the *gomo*, (sarki). Around the chief were other privileged titled members in the society, including priests of religious cults such as *Gomvun M'gilø* (chief priest of the M'gilø among the Dakarkari) and *Bakin Dodo* (his equivalent among the Dukawa), clan heads, chief farmers and head hunters. These people wielded power, authority and influence in the society. Below them was the bulk of the population

---

[84] *ibid.*

[85] S. Mohammed, *Op.cit.* p.17.

which was generally organised in age-sets known among the Dakarkari as *skeme* or *skemo*. There were also elements of servile status kept especially by chiefs and their officials and other well-to-do in the society. Women were generally subordinated in the social structure although they performed very vital functions in reproducing the society, performing household chores, assisting in agriculture and undertaking petty trading.

## 6. Conclusion

The above survey reveals the complex nature of the history of Zuru Emirate. As the survey has shown, the problem of reconstructing Zuru history is not so much one of lack of data, but rather that of meaningfully employing the data to properly reconstruct the dimensions of the evolution of the society. The survey has further revealed that the communities of Zuru, as with other areas around them, were not static and that important changes had taken place among them even before the century such as the transition from Stone Age to Iron Age and from hunting to agricultural societies. The societies were also far from being isolated in so far as there were constant movements of people in the region and the development of various forms of cultural, economic, religious and political interactions among them as well as between them and their neighbours. The societies also developed hierarchised political systems with some elaborate social structure of unequal elements in the society. It was upon these complex social and political structures that the British colonialists imposed their domination early in this century and sought ways and means of building up a unified administrative and political structure. The making of Sakaba Emirate, Dabai emirate, Zuru Federation, Zuru xNative Authority, Zuru Division, and now Zuru Emirate are all part of the dynamics of the long history of the area.

Chapter Six

# Transition And Changes In Religions And Belief Systems In Zuru Emirate.

*by*

**Ahmed Bako**

## Introduction

This chapter is an attempt to provide an account of the religious history of the people of Zuru Emirate. The paper will investigate the past and the present religious practices of the inhabitants of the region in order to understand the social forces that made or are still making religious changes possible.

Furthermore, the paper will show that the people occupying the Zuru Emirate have a religion of their own and that religion has been embedded into the core of their material as well as spiritual lives. Also, the paper will examine how the religions of Islam and Christianity affected and changed the religious lives of the inhabitants of the Zuru region.

In a sense therefore, this part of the book is fundamentally going to deal with interaction of three different religions: viz; Traditional Religion, Islam and Christianity. The sense in which one can deal with the purely religious aspects of the interaction of these three religions is difficult, for other factors (education, mechanization, migration and certainly politics) are powerful forces for change, that to observe religion exclusively in studying religious history is impossible. Yet no study on the subject which we have set out to deal with could do justice to all these dynamic forces around which, and within which, religion takes its shape.

## Pre-Colonial And Colonial Economic Activities And Social Relations.

Since previous chapters have already discussed both the geography, people and the pre-colonial and colonial economic activities of Zuru region, I do not wish to say much on this here. What must be emphasized, however, is that unlike other parts of Sokoto State, Zuru Emirate is situated in a hilly terrain and it enjoys a fairly heavy annual rain that lasts for about six months, from April to late October. And due to this important factor (i.e heavy rainfall), agriculture has become a successful venture as well as the predominant occupation and economic activity of the people of the emirate. Peasant production was the dominant form of agricultural production, and the peasantry controlled directly its means of production-land. Labour operated in Communitarian units and it was controlled by *Masu Gidaje* (household heads). During the pre-colonial period agricultural activity was dominated by a grain economy based on the production of millet and guinea-corn, for food and beer. Other crops that were cultivated included tubers (yams, cassava and cocoyam).

It is important to point out that production of agricultural goods in pre-colonial Zuru society was geared mainly towards the production of use-values. This is not to say that exchange did not take place. There was exchange between the produce of peasant families and the commodities of non-peasant households who specialized in the production of agricultural implements and other necessities which were fundamental in the workings of family units.

Animal husbandry was practised side by side with crop cultivation, even though on a limited scale. The people of Zuru Emirate depended largely on the pastoral Fulani for meat, milk and butter.

Hunting was the second important economic activity after crop cultivation. Hunting was regarded as a supplementary occupation and was carried on throughout the year because it provides a means of getting meat for consumption. It also serves as a source of obtaining skins of animals for shoes, warfare robes, sash for carrying children and for making local drums. Hunting expedition was done in different ways in accordance with the changing times. For instance, in the wet season when people were busy on their farms, it was done by means of large traps by individual farmers or families. But during the dry season when people are less busy and when the country side was more open, people hunt in groups with bows and arrows as well as hunting dogs.

Other important economic activities are local handicrafts like pot-making and weaving by women and blacksmithing by men. Though peasant units did engage in hand craft production, there existed specialized groups, who engage in industrial production on a permanent basis. Blacksmithing was the most important craft, for those who engage in it provided the society with tools for production. Blacksmiths make hoes and ploughs for the farmers, knives and cutlasses and arrows for the hunters.

## Colonial Conquest, Economic Activities And Social Relations In Zuru Emirate.

The economic activities of Zuru Emirate like that of other societies in Africa, underwent far reaching transformation under the impact of colonial rule. After the colonization of Zuru Emirate in 1910,[1] the colonial state and traders jointly used price mechanism, exorbitant taxation policies, religious ethics and force to extract surplus value from the hitherto independent peasantry of the region. Since the purpose of colonial domination of Zuru region was to stimulate the production of raw materials needed by British industries and to create markets for the products of these industries, the colonial authority in Zuru encouraged the cultivation of groundnuts and cotton as cash crops. Also because of the British land and labour policies in Northern Nigeria, other changes became inevitable in the economy of Zuru Emirate. The appropriation of uncultivated lands had significant effects on agricultural producers, who could not expand their acreage or acquire new farmlands.[2] These new policies greatly led to land hunger along with other related consequences such as poverty and malnutrition. It is important to note that the British colonizers did not mechanize agriculture in Zuru region before they left in 1960.

## Economic Activities, Social Relations And Religion.

It is within the context of the above economic and social relations in pre-colonial and colonial Zuru society that we will study religious changes in the region. Our fundamental argument is that religion in Zuru Emirate (especially pre-colonial Zuru) was intricately related to the material life of the people: viz: Agriculture, Rainfall, Hunger, Drought, Disintegration etc. What we are saying in this regard is that religion as part of the superstructure of the society is shaped by the infrastructure. Thus, changes in nature of production and social relations will ultimately lead to changes in religious beliefs and practices.

We have already indicated that in pre-colonial Zuru society economic activities were based on the production of use-values, and social relation was based on simple form of community exchange and not on labour exploitation and unequal exchange. Our argument is that in simple societies, like pre-colonial Zuru region, traditional forms of

---

[1] Mohammed Abdullahi, "Political and Economic Development of Colonial Northern Nigeria: Case of Zuru" *B.A. History Thesis*, University of Sokoto 1985, p. 14.

[2] Mansur I. Muhktar, "The Significance of Colonial Labour policies in the Re-Orientation of the Economy of Kano in the first half of the 20th century" *Second International Conference on Kano History* p. 4-6.

worship were the main forms of religions and belief systems. Also religion in such kind of societies organize people politically. That is to say that political institutions were organized around religious institutions, and the social order of such kind of societies was harmonized, sanctified and expressed in religious ceremonies.

Transition from traditional religions (which are family centred religions, clan centred religions etc) to Islam and Christianity in Zuru region was the result of the disintegration of the older values due to increasing class differentiation; occupational sophistication and grouping; concentration of wealth in the hands of private groups; external migration and colonial conquest. As the older values disintegrated, social and economic conflicts became too intense and too complex to be mediated by traditional forms of worships. It was in this context that the need to replace or at least to supplement individual gods with the Universal God arose. Islam and Christianity entered and spread in Zuru region at the time of these needs. The two religions replaced the traditional religions in some parts of the emirate, and in other parts they only supplemented the traditional modes of worship.

In the pages below we discuss the three religions and the interrelation between them. We start by examining the pre-Islamic and pre-Christian religious practices of the region. The second and third parts of the paper examine how Islam and Christianity (respectively) entered Zuru region and interacted with traditional belief systems. Once again our fundamental argument in the paper is that religious changes and transitions in Zuru society was the result of economic transformations and changing nature of social relations that came about due to migration, urbanization, colonization etc.

Indeed, in our effort to write this paper, we have encountered some problems. First, there was the problem of dearth of sources due to the fact that the region (i.e. the Zuru emirate) did not have a highly developed traditional life. The other problem is the difficulty in deciding which tribe or sets of tribes to select among many other tribes in the emirate as case studies. Indeed, it would be sheer presumption for anyone to try to cover all the tribes in the emirate. In this paper attention was given to the major tribes in the emirate, viz:- Hausawa, Dakarkari, Fakkawa, Dakkawa, Gelawa, Achipawa and Bangawa. The selection is based on various geographical and historical factors which have bearing on their religious similarities.

## Section One: *Traditional Religious Practices In Zuru Emirate.*

Historically we know little on all the types of religions that the people occupying Zuru region practiced before the spread of Islam and Christianity. What is however certain is that before Islam and

Christianity, the inhabitants of Zuru area believe that there is a supreme 'God', a *superenti* to whom people direct prayers and in whose names blessings are invoked. Indeed, God's name is called in the people's daily activities and God is believed to be Masculine.[3]

In general terms, the religious practices of the inhabitants of Zuru emirate before Islam and Christianity are called traditional religions, for they have been handed down from fore-fathers, and each generation takes them up with modification suitable to its own historical situation and needs.[4] One interesting thing about traditional religions in Zuru area is that each (of the religions) arose in one cultural area, and as they spread they served as vehicles for the diffusion of social institutions and cultural values. Religious practices, including those with the same or similar names are being practiced differently in different parts of the emirate. In other words, local variations exist in the traditional religions of the Zuru people.[5] In this sense one can say that it is difficult to systematize the belief systems of the people of Zuru emirate before Islam and Christianity. Religion in pre-Christo-Islamic Zuru region is characterized by lack of rigidity. For instance, no definite list of gods may be given since new ones seem to be constantly invented.

Among many of the traditional religious acts that are being practiced by the people of Zuru area are: Ancestor worship, *M'gilø*, *Uhola* and *Dibiti*, *Wøh* and *Golmo*.[6] Some of these religious practices as already indicated are also considered to be festivals. The traditional religion demands festive atmosphere in which truth can be played out. Before any of these practices/festivals take place there must

---

[3] I am indebted to M.S. Abdulkadir of History Dept., Bayero University Kano whose paper "The Jihad in Igalaland" November, 1985 increased my knowledge to the understanding of Traditional Religion in African Societies. Although his paper fundamentally treated Igalaland, his findings are more or less similar to what I found druing my field work in Zuru,

[4] For a brief summary of all the religious practices of the Zuru people, see S. Mohammed, "Some Aspects of the Culture and Institutions of the Dakarkari people examined in the light of their contiguity with the Hausa people". *M.A. Thesis*, Dept. of Nigerian Languages, Bayero University Kano 1982, pp 17-31; 51-63 and 106-17.

[5] Mallam Salihu an elderly man in Zuru town confirmed this information to be during the first Workshop of Zuru History Project, November 1986. Also my informants in Ribah 24th December, 1985, Dirin Gari 25th December, 1985 confirmed the view.

[6] These Religious practices are not being practiced by all Zuru people. Some areas accept and practice them all and other areas practice only one or two. Dirin Gari and Ribah practice all. Wasagu District Practice only Uhola and Makoki Wøh. (Oral information gathered during my field work in December, 1985).

be sacrifices.[7] Although the people of Zuru area have not clearly articulated their theological beliefs about 'God', some people claimed that sacrifices (during any of these religious practices and festivals) are directed to God, who is considered the Almighty.

## Ancestors As Leader-Figures In Traditional Religions.

Respect to Ancestors known as *Øknu* in *Dakarci* language is one of the most important forms of worships among the followers of Traditional Religions in Zuru Emirate. Ancestors come under an all embracing spirits and are considered to be intermediaries between the living and God. Like the spirits, ancestors are channels through which devoted worshippers convey their prayers to the Supreme Being.

To qualify as an ancestor in traditional Zuru belief systems, a person must attain certain socially approved objectives while still alive. An Ancestor must for example, have lived to old age; must have led a good unblemished life; and must have children surviving his death to ensure the continuation of the tribe or family. Commenting on Ancestor worship in African societies, Onige and Ogionwu explained that:

> Ancestor worship is a form of religion commonly found in Africa .... most people, particularly those who put in value on unilineal descent, believe in the worship of ancestors.[8]

In the past and to a certain extent up to the present, it is believed by the Zuru people (especially *Dakarkari, Kambari, Achipawa,* and *Fakkawa*) that Ancestors can influence events in the lives of the living descendants. An informant explained that sacrifices are made to ancestors periodically at certain shrines that were evidently open to all.[9] Such sacrifices are meant to feed the ancestors, and they are not routine, but were offered especially when things were not going well. When sacrifices are made to the ancestors they served as symbols of fellowship, a recognition that the departed are still members of human families. Sacrifices to ancestors also are acts which renew contact between God and man, the spirits and man i.e., the spiritual and physical world. Some of my informants emphasised that 'Ancestors intercede to bring good things and are never responsible for

---

[7] During any of these sacrifices dogs or goats are slaughtered. The Dakarkari people slaughter dogs on most occasions. Elders eat the meat of the animal slaughtered and the blood is sprayed on Shrines.

[8] Ottite Onigu and Ogionwo, W. *An Introduction to Sociological Studies P. 160* (Quoted in Chidobelu Ofia, *Bafasido Religion The Search for a Suitable name for the Aboriginal African Religion.* (1987) p.11.

[9] An information in Dirin Gari during group interview, 25/12/85.

misfortune'.[10] Commenting on ancestor worship in African societies, Mbiti has this to say;

> Ancestors (the living dead) occupy the ontological position between the spirits and men, and between God and men., They (i.e Ancestors) in effect speak a bilingual language of human beings whom they recently 'left' through physical death, and of the spirits to whom they are now joined, or of God to whom they are now nearer than they were in their physical life. Because of this unique position, the living-dead constitute the largest group of intermediaries in African societies.[11]

Indeed, the truth about the ancestor worship as Glyn Leonard observed is that all of us, regardless of creed, nationality, religion or culture respect our ancestors. Even the Christians and Muslims not only look forward to meeting those who have brought them into this world but believe that their ancestors are looking over their activities.[12]

## M'gilø: The Most Ancient Religious Cult

M'gilø is the most ancient and powerful religious cult in Zuru Emirate,[13] P.G. Harris believes that the cult of M'gilø is widespread, and states that it originated in Kotorkoshi, Sokoto Province. Furthermore, Harris argued that traces of M'gilø are found in Argungu as well as Yauri and Kontagora.[14]

The M'gilø celebration developed out of the worship of the spirits of the ancestors. This fact explained why all villages, districts and towns in Zuru Emirate constructed huts where M'gilø dwells. M'gilø is considered to be intermediary between men and God, and M'gilø gives and takes, punishes and rewards, hence the sacrifices and appeasements. Disputes are settled by M'gilø cult members who act as courts of law, hearing disputes over the use of land and cases involving fights.[15] The fact that M'gilø cult members settle disputes is an indication that pre-colonial or pre-Christian-Islamic religion in Zuru society was related to the socio-political institutions.

During M'gilø festival which takes place annually, dogs are slaughtered and a special wine (Mkya) made from guinea-corn flour is

---

[10] ibid.

[11] J.S. Mbiti, *African Religion and Philosophy*, P.90.

[12] Major A. Glyn L, *The Lower Niger and Its Tribes* P. 90.

[13] Ahman, H, "Zuru-Dabai Relations: A Case Study of the rise of political institutions in Zuru Emirate", *Unpublished B.A. Thesis*, University of Sokoto, 1983, p.11.

[14] H.D. Gunn & E.P. Conant, *The Dakarkari and Dukawa Peoples*, p. 17.

[15] Yusuf, M. Dandikko, "Traditional Medicine among the Dakarkari speaking peoples in the 20th century", *B.A Thesis History*, University of Sokoto, 1986 p.22.

prepared. According to an informant only those men who are well versed with the traditional rights and obligations prepared the wine.[16]

No woman is allowed to sing, dance or play during the *M'gilø* festival and this according to the belief of Zuru people is because a woman could not and would never become an intermediary between God and the people. It is believed that any woman who sees *M'gilø* will die instantly.[17] Flute and drum are the only two instruments that are used during the M'gilø celebrations, and whoever plays any other instrument or performs wrong acts would have to be punished by God through the *Gom-vu-M'gilø*. The offender many be asked to surrender a goat, a dog or some chicken to the deity. As a rule M'gilø mixes little with mankind.

Beside dancing, singing, sacrifices and drinking, young men of between seven to nine years of age are initiated into the traditional society during the *M'gilø festivals*.[18] The initiation of the young is a key moment in the lives of the individuals, for with the initiation, the youth are ritually introduced to the art of communal living and state of sexual and social responsibilities. With the initiation, the young was introduced into adult life and was allowed to share all privileges and duties of the community. Moreover, initiation rites have a great educational beginning of acquiring knowledge which is otherwise not accessible to those who have not been initiated. According to D.S. Magaji, initiation was and is still a very important religious practice during the *M'gilø* festival.[19]

During the initiation, boys are taken to the *Gidan M'gilø* i.e *Køb-dim'gilø* naked by his parents or parents' friends, and they are whipped and forced to work hard.[20] *Køb dim'gilø* is looked upon with considerable awe by youngsters. Any of the boys who cannot endure the hardship during the initiation rituals is sent away. The idea of this custom is to give young men courage so that they become brave men. After this ceremony a youth is allowed to put on *Ubada* (loin-skin) which hangs down behind. He is now supposed to be entering manhood and for the next two years assists his father in farming.

---

[16] Mallam Salisu Zuru, A Middle Aged Western Educated person, 22nd Nov. 1986.

[17] See Bitrus Nagode, 'The Development of Christian Churches in Zuru 1925 to 1983' (N.C.E. Dissertation, College of Education, Sokoto, 1986) p.2.

[18] Information from Usman Gele during the first Workshop of Zuru History Project, November, 1986.

[19] D.S. magaji, An Informant during the 2nd Zuru History Project Workshop, August, 1987.

[20] Bitrus Nagode, *Op.cit.*, p.3.

## Uhola And Dibiti Festivals And Sacrifices

*Uhola* and *Dibiti* are important traditional religious festivals among the people of the Zuru Emirate. These two festivals are the major seasonal rites and are both associated with Agricultural activities. In a society passionately devoted to the cultivation of the soil and crops, one must expect such kind of celebrations and communal rites specifically associated with such kind of agricultural operations as sowing, transplanting or harvesting. As we have already indicated, Agriculture in Zuru Emirate was and is still highly ritualized. The beginning, middle and ending of the farming season (the date of which varied from one part of Zuru region to another for ecological reasons), was a formal occasion marked by festivals and rituals. *Uhola* and *Dibiti* which we are going to deal with in this part are typical examples of such kind of ritualized festivals.

It was not only the practice of agriculture that was ritualized, but also the crops, especially guinea-corn and millet which constituted the backbone of the economy of Zuru region. Its spirit force was believed to be very powerful and they must be fed with Guinea-corn made beer through the *M'gilø cult* at the end of each farming season.

The celebration of Uhola takes place after agricultural products have been harvested. The fundamental aim of *Uhola* is to thank God for providing rain and the energy that was used in both the planting as well as harvesting of crops. *Uhola* therefore, is celebrated to send-off the rain by expressing gratitude to the god of rain through its shrine, known as *Købdin Menke* in *Dakarci* language.[21]

Before the *Uhola* festival, *Dibiti* (i.e mid of the year festival) must be celebrated. *Dibiti* is celebrated when crops are fully grown but not harvested. The aim of *Dibiti* is to pray to the god of rain to provide adequate atmosphere: viz: rain, wind, sunlight, etc, for the plants to grow well. It is believed that too much rain is not good for the crops. According to my informant, '*Uhola* is just like *Id-el-Kabir (Babbar Sallah)* in Islamic religion and it marks the end of the year, and *Dibiti* is like *Id-el-Fitr (Karamar Sallah)* which marks the beginning of the year.'[22]

The principal public functions in both *Uhola* and *Dibiti* are processions of men and women, boys and girls dressed up in their best, singing and dancing. Moreover, during these two festivals boys show their skill and power in wrestling.

---

[21] Rebecca, M.Y. (Mrs), "Development of Christian Churches in Zuru 1920-1983", *NCE Project*, College of Education, Sokoto. 1983. p.4.

[22] Id-el-Kabir is celebrated in the month of Dhul-Hajj, i.e. the month in which muslims all over the World gather together for pilgrimage. Id-el-Fitr is performed on the first day of Islamic Calendar.

A champion wrestler is considered to be a great man, and on his death his grave is adorned with a large *Ugamba*, a 'Y' shaped piece of wood, standing several feet high. The wrestling during *Uhola* or *Dibiti* is always attended by a large concourse of people. According to C.E. Boyd, 'wrestling is a great feature of a youth's training until about the age of fourteen when he usually commences his *Golmo*.'[23]

*Cɑ́ gamba* (singular - Ugamba) "Y" shaped instrument which is used to adorn the grave of a champion wrestler.

The Religious side of both *Uhola* and *Dibiti* consists mainly of sacrificial rites performed separately by different village clans, but intended for the general welfare of the people. The priest or an elder representing his clan or village performs these by sacrificing an animal, goat or a dog.

The social implication of *Uhola* and *Dibiti* are more easily observed than the religious. The time of any of the two festivals is an occasion for entertainment and great joy. Youths get very excited as they look forward to the day of the celebration. But for parents the period before *Uhola* or *Dibiti* is a hard time because it is their responsibility to

---

[23] C.E. Boyd, *Gazetteers of the Northern Provinces of Nigeria; The Central Kingdoms* p.57.

provide ceremonial requirements such as foodstuff and dresses for their children and wives.[24]

Indeed, there are no other seasonal rites comparable to *Dibiti* and *Uhola* and Zuru town being the headquarters of the emirate always starts celebrating these festivals before any other place.

## Makoki And Gólmo

*Makoki* or *Wøh* and *Golmo* are two other important modes of worship among the people who practice traditional religious activities in Zuru Emirate. *Wøh* is a funeral ceremony and it is conducted by the family of the deceased after the first year of his death. The importance of this ceremony in the rituals of the traditional religions in Zuru region cannot be over emphasized. *Wøh*, the soul, when it leaves the dead body cannot pass along the road that leads to its destination. In a spiritual sense therefore, *Wøh* is a special memorial service held over the deceased in order to release him from the thralldom of the region of the dead in which all souls are confined.

Before the *Wøh* takes place and the nearest relatives of the deceased meet at the house of the deceased to discuss the arrangement, a notice to the effect is publicized amongst the community. Every relative, or even connection by marriage, is bound by custom and law to contribute a share towards the *Wøh* expenses, consisting principally of eatables, drinkables, and the sacrificial offerings.

*Golmo* on the other hand is a traditional way of paying dowry or bride price by young men. It is the basis of marriage contract. During the Golmo period young men work on a future father-in-laws' farms for a number of years usually between five to seven years. A young man does not take his wife to his own house until he had completed the agreed number of '*golmo*' years. Furthermore, the future husband is not supposed to have anything to do with the girl until the *Golmo* period is finished and she has finally come over to his house. Golmo is always arranged on well organized lines by *Gom-vun Golmo* who is selected by the senior *golmo* peers.[25]

The above survey on the traditional religious practices and festivals ranging from ancestor worship to *Golmo* reveals that pre-Christo-Islamic religions of the people of Zuru Emirate is intricately interwoven with their culture. Most of the religious practices were associated with the material well-being of the people i.e. agriculture, shelter, social relations and achievement in life. In this sense one can argue that it is true as Walter Rodney emphasized that in all traditional

---

[24] *Ibid.*, p. 55.
[25] *Ibid.*, p. 57.

African societies religious beliefs were associated with the mobilization and discipline of a large number of people to form states' struggle for social justice and to produce.[26] Although these practices still exist hand- in-hand with Islam and Christianity, they have been radically changed, modified or eroded in some area. My informant in Dirin Gari emphasized that people did not like to leave their customs, festivals and practices when Islam and Christianity came.[27] Perhaps, one may argue that the spread of Islam and Christianity is a turning point in the religions history of Zuru people. The spread of these two new religions represented fundamental transformations in the history of the civilization of the Zuru region. These religions provided changes which were to leave a lasting impression on the popular culture of the inhabitants of the region. Our task in the sections below is to analyze the process by which Islam and Christianity spread and show their impact upon the areas in which they spread.

Our hypothesis in explaining why the inhabitants of the Zuru region accepted Islam and Christianity is that the religions and intellectual leadership in the older centres failed to create new ideas or articulate moral doctrines that would have been meaningful in the conditions of the time.

## Section Two: *Islam And The Rise Of Muslim Communities In Zuru Emirate.*

In this section, I shall examine the process of Islamization in Zuru region by briefly considering the various channels or methods by which Islam has penetrated and affected the inhabitants of the Zuru region. Indeed, an important factor that we will consider in our discussion is that the expansion of Islam was characterized by tolerance and a highly pragmatic approach to the problem that emerges because of the spread of Islam is that Islam interacted with traditional life in a highly positive and mutually beneficial manner.

Beyond any doubt, the people of Zuru Emirate like many other societies in Nigerian Region were familiar with the religion of Islam before Christianity. Perhaps, the earliest influence of Islam in Zuru region could be traced back to the 15th century as the result of the migration of Southern Katsina people to Wasagu and other small-scale polities in Zuru region.

The Katsinawa were attracted to Zuru region because of ecological as well as socio-economic reasons. Ecologically, the Zuru area is fertile and agricultural potential was enormous. Also a modest number

---

[26] Walter Rodney, *How Europe Underdeveloped Africa*, P. 43
[27] Group Interview in Dirin Gari, 25th December, 1985.

of livestock could be maintained at very little cost, pasturing in fallow land. Wild game hunting was also very lucrative even though it increasingly became difficult as the inhabitants of the area claimed the overall ownership of the hunting fields. Economically, Zuru region linked the trading centres of Kano, Katsina an d Zamfara areas in the north with Yawuri, Jega and Nupeland in the South.[28]

Already there was an intensive discussion on the migration of Katsina people to Zuru area by my colleagues who have studied the historical evolution and development of Zuru Emirate, so there is no need to go into this issue again. Notwithstanding, I will like to emphasize that the migration of Katsina people to Zuru region continued (from the 15th century) to the late 19th and early 20th centuries. In the 19th century, what pushed the Katsina people to migrate to Zuru area was the decline of Katsina as a commercial centre. According to Mahdi Adamu,[29] Katsina declined not because the town was physically destroyed when it was captured by the Jihad forces in 1807, but because of the raids and counter-raids of the ousted Hausa dynasty that threatened the peace and security of the city. For that reason many of the principal merchants resident in the city transferred to Kano where normalcy was restored as soon as the change of government (from Habe to Fulani) was achieved. Other areas beside Kano where Katsinawa merchants transferred to were Yawuri, Jega, Birnin Gwari and Sokoto. The city of Katsina ceased to be the destination of trading caravans that previously reside the exchange commodities.

Undoubtedly, the waves of Katsina migrants to Zuru region brought not only commerce but the religion of Islam. In a very real sense, this economic class could be described as a group of 'Merchant-Cleriks', for many of its members clearly served in a dual capacity, their aims were two-fold: the control of trade and trade routes and the introduction of material elements of Islamic culture to individuals or groups. Bravmann, A.A., supported this view by emphasizing that:

---

[2] These North-South trading centres were exchanging different commodities which included cotton, tobacco and indigo. from evident collected by various travellers, cotton was the most widely grown cash crop in Nupeland. Tobacco was extensively cultivated at Kabakawa, Northern Katsina. A recent study confirm that Kabakawa was the most renowned tobacco growing centre in North-Central Hausaland. See G.O. Ogunnemi "The Pre-Colonial Economy and Transportation in Northern Nigeria" in Akinjogbin and Osoba (eds) *Topics on Nigerian economic and Social History* pp. 96-97

[29] Mahdi Adamu, "Distribution of Trading Centres in the Central Sudan in the 18th and 19th Centuries" in Yusuf Bala Usman (ed) *Studies in the History of Sokoto Caliphate*, P. 86 .

traders have not always been given their due in the historical and ethnographic literature on West Africa, especially in acculturation studies, they can be neither slighted nor ignored when dealing with the phenomenon of Islam.[30]

According to my informants, the parents of the present Imam of Zuru town came from Katsina. They first settled in Dutsin Mahi and from there to Zuru town where they built a mosque in the present site of Zuru *Jumma'at* mosque.[31]

Indeed, from what was structurally obtained in Katsina society during the period from the 15th to 19th centuries, one may expect these migrant groups to spread Islam. Since the beginning of the 15th century, Katsina was a famous centre of Islamic learning. Most of the pilgrims from Mecca as well as scholars from Sankore University, Timbuktu, visited Katsina bringing with them books on divinity and etymology.[32] In the 17th century, Katsina produced native scholars like Muhammed Dan Marina (d.1655) and Muhammadu Dan Marina (d.1655). According to Hamidu Alkali 'learning developed among Katsinawa people, producing an intellectual community which continued to exist until the coming of the British Imperialists.'[33]

Besides the migration of the merchant class, the migration of other occupational classes (farmers and hunters) as well as private individuals helped in spreading the religion of Islam. Hashimu Abubakar Ladan argued that Islam entered through as the result of the activities of migrant communities from Argungu who entered Zuru through Fakai.[34] Mohammed Bello Isa believed that Mallam Audu who came to Zuru with Sakaba Banufe was responsible for spreading the religion of Islam. Mallam Audu according to Mohammed Bello Isa established a Quranic school and a mosque.[35]

Although Islam penetrated into what we throughout this work referred to as Zuru Emirate or Zuru region, it is pertinent to point out that the religion was largely practiced by Katsinawa and other immigrant groups (perhaps Kebbawa) as well as the ruling class of Zuru Emirate until the beginning of Shehu Usman Dan Fodio's Jihad in 1804. Although the Jihadists did not reach the Zuru area, it is argued by some studies that after the death of Shehu, Abdullahi (his

---

[30] Rene, A., Bravmann, Islam and Tribal Arts in West Africa, Cup 1974 p.7.

[31] Information from Limamin Zuru and other people who participated in the 1st Workshop of Zuru History project, November, 1986.

[32] Babs Fafunwa, *History of Education in Nigeria* p. 54.

[33] Hamidu Alkali, "A Note on Arabic Teaching in Northern Nigeria" Quoted in Baba Fafunwa Op.cit P.54.

[34] Informant during the 2nd Zuru History Workshop, august, 1987.

[35] *ibid.*

brother) went to Zuru through Gummi.[36] Abdullahi was said to have left some scholars in the persons of Mallam Abubakar, and Mallam Abdullahi to spread Islam in Zuru.[37] Hence, the spread and diffusion of Islam among the followers of traditional religions was set in motion, and by the end of the 19th century a substantial number of the indigenous people became Muslims. This argument was supported by Mahdi Adamu who argued that:

> ... the Sokoto Jihad was a vehicle of expansion in West Africa. Because of the Jihad, classes of Hausa people viz: Warriors, administrators, Quranic teachers, traders, craftsmen., and refugees emigrated to different parts of West Africa.[38]

In addition, by the time of colonial rule the entire region of Zuru area came under the control of Muslim rulers because of the deliberate policies of colonial administrators to put all non-Islamize tribes and communities of Northern Nigeria under the Muslim rulers. Such kind of policies, i.e. of imposing Muslim rulers over non-Muslims consciously or unconsciously converted many individuals to the religion of Islam. Also after the colonial conquest Islam was spread by private individuals who were interested to Islamized the whole of Northern Nigeria. Furthermore, because of colonial economic policies, Zuru town became an urbanized area where physical proximity of Muslims and non-Muslims became a factor in disseminating the religion of Islam. Close contact between Muslims and non-muslims was common in all colonial West African urban centres.

The spirit of Islamization in Zuru emirate was recorded around 1969 when more immigrants (viz: late Mallam Dangurgu, Mallam Dogari, and Mallam Balarabe) stormed the town in large numbers. Many *parlours* were converted to Quranic schools because of these immigrant communities. In the early 1960's to the present time a number of movements such as *Izala* intensified the spread, preaching and reforming Islam.

Indeed, one can see from the above survey that the process of Islamization in Zuru area was one of the gradual acculturation to Islamic life-style. The manner in which the religion expanded was essentially non-disruptive in nature. In general, Islam spread rapidly because it possessed a deep and pervasive appeal that went far beyond anything that the people of Zuru region had known prior to that time. By way of contrast with the traditional belief systems of Zuru people, Islam was a religion open to all people, irrespective of sex, tribe or social background. In other words, Islam had a sort of egalitarian

---

[36] Daniel Jibo, Op.cit P.19
[37] *ibid.* p. 19
[38] Mahdi Adamu, *The Hausa Factor in West African History* A.B.U. Press 1987. P.91.

component, not always very obvious to the outside observer, yet a factor of some importance in determining the nature of social relationships.

**Section Three:** *Missionary Endeavour And The Institutionalization Of Christianity In Zuru Emirate.*

Although the main impetus for the imperialist conquest of Zuru emirate in 1903 comes from economic interest of Western Europe, the Europeans in Zuru (as well as imperialized societies in Africa) realized that they had to expand their activities beyond commercial adventures, at least to cover their economic interest with religious moralism. From the onset therefore, European activities in Zuru were not only limited to commerce, but was also extended to religion. The colonial government fostered and assisted missionary enterprise, provided that it was confined to those districts and villages which were sufficiently under control. From about the second and third decades of the 20th century, the missionary endeavour progressed at a slow but successful pace. The people of Zuru area accepted Christianity because traditional forms of worships which so many people were still attached to could not fit into the new society that the colonial capitalism created. Colonialism created a new mode of social relationship which brought together different ethnic groups and tribes. Because of these changes the traditional religions failed to create new ideas or articulate moral doctrines that would have been meaningful in the condition of the time. Missionary activities therefore, became necessary, and today missions are established throughout Zuru emirate, especially Zuru town, where the headquarters of all the Christian churches, United Missionary Society (U.M.S.), Roman Catholic Mission (R.C.M.), Christ Apostolic Church (C.A.C), Evangelical Church of west Africa, (E.C.W.A.), and Apostolic Church (A.C.) are situated.

The United Missionary Society (U.M.S.) from America was the first missionary organization to come to Zuru. The U.M.S. came under the leadership of Joseph and Paul Ummel in 1925.[39] Joseph and Paul Ummel were men of high character, undoubted piety, and thorough devotion to their mission. Their activities in Zuru Emirate is comparable to that of Miss Mary Slessor, a Presbyterian Missionary who lived among different African societies from 1876 to 1915 and

---

[39] Oral information from Alhaji Isa Illo, a 79 years old traditional title holders in Zuru town, I am indebted to Mohammed Abdullahi who collected this information during his research in 1985. See Mohammed Abdullahi, "Political and Commercial Development of Colonial Northern Nigeria: A case of Zuru Town, 1910-1960" B.A. Dissertation, University of Sokoto, 1985, p. 14.

devoted herself to saving twins and their mothers from the death of which a cruel superstition would have doomed them.[40]

Undoubtedly, conversion to Christianity necessarily involved weaning the people of Zuru away from traditional religions as well as from their traditional social values. Also, in order to permanently convert the people to the Christian faith, there is the need to raise an indigenous class of people who would be able to carry on the work of evangelisation. Moreover, the U.M.S. members strongly believed that the chief instrument of effecting widespread evangelization was the spread of western education. United Missionary Society, therefore started the business of educating the natives, at least in 3 Rs - not because the mission regarded education as good in itself, but because it found that it could not do its own proper work without giving its adherents, and especially the clergy, as much of the formal learning as required for the study of the sacred writing and for the performance of their religious activities.

In 1933, Joseph and Paul Ummel recruited the services of two brothers Sakaba and Zomi Rikoto who joined the U.M.S.'s school in order to learn how to read and write.[41] Sakaba and Zomi together with one of the earliest converts, Gujiya helped the U.M.S. mission in establishing Christian religious centres in the following areas during the period from 1933 to 1940.

| | | | |
|---|---|---|---|
| 1. | Rikoto | 2. | Dabai |
| 3. | Tungan Bede | 4. | Bajida |
| 5. | Magoro | 6. | Ubege |
| 7. | Senchi | 8. | Bedi |
| 9. | Ribah | 10. | Dirin Daji |
| 11. | Sabon Garin Ushe | 12. | Tungan Magajiya. |

In addition to these centres, a church was constructed in a place now known as mission quarters in Zuru town in 1945.[42]

It is pertinent to note that evangelization by the U.M.S. mission encountered a lot of problems. Early converts were mocked and members of the mission molested. In fact it was not until after the Second World War when Ex-service men returned home that the process of evangelization became safe to the U.M.S. mission.

---

[40] For detailed explanation of the activities of Mise Mary Slessor, see *The Nigerian Gazetteer* or January 21, 1915.

[41] Sakaba and Zomi Rikoto, *Tarihin Eklesiya a Kasar Zuru Farkon Zuwan Maganar Allah a Kasar Dakarkari a Zuru daga 1925.* (November 1977) p.1

[42] *bid*, p.1, Informant in Dirin Gari (December 1985).

The Ex-service men did not only have interest in Christian religion, but have also got the "gun" to challenge those who rejected Christianity or physically attack the missionaries.[43]

Apart from the United Missionary Society (UMS), the Roman Catholic Church (R.C.M.) was another Christian church that proliferated Christianity in Zuru Emirate. The Roman catholic Church was first established in 1951 by an Irish Reverend Father who came to Zuru from Minna.[44] Minna by this time was the Headquarters of all the Roman Catholic Mission Churches in Northern Nigeria. John Macarthy was the first Roman Catholic priest in Zuru.[45]

The Roman Catholic Mission did not encounter much problems like the U.M.S. This was because the U.M.S. had already gained ground in Zuru as Christians. Members of the Roman Catholic Mission did not face the problem of persecution like that of the U.M.S., notwithstanding, the Roman Catholic Mission faced the problem of where to get a place to construct their church. Also the Roman Catholics faced the problems of how to get converts, for by the time they came to Zuru, U.M.S. had already converted and indocrinated the people of the emirate.

Due to these two major problems therefore, the activities of the Roman Catholic Mission were at first mainly on Sundays. But as time went on the activities were spread to cover the whole week. The weekly activities are as follows: Sunday service which takes place in the Church; baptism and confirmation both done twice a week; Women Fellowship, Catholic Truth Society; Men's Fellowship and Catechism are done thrice a week.

The Roman Catholic Church has now expanded its membership and has constructed churches since the early 1960's. The church members have cordial relations with other churches. At the time of writing, Mr. Kuba Joseph is the President of the Roman Catholic Association.[46]

## Other Christian Missionary Bodies In Zuru Emirate.

Only two denominations (U.M.S. and R.C.M.) were in Zuru when the Apostolic Church (A.C.) came in 1966. Pastor Oludogu came from Kontagora and established the church.[47] The first place of worship of

---

[43] *ibid*, Sakaba and Zomi Rikkoto, p.3

[44] See Bitrus Nagode, "The development of Christian Church in Zuru, 1925 to 1983", *NCE Certificate Project*, College of Education, Sokoto, 1986, p.11.

[45] Rebecca, *Op.cit* p. 17

[46] Bitrus Nagode *Op.cit* p.12 & 19 and Rebecca Musa *Op.cit* p.18.

[47] Rabecca, *Op.cit* p.18.

the Apostolic Church was outside Mr. E.A. Anigbadu's house in Unguwar Yarabawa.[48] The Apostolic Church had to face problems more than the Roman Catholic Church, for there were many attempts to stop them from worship or preaching. The first church they built was in 1968, and by 1981 had built a bigger church which they now use as the Headquarters of all Apostolic Churches in Zuru Emirate. Like other churches previously discussed, the week is full of activities for the members of the Church. On Mondays, they have thanks giving praises and prayers. On Tuesday they have the Bible teaching programmes, and Thursdays are meant for teaching church doctrines to the members of the church.

## The ECWA, Emmanuel Baptist Church And C.A.C.

The Evengelical Church of West Africa (ECWA) was introduced to Zuru by some Christianized Yorubas, viz: Mr. John Samuel, Mr. Joshua Ofafin, and Victor kalawole.[49] The attendance to the ECWA Church was at first very poor because Yoruba was the language that was used in preaching. Later, however, Hausa was introduced to be the means of communication and followers started to increase in the church. Services by the ECWA mission was done in Zuru Primary School up to 1982 when a permanent building for the church was constructed.

Other Christian Missionary churches which were established in Zuru were the Emmanuel Baptist Church which was introduced in 1970, and the Christ Apostolic Church (1972). As at 1988, these two churches have followers ranging from 500 to 1000.[50]

An important thing that we should note about the activities of Christian missions in Zuru is that, the missionaries introduced western education together with the gospel. Missionary education is inextricably related to Christianity. Bible readings, religious instructions, and church attendance are required of all western school students. What is written is absorbed uncritically, and the Bible is presented as the book among books. All the missionary organizations therefore built primary schools. After primary education, the students were sent to Teachers' Training Colleges outside Zuru in either Minna or Mokwa. All these mission schools have now been taken over by the government. The present Government Teachers' College Zuru was for

---

[48] *ibid*, p.18.
[49] *ibid*, p.25.
[50] Oral information during the first Workshop of Zuru History Project, November 1987.

example, initially a Secondary School of the Catholic Mission, but the Government of North Western State took over the school in 1973.[51]

## Conclusion

In this chapter, an attempt has been made to reconstruct the religious history of the inhabitants of Zuru Emirate before and after the proliferation of Islam and Christianity. As a preamble to the study, we discussed different modes of religious practices and how these practices changed as a result of cultural fission and fusion among different polities in the region. Islamization and christianization saw the emergence of a society with different norms and values. Those traditional religious institutions that were accorded much recognition were either replaced or modified by new ones. For instance, the institution of *M'gilø* cult which was obtained during the Christio-Islamic days became abandoned by so many people. *M'gilø* had little place in the new society's religious belief system. But with all the changes that Islam and Christianity brought, the original religious instinct of ancestral fear and veneration still remain and ancestor worship is established in the social values of most tribes in Zuru emirate.

Finally, I will like to emphasize that the experiences of the Islamized and Christianized people of Zuru Emirate no doubt reshaped the face of their history, and accorded them with a different world view in which they found themselves.

---

[51] Zuru File No. His/1/32/355 Historical Backgroung of Zuru Division 1971 - 74 p. 12.

**Alhaji Musa Mohammed.**
District Head of Wasagu
*(Installed Jan 13, 1961)*

Chapter Seven

# Some Aspects Of Traditional Marriage Systems In Wasagu And Fakai Districts Of Zuru Emirate.

*by*

Mal. Balam Birged Muhammad

## Introduction

Paucity of literature on the social structure of Zuru Emirate tended to posit the culture of the Dakarkari (the dominant group) to be the representation of the total sum of way of life of the emirate without regard to sub-cultural groups. This is in a way denying the existence of the sub-cultural groups in our area. This paper, therefore, attempts a survey on the nature of the social structure in the emirate especially, the traditional marriage systems, and the traditional belief systems among the sub-cultural groups in Wasagu and Fakai districts vis-a-viz the ones of the Dakarkari.

The chapter is divided into four parts: a brief historical account of the two districts namely Wasagu and Fakai; traditional marriage systems of the districts; and change(s) and continuity in the traditional marriage systems.

## Wasagu

Wasagu is one of the five districts of Zuru Emirate. It occupies the North-Eastern part of the Emirate. The district is surrounded by five villages, namely, Bena, Ribah, Kanya, Waje and Macika. The major ethnic groups of the district are the Katsinawanlaka and the Lélna.

The Katsinawa were said to be the earlier settlers of the district,[1] and, were believed to have migrated from the southern part of Katsina and settled in the present day Wasagu.[2] They were said to have chosen their present settlement because of two important fortunes attached to it, these are: fertile agricultural land and opportunity of good hunting grounds.[3] Other factors include the provision of a commercial link

---

[1] Augi A.R. - 1987 "A survey of Social and politcal History of Zuru Emirate before 1900 A.D.", *Unpublished Seminar paper*.
[2] *Ibid* P.40.
[3] *Ibid* P.40.

between the new settlement and some regions particularly Katsina, Zamfara, and Nupe (due to the advantages that were accruing as a result of the iron work).[4]

At first, the Katsinawan Laka were said to have settled at the 'Kangon Wasagu' and later moved into Wasagu proper.[5] Reason for the movement was largely attributed to the desire for territorial expansion for political purposes.[6] The fortunes that accounted for the settlement of Katsinawa at the present day Wasagu were shared by the inhabitants of Ribah who were also said to have migrated from Katsina and settled in Ribah.[7]

There are two views as to the origin of the Lélna speaking people of Ribah. On the one hand, the Lélna of Ribah contended that they migrated from Katsina and settled in the present day Ribah. While on the other the Katsinawan laka denied this Katsina origin of the Lélna of Ribah as false and went further to explain that they migrated from Zamfara.[8]

Historically, it was explained that when the original inhabitants of the present day Ribah first migrated from Katsina, they settled in a village located in the Northern part of Gusau called Ribe. Perhaps, the association of the origin of the Lélna speaking people of Ribah to Zamfara by the Katsinawan laka of Wasagu may not be unconnected with the place they first settled.[9] However, both the Katsinawan laka of Wasagu and the Lélna of Ribah had a common cause for migration.

## Fakai

The inhabitants of Fakai otherwise known as Fakawa (which refers to the royal house) migrated to their present settlement from Birnin Kebbi.[10] Harris, explained that, the inhabitants of Fakai migrated from a place called Faka in the Yabo District and settled in Kebbi, until they were driven away to Fakai by the Gimbanawa.[11]

There appears to be a disharmony between what Harris reported to have been the cause of their migration to Fakai and what was explained by the Fakawa. Accourding to them, it was during one of their engagements in slave raids, which took them to the present Fakai to

---

[4] *Ibid* P.40
[5] Group interview in the palace of the District Head of Wasagu (1988).
[6] *ibid.*
[7] Group interview with the Village Head of Ribah in (1987).
[8] Group interview in Wasagu *op.cit.* 1987.
[9] Group interview in Ribah *op.cit.* 1987.
[10] Group interview in the palace of the District Head of Fakai in 1987.
[11] Harris P.G. 1938. *Sokoto provincial Gazetteer..*

**Alhaji Isah Mohammed Wamalle**
District Head of Fakai
*(Installed February 1, 1976)*

look for drinking water for their horses and themselves. Consequently, the area became 'colonised' and provided the avenue for them to establish hegemony over the existing tribal groups via the handwork of Musa Dan Dunguzu who is believed to be the first leader of Fakai.

However, the original inhabitants of Fakai are from Gele, Zussun, Birnin Tudu and Rafin Kaya. The settlement of Fakawa (where they live presently) took effect prior to the period of colonialism.[12]

## Marriage Systems

From a simple definition, marriage, refers to a union between two or more persons of the opposite sex, whose period of relationship is expected to go beyond the period of gestation and the birth of children.[13]

Different societies practice different forms of marriages. In the areas under research (Wasagu and Fakai), marriage is regarded as a legal institution and forms the integral part of their existence especially in relation to child bearing, rearing, regulation of sexual behaviour (incest, taboo), maturity, bravery, strengthening of affinity, relationship etc.

However, despite the above mentioned importance of marriage, the prerequisites of marriage do not entirely cut- across the two areas under study. The study does not also rule-out the existence of semblance of pre-requisites of marriage between the two areas.

In the days gone, parents were in the forefront of marriage arrangement of their children. This was done in accordance with the customs in order to, among others; chose an ideal partner for either the boy or the girl; to ensure that neither the boy nor the girl marries from a family that has a record of stigma; to ascertain that very close relations do not marry one another, etc.[14]

In some situations, the decision of marriage (which was rarely reached) by either the boy or the girl was not informed to the parents directly, but through some relations (especially males) for their consent and acceptance, without which marriage hardly takes place. By implication therefore, it means that both the boy and the girl must have met and agreed prior to the knowledge of their parents.

It is reported that the stage of betrothal began in the following forms; that at first the boy will keep secret his relationship with the girl except to the women in his house who would confirm to the boy

---

[12] Group interview in Fakai *op.cit.* 1987.

[13] Stewart E.W. etal - *Introduction to Sociology.*

[14] Group interview in Fakai and Ribah *op.cit* 1987.

whether the girl reciprocates[15] the same feelings after which they report to his parents.

The revelation of the affair to the parents of the boy will be thoroughly discussed at his own family level, after which a representation consisting of his relations (especially his aunt or uncle or both) would be made to the girl's house, to meet and discuss with similar representation of the girl.[16]

During this visit a gift is given to the girl. The acceptance of the gift is a testimony of the acceptance of the boy by the girl and her family. Harris reported that during the visit, the leader of the representation offers a ring to the girl. If she consents she will collect the ring and throw it to either her mother or aunt, who are by custom expected to place the ring in one of their fingers.[17] On receiving the good news, the boy sends 20 cowries through the same delegation to the mother of the girl. Consequently, a detailed arrangement for the marriage would be worked out including "Golmo".[18]

To the Lélna speaking people of Ribah in Wasagu district, the acceptance of marriage proposal by the parents of the girl is marked in the following traditional manner: twenty cowries known as *d-kweze* (Marriage dowry) is taken inside a calabash to the girl's house before sun set.[19] The cowries would be thrown on the ground for the girl to collect or reject them. If she collects the cowries from the ground it signifies final acceptance of the proposal made by the boy. But, most often than not the collection of the cowries from the ground was not done directly by the girl, but by her relations (mother or aunt), who would present to her for her acceptance or rejection.[20]

What was normally presented to the parents of the girl by the parents of the boy for the acceptance of marriage proposal among the Fakawa, was at variance with what was obtained among the Lélna of Ribah.

Among the Fakawa; tobacco (*taba*), thread (*zare*), alimony (*kwalli*) and mirror (*madubi*) is presented to the parents of the girl for the acceptance of marriage proposal.[21] The use of cowries was said to be less significant. The pattern of presentation was the same with the

---

[15] group interview in Fakai and Ribah *op.cit* 1987

[16] Harris, P.G. 1938, "Notes on the Dakarkari peoples of Sokoto province, Nigeria, *Journal of the Royal Anthopological Institute.* Vol.ixviii p. 138

[17] *Ibid* P.138

[18] *Ibid* P.138

[19] Group interview in Ribah *Op.cit.* 1987

[20] *ibid*.

[21] group interview in Fakai *op cit* 1987

Lélna of Ribah. Therefore, the acceptance of any of the above mentioned gifts served as victory for the boy and, lack of acceptance indicated a rejection of the proposal.[22]

Areas of similarity exist between the Fakawa and the Lélna of Ribah. One of such similarities was in the area of presentation of gift to the girl's parents, for the acceptance of marriage proposal. It is observed that neither the boy nor the girl was made to be directly involved in the presentation of the marriage gift, but by representations.

Further, among the Fakawa and the Lélna of Ribah the parents of either the boy or the girl reserve the right to determine who should marry who and who should not. It is logical therefore, that the collection or otherwise of the cowries, *taba,* or *tandu,* from the deputation of the boy was greatly determined or influenced by the interest of the parents which may or may not tally with the wishes of either the boy or the girl.

After the outlined presentations have been done, the boy becomes bethroted to the girl. The custom allows the boy to continue to pay visits to the girl. He (the boy) reserves the right to challenge anyone he finds making overtures to her.[23] The procedures mentioned above are done before the girl reaches puberty. The moment she is identified as a mature person the boy joins *golmo*.

## Golmo

When it becomes certain that the girl is bethrothed to the boy he joins Golmo. It refers to "the contract of agricultural service each year".[24] In otherwords, *golmo* also refers to an institutionalised agricultural service by the suitor (*tuku*) to the parents of the girl *Ladi*.[25]

Harris[26] revealed that the usual period of *golmo* was six years but sometimes it is extended up to seven years. It is further explained that there are advantages attached to the seven years period of *golmo*. That, when the man that engages in the seven years period of *golmo* fathered "marriageable daughters", he is by the Lélna custom expected to demand for the same seven years he had served during his period of

---

[22] *ibid..*
[23] Ribah, L.M. 1987 "A popular theatre of Zuru people a case study of their customs and traditional beliefs" *Unpublished Project work.*
[24] Harris, 1938 *Op.cit* P.139.
[25] Harris, *Op.cit* 1938 P.139.
[26] *ibid.*

*golmo*. The situation is described by Harris as "a form of insurance, returning a very good bonus in old age".[27]

To most of the Lélna, *golmo* inculcates in the minds of the participants a spirit of discipline, loyalty, bravery, patience and independence.

The recruitment or initiation into regular agricultural service of seven years otherwise known as *golmo* is not done at anytime of the year. It is normally performed during a particular traditional festival called *Dibiti*.[28] The festival d*ibiti* is dominated largely by members of *golmo*. Similarly, new enteries into *golmo* join the older members during the same festival. The festival, attracts colourful activities which include, dancing, wrestling, eating and drinking of local liqour. Consequently, the new members of *golmo* must be certified that they attain the age of sixteen, without which, they would not be allowed to engage or participate in it.[29]

After the recruitment of the new *Yan Golmo*, a place of meeting will be announced by the *Sarkin Golmo*. It is in the place of meeting that a *golmo* work schedule would be worked out by the *Sarkin Golmo*. At the same time, a register of names would be taken in order to find out the absentees.[30]

Before the commencement of the work, it is required of the *yan golmo* to carry along to the ground of meeting about one hundred roasted rats each, out of which, only one is expected to be consumed daily. Food, prepared from guinea-corn, (*tuwon dawa*), is offered to the *yan golmo* before they begin to work.[31]

When *Sarkin Golmo* shouts up - to three times the *yan golmo* will run down to the farm and begin weeding. Once they began none is expected to stand up until when six or more ridges have been completed or weeded.[32]

At the end of the day, members of *golmo* retire to their respective homes. But, before their final departure, the owner of the farm (father-in-law to any of the *golmo* members) will provide them with food.[33] This service continues until the exit of farming and harvesting periods

---

[27] Group interview in Fakai and Ribah *op.cit* 1987.

[28] Mohammed S. "Some Aspects of the culture and institutions of the Dakarkari people examined in the right of their contiguity with the Hausa people", *M.Sc. Thesis Unpublished.*

[29] *ibid* p.36.

[30] *ibid* p.37.

[31] Group interview in Fakai and Ribah *op.cit* 1987.

[32] Harris *op.cit* 1938 p.140

[33] *ibid* P.139-140.

or seasons when also some of the *golmo* members would be graduating.

It should be noted that the practice of *golmo* does not continue throughout the stipulated six or seven years. This is because, at the end of planting and harvesting periods, the *yan golmo* will go to the houses of their in-law and ask if their huts need new thatches. Consequently, for the re-roofing of a hut with new thatches, *Sarkin Golmo* will be consulted, who is by custom be required to take action by drawing a time- table that would set *yan golmo* into action.[34] But if the repairs are minor, the work can be undertaken by a *tuku* (suitor), independent of the group of *yan golmo*.[35] At the end of the exercise (re-roofing or repairs of huts, the *golmo* for that period or season in question is said to have come to an end.

Consequently, once again, yan golmo are back to their communities and normal interaction with members of the community except their bethroted wives resume. It is explained that during the first agricultural service year, cohabitation cannot take place between a suitor and a bethroted wife.[36] But it can be allowed only when a bethroted suitor spends two or more years in golmo service.[37] At this stage it is the father in-law that will prepare a hut in his house for the suitor and the bethroted wife.[38]

At the end of golmo period the bethroted wife joins her suitor in accordance with the customs. At this juncture, final initiation is made into a status of a full-fledged married woman. The negotiation and preparation for making the final stage of marriage of a bethroted girl is carried out during the festival of *uhola*. During the festival, a bethroted girl will be presented as *yadato*, meaning that she is married now, therefore, she can no longer stay with her parents.[39] The lady will be well dressed in her attire while drummers and singers will be showering praises on her beauty and her family members. The festival lasts between three to four days.

At the end of the festival, the parents of the bridegroom will seek for permission from the parents of the bride to allow her to spend a day with them. When the request is granted, the bride and her friends

---

[34] *Ibid* P.140.
[35] Mohammed *op.cit*. P.34-35.
[36] Harris *op.cit* 1938 P.140-141.
[37] Harris *Op.cit*. 1938 P.141.
[38] Group Interview in Fakai and Ribah in 1987.
[39] *ibid*.

will sleep in the house of the in-law only to leave very early in the morning, after fetching water for the parents of the bridegroom.[40]

The departure of the bride and her friends from the house of the in-laws is marked with yet another ceremony. The parents of the bridegroom would prepare food and liquor in abundance specifically for the parents of the wife, in which also friends, relations and well-wishers will be invited to come and grace the occasion with them.[41] The last stage of the marriage is a request to the parents of the bridegroom for the bride to be taken to her husband's house. The period between the request and its acceptance does not normally take a long time. It all depends on how prepared are the parents of the bride, which is determined by their financial viability. When the bride is finally taken to the husband's house, she is accompanied with household utensils which include calabashes, pots, foodstuff etc.[42]

## Divorce

This refers to separation of marriage, which vary from one culture to another. In the traditional marriage systems of both Fakawa and Lélna of Ribah, divorce is rare. It is believed that the type and nature of marriage arrangement discourages divorce. This is inorder not to sour affinity relationship that exist between the two families that are involved in a marriage contract.

As explained, the chances of divorce were higher before than after the completion of *golmo*. Some causes of divorce during and after *golmo* are attributed largely to extra marital sexual relations (which is an acceptable act) by a bethroted girl. The engagement in extra maritual sexual relations of the bethroted wife comes about due to the long absence of a suitor from home especially for military service. Consequently, divorce becomes obvious when it is discovered that a bethroted wife engages in cohabitation with another man other than her bethroted husband.[43]

Under divorce situation as reported, the "lover" of the bethroted wife (whom she cohabits with secretly), if he so wishes to marry her, is allowed by the custom to complete the rest of the agricultural service years (golmo) and pay some money as compensation to the former bethroted husband for the years he spent in *golmo*.[44] Similarly, if by any cause the lady decides to leave her "lover" husband and go back to

---

[40] Harris *op.cit* 1933 P.142 and Group Interview in Fakai and Ribah in 1987.

[41] Harris *op.cit* 1938 P.142 and Group Interview in Fakai and Ribah in 1987.

[42] Harris op.cit 1988 P.142 and Group Interview in Fakai and Ribah in 1987.

[43] Group interviews in Fakai and Ribah *op.cit* 1987.

[44] Augi *op.cit* 1987 p.52.

her former bethroted husband, the former bethroted husband is by custom required to pay some money as compensation to the later bethroted husband for the years of service (*Golmo*) he has completed.[45]

On the other hand, if divorce occurs after the completion of *golmo*, for similar or other reasons, children born by another man other than a bethroted husband belongs to the former. And neither the later nor the wife will claim ownership of the children, as line of descent is traced through the male line.[46] Therefore, the custom recognises the existence of a "pater" (Social father), and a 'genitor' (biological father). In this case, the bethroted man will continue to be the biological father, even after the wife might have left his house. While, the "lover" husband would be regarded as a social father to the children and social husband to the wife. Other reasons which can lead to divorce include, lack of maintenance and infertility of either of the couples.[47]

## Katsinawan Laka

The Katsinawan Laka of Wasagu, on the other hand present a more or less different picture of marriage arrangement. This is because Katsinawan laka migrated from an area where the religion of Islam has been introduced as far back as the 15th century.[47] Furthermore, the "immigrants" explained that the religion of Islam has made a tremendous impact on them, and that, they migrated to the present settlement after their conversion to Islam. Consequently, they discarded their former norms to the ones acceptable to the religion of Islam.[48]

A type of marriage that does not exist among the Lélna of Ribah and Fakawa, except those who embraced Islam, is "gift marriage" or "Sadaka". In this type of marriage, the parents of the girl "marry off" or give out the hand of their daughter in marriage to certain categories of people namely, the learned and the poor ones. This marriage does not require giving material benefits to the parents but it is based on pious intentions.[49] Consequently, the parents of the girl shoulder the entire responsibility of the marriage from its very beginning until its end. What may be required of the husband is to give out an unspecified token amount of money to the friends and relations of the

---

[45] Group Interview in the palace of the District Head of Wasagu in 187.
[46] Augi *op.cit* 1987 p.52.
[47] Group Interview in Wasagu in 1987.
[48] Madauci etal, 1968 *Hausa Customs*, NNPC Zaria, P.20.
[49] *Ibid* P.20.

bride on the day she is brought into his house with a meagre bride wealth which is to be in accordance with what is stipulated by Islam.[50]

Under the types of marriages organised by parents among the Lélna and Fakawa, certain rules of marriage are taken into consonance. They are exogamy and endogamy.[51] Among the Katsinawan laka a girl can be married off or given out of a certain family with whom they do not share common kinship. In otherwords, a girl can marry someone that they are not in any way related. While on the other hand a girl can be married to someone with whom she shares common kinship but whom she does not share the same "putative or fictive consanguine" blood relationship like, sister, brother, etc.[52]

Unlike the Lélna and Fakawa, the Katsinawan laka present as a marriage gift, a locally made box called *adudu* containing few clothing materials, a pair of shoes, *kwalli* etc, which are given to the girl by the parents of the boy as *lefe* after she has given her consent to the boy. On giving her consent, the girl becomes bethroted to the boy.[53] It is the custom of most Hausa people that the preparation of *lefe* is done by the parents of the boy, especially on an occasion of first marriage.

As is the practice among the Lélna and Fakawa, the presentation of *lefe* is not done by the boy, but by a team of deputation of the boy, mainly old women. The women take around town or village the *lefe* to relations of the girl and well wishers for their confirmation and blessings. Consequently, once *lefe* is accepted by the family of the girl, the boy to a certain extent can deter his rivals from coming to the girl, (it is like when a marriage gift is accepted among the Fakawa and the Lélna).[54]

The next stage is fixing the date for the marriage which is popularly called *baiko da sarana*. On this occasion, Kola nuts will be distributed to both family members as an invitation to witness the occasion. The occasion does not normally attract a crowd. During the occasion, representatives of both sides (the boy and the girl) otherwise known as *waliyai* will meet and decide on the appropriate date for the marriage. Also, in the arrangement, the representatives will discuss the amount of money to be paid as bride wealth, which is subject to negotiation guided by Islamic injunctions.[55]

---

[50] Wilkin Elizabeth J., *An Introduction of Sociology*
[51] Group Interview in Wasagu *op.cit* in 1987
[52] *Ibid.*
[53] Madauci, *op.cit* 1968 p.20-22
[54] Group Interview in Wasagu *op.cit* in 1987.
[55] *Ibid.*

As from the period of *baiko da sarana*, the husband-to-be assumes ownership of the girl. Just like his counterparts among the Fakawa and Lélna, he challenges anyone he sees making overtures to her, especially his rivals, because this arrangement points to those willing to contest for the girl to stay away from her. Furthermore, parents of the girl loose respect from their community if they allow back door competition after *baiko da sarana*.[56]

In contrast to the Lélna and Fakawa, among the Katsinawan Laka when *lefe* is accepted, no type of labour, either in form of farming or in other forms are required from the bethrother husband. Instead, bride wealth in form of cowries is paid to the family of the girl.[57]

The period of *baiko da sarana* expires when the actual marriage takes place. During the ceremony, both families and their relations, as well as well-wishers will be in attendance. An Imam will be invited to tie the knot for the marriage under the following conditions: that 'the husband accepts responsibility of feeding the wife; that he agrees to provide shelter and clothing for her.'[58]

On the part of the wife, marriage activities commence a day before the day of the marriage. This part involves the girl and her friends (mostly age mates) leaving her parents house, to make visitation to a couple of places, after which they retire to a house unknown to the ladies or women that will accompany her to the husband's house. This process, is referred to by some as *yawon gudu*.[59] It should be noted that the wife is taken to the husband's house in the night of the day the marriage takes place. Consequently, when their hiding place is discovered, some payment of unspecified amount of money for what is called *bude "kofa"* (allowing access to where the bride is hidden) will be made by the relations of the bridegroom. When such payment is made, the bride, while crying with her friends for departing from an unmarried life, will be conveyed, accompained by relations, friends, and well-wishers to the husband's house. This part of the ceremony is normally accompanied by drumming, singing and dancing by both the girls and the married women, [60] and it continued in this way for three days. Food, prepared by the two families, is served free of charge.

On the last day of the event, properties brought from bride's parents home are used in decorating her room. The properties which include calabashes and pots, etc are brought in a procession,

---

[56] *Ibid*.
[57] *Ibid*.
[58] Madauci *op.cit* 1968 P.22-23.
[59] Group Interview in Wasagu *Op.cit* in 1987.
[60] *Ibid*.

accompanied by drumming and singing. After the decoration, a few girls will be left with the wife (normally her friends), until the arrival of the husband and his friends.

On the part of the husband, his friends (mainly his age mates) will organise a wrestling contest on the marriage day as a sign of honour and that of their contribution to the occasion. The friends will find and arrange a suitable place for the groom where he will receive well wishers. After three days of such event, in the night of the third and final day, the husband in company of friends, will move into his room, where his wife has already been taken. On reaching the door (normally late) the wife with her friends will pretend to be sleeping, and will refuse to open the door initially until after repeated knocks. Once inside the room the groom's friends will start making jokes by way of story telling in order to make the bride laugh. This normally takes a long time to accomplish. This custom is called "Sayen Baki".

By custom, cohabitation is expected to take place the night the husband and wife meet. As explained, a white cloth is laid on the bed that night, and once the husband succeeds in disvirgining the wife, some stains of blood is expected to be found on the white cloth after which early in the morning the husband is, by custom, required to leave the house.

When the news eventually reaches the parents of the bride, they feel happy that their daughter has been a decent girl before marriage. Consequently, she is said to bring respect and decency to her family. Several gifts including slaughtered animals will be presented to her. And she is said to command respect from her in-law.[61]

On the other hand, if the husband discovers that the wife is not a virgin, the story will be communicated to both his and her parents. This discovery may be a source of stigma to her family, as it is regarded as a disgrace. While, to the parents of the husband, they may feel cheated that they had married a "remnant" to their son. This may lead to divorce as there will be pressure from his parents even though he may still love his wife.[62]

Also, like their counterparts, the Katsinawan laka frown at pre-marital sexual relations, especially from a female. If the relationship is discovered by the husband, he reserves the right to send the wife away and report the "lover" to the local chief.[63]

Other reason for divorce include, infertility, witchcraft, lack of maintenance, long period of absence from home etc. When divorce occurs, the wife has no right to claim the ownership of the children.

---

[61] *Ibid.*
[62] *Ibid.*
[63] *Ibid.*

The children are said to belong to the husband, as the system (patriliny) allows inheritance and ownership of children by the male.

## Changes And Continuity

Most of the procedures of the traditional forms of marriage of the Lélna, the Fakawa and the Katsinawan laka have either withered away or are on the verge of disappearance. Several reasons were cited for this. These include new forms of occupations, education, introduction of Islam and Christianity.

The decision of who to marry is no longer under the total control of the parents. Parents are said to play little or no role in the marriage proposal of their children. What obtains presently is that once there is mutual agreement between the boy and the girl their parents are informed and they are expected to offer their blessing.

The independence in the choice of a marriage partner is largely attributed to a decline in interest in agriculture by the younger generation. According to them, the decline emerged due to the rise in aspiration of the young ones and existence of new forms of occupations that are found in the cities. Therefore, lack of dependence on the traditional forms of occupations like farming, pastoralism etc which are to a large extent controlled by the parent is tantamount to an erosion of certain level of control of the children.[64]

Therefore, with the emergence of, and the discovery of new forms of occupations by the ruralities, they migrate to the cities so as to reap the benefits of the new occupations. With new occupations, a migrant is rarely expected to look for financial assistance from his parents. As a result, little or no financial dependence gives the men the freedom to determine who to marry and how to go about the marriage.[65]

Coupled with the financial independence as a result of urbanisation and engagement in new forms of occupations and influence of city life, it is revealed that, when their children migrate to cities, they maintain a certain distance from their parents. Consequently, when they become exposed to Urban life where there is the absence of parental guidance, they take decisions (including that of marriage) independently.[66]

With the introduction of the school system, an avenue is created for the rural children to move out in search of education to places other than their places of origin. This provides the rural children with the opportunity to interact with their colleagues from different geo-cultural environments. Consequently, educational institutions serve as an area

---

[64] Group Interview in Wasagu and Fakai Districts *Op.cit* 1987.
[65] *Ibid.*
[66] Group Interview in Wasagu and Fakai Districts *Op.cit* 1987.

where students from different geo-cultural environments meet, and to a large extant, their interaction curtails some parental function(s) in relation to selection of marriage partners.[67]

Also affected as a result of migration and new occupation is the traditional practice of golmo. It is explained that due to the above mentioned reasons, the practice of *golmo* has faced and still faces a serious decline, except for those who are still confined to the rural areas.[68] Consequently, those who have moved out from the villages for reasons of migration, into the army and education etc, pay money as bride price to the parents of the girl. Furthermore, for those who cannot afford to pay money as bride price they partake in *golmo*. But to some, even among those that have not seen "the light" but have some money, they are allowed to pay the bride price in form of money. The acceptance of the later practice has also been attributed to the introduction of Islam which encourages payment of bride price in form of money as against labour. Thus, the payment of bride price in form of money will enable the father-in-law to use the money for the payment of farm labour.[69]

Regarding the influence of Christianity, marriage started to be contracted through the church. It has also put a limit to or regulated the number of wives its followers should have. In effect, if an individual is refused marriage of a certain girl customarily, the church can perform or take over the role of his family.

The religion of Islam has also in many forms affected the traditional procedures of marriage. With its introduction, it has among others, regulated the amount of money to be paid as bride price instead of *golmo*. It has also regulated the number of wives its followers should have. Coupled with the above mentioned functions, it also performs the function of the family especially the ones concerning marriages. This institution arranges marriages for couples in situations of opposition from either of the parents.

It should be noted however, that the changes that occurred as a result of the introduction of the above mentioned institutions, (i.e. Christianity and Islam), did not affect non-adherents. To the non-adherents, the former practice is retained except for changes that might have occurred due to migration and education.

---

[67] *Ibid*.
[68] Group Interview in Fakai and Ribah *op.cit* 1987.
[69] *Ibid*.

## Chapter Eight

### Socio-Economic Transformation In Colonial Zuruland 1901 - 1950: A Preliminary Investigation

*by*

**Dr. I.L. Bashir**

## Introduction

The main Objective in this section is to provide a brief but useful background to colonial Zuruland with the view to appreciating the consequences of colonialism on the people. The pre-colonial history of Zuruland, like most of Africa, was a history punctuated with intra-ethnic co-operation and peaceful co-existence. This statement is corroborated by Mahdi Adamu's finding and other archival documents. According to an archival source, Dabai Emirate which encompassed the whole of Zuruland of today, "was raided several times by the Emir of Kotagora, Nagwamatse and his son Ibrahim.[1] This was presumably for slaves and as counter offensives against personalities like Danduguzu; the Dakkakari Chief of Fakkai. As a result of the activities of this personality there was serious political instability in the Zuruland-Kotagora complex.[2] Danduguzu raided his neighbours for booties and captives and was counter raided especially by his Hausa-Nupe neighbours.

This political instability and the consequent air of insecurity, greatly determined the settlement pattern in Zuru land during the period in question. As a result of the sense of insecurity created by such wars for example, a large population of the inhabitants of this area, especially the Dakkakari, dwelt in the hills and other places where they were secured, while the plains and valleys were rather uninhabited or sparsely populated until the establishment of colonial rule.[3] This confused socio-political atmosphere was intensified in 1888 when Abarshi was despatched by one Gallo on punitive expedition against

---

[1] C.O. 446/4 Dispatch No. 111 of 23rd March, 1899, Sokoto Prof. 1482 (*Sokoto Prof. Administrative Division*) P.12.

[2] Adamu, M., *op.cit.*, P.313.

[3] Harold, D. Gunn & F.P. Conant, *Peoples of the Middle Niger Region of Northern Nigeria.* International African Institute, London, 1960, P.30 and 37, see also *Report on Land Tenure, Niger Province*, P.42.

Zuguntane. While this was happening, Danduguzu and some warriors from Kebbi and Gummi surprised and attacked the Yawuri forces. Mahdi Adamu, nor any other source does not seem to tell us the outcome of this encounter. However, counter offensive and hence insecurity seems to have persisted, for in 1896, eight years later, Danduguzu entered Yawuri to raid for slaves. At night, Abarshi rallied his forces and captured 44 horses from the intruding enemies.[4]

## Zuruland and British Imperialism

The activities of Danduguzu, Abarshi and others as we have seen, created an atmosphere of insecurity which were of serious consequences to production and commerce, both of which explained the presence of Britain in the region. At this time British imperial interest in the Niger-Yelwa-Yawuri-Zuruland and Kontangora complex was fast growing and such political instability was therefore inimical to such imperial interest. Furthermore, under one Decour, the French were advancing towards this region from Say, while one Toutee was to travel from northern Dahomey to link up with Dacour at Bajebo, below Bussa to carve out an imperial possession for France. In 1895, Toutee established a fort at Bajebo which was named Fort De Arenberg. He then moved up-stream to sign treaties with all the chiefs of all towns on both banks of the Niger after which he moved further northwards.

Fearing the French monouvres and the existing political instability in this region, British imperial agents on the spot, the Royal Niger Company, in 1886 arrived at Yelwa with troops stationed at Jebba. Jebba was therefore to be the springboard of British imperial expansion in this region. In 1898 a further move was made to Jega by one Arnold, another British imperial vanguard.[5] At Jega, Arnold met a resistance from Ibrahim Sarkin Sudan who on the instruction of the Sultan should push the Europeans back to where they started from. Without much attempt at aggression, Arnold moved back to Jebba.

Meanwhile trouble was brewing between Zuruland, represented by Dakarawa, and the British. When Col. Moreland left Yelwa, the Dakarawa Chief of Fakkai, Danduguzu threatened to destroy the town. He blocked the road to Yelwa from the east and this disrupted the supply of food-stuffs to the British from towns and villages lying to the east. Next, he attacked the chief of Kele who supplied the British troops with cattle and other food-stuffs.[6] In the war that ensued, the British troops in Yelwa inflicted a paralyzing defeat on Danduguzu

---

[4] Adamu, M, *op.cit*. P.406.

[5] *ibid*.

[6] C.O. 446/4 Despatch No. 111 or 23rd March, 1899.

who lost from thirty to one hundred men. In addition, eight of the towns/villages under him were burnt, fifteen herds of cattle, five ponies and four hundred sheep were captured.[7] With the defeat of Danduguzu as Mahdi Admau concludes, sanity and political stability or their likes seemed to have come to this region.[8] With this also, the British presence came to be felt by Zuruland and effective occupation was only a question of time.

### The Establishment of Colonial Rule in Zuruland

As has already been seen, British expansionism in this region from the late 19th century gathered momentum year after year and by 1901 Kotangora had fallen to Britain. This development largely means the fall of towns and villages around like Zuruland. With this development, the province of Kotangora was immediately created and Abdulahi Abarshi was appointed the first Sarkin Sudan ruling over Kasar Yawuri and all surrounding ethnic communities such as Dakarawa and their neighbours.[9] Zuruland's first experience of the British rule was therefore to be through Kotangora under the rulership of their traditional enemy, Abdullahi Abarshi, formally Emir of Yawuri but then Sarkin Sudan of Kotangora.

### Administrative Reforms

After conquering the whole of Northern Nigeria, Lugard settled down to restructure the feudal caliphal administrative machinery. The restructing which transferred Zuruland from one place to the other, continued throughout the period from 1901 to 1950. The frequency of these transfers as we shall see was undoubtedly counterproductive to any political and administrative development. To illustrate this point, Dabai division which encompassed the whole of Zuruland throughout most of colonial era, oscillated between Kotangora and Sokoto provinces and between Gwandu and Sokoto Divisions.

Colonial restructuring of Zuruland started about April 1903 when the emirate of Sakaba was created with a second class chief.[10] This brought together people who hitherto were autonomous to be administered and governed under one political or administrative umbrella. The first chief was Brama (Ibrahim) the son of Mohama, who was a Nupe man and hitherto a slave in the house of the Emir of Yauri. The jurisdiction of the new administrative unit was that part of

---

[7] *ibid.*

[8] Adamu, M. *op.cit.*, P.313.

[9] *ibid*, P.319.

[10] John Ralph Wills (ed.) *Gazetters of the Northern Provinces of Nigeria III The Central Kingdom* Frank Gass.

Kotangora lying north of the river Malendo and included also Rijau District. In August, 1912, Dukkawa towns of Danrangi and Ungwan Tsamiya were included in this emirate.

The Dakarkari and Dukawa of the newly created emirate refused to recognize their new ruler because of his slave background. To these groups, the appointment of a foreigner was an intolerable imposition and worst still when such a ruler was of slave descent. This protest was further ignited by the extortionate nature of Brama's administration. As an oral informant said, the Emir was removed due to his moral bankruptcy manifested in all his behaviours.[11] The pangs and pains of all these were not helped by the type of people the ruler surrounded himself with. He had around him, Nupe and Yoruba chiefs as tax collectors whose aspirations were not in consonance with those of his subjects. These men engaged in enriching themselves at the expense of the poor tax payers. Consequently, from 1904 to 1908 protests continued to be a feature of the Anglo-Zuruland relationship and this was a matter of concern to the British administration. Such acts of protest eventually necessitated punitive action which culminated in the July 1908 punitive expedition which seems to have silenced protests against the colonial establishment in the division, Zuruland.[12]

It appears that generally, dissatisfied with the administration, the government had to review its policy and so the emirate was in September, 1911, divided into eight administrative areas to effect administrative efficiency.[13] In spite of this, however, bureaucratic corruption continued to be the bane of the administration. Consequently, Sarkin Sakaba was removed from office in 1913. After this, the six districts which comprised the emirate-Kumbashi, Dabai, Donko, Sakaba Fakkai and Wasagu - were made independent confederal units under their own ethnic chiefs with a central treasury controlled by the District Officer (D.O.). Under their various ethnic chiefs now, the various groups were happy and contented. Six years later, in 1919, the division was once more organized under a Paramount Chief with its Headquarters in Zuru, thus creating for the first time, the emirate administrative structure in line with the older emirates of the province.[14] This time instead of imposing an "alien" on the people of Zuruland, they were allowed to select their own leader in the person of Andi Gambo, the chief of Dabai, who himself was a

---

[11] Interview with Mallam Audu Gobo, August, 1987.
[12] ibid., See also Horald D. Gunn & F.P. Connant, *Peoples of Middle Niger*, op.cit., P.31.
[13] ibid., P.34, See also Horold & Co., *Peoples of Middle Niger*, op.cit. P.33.
[14] ibid.

Dakarkari man[15]. Andi Gambo died in 1926 and was succeeded by his fourteen year old son Bahago who ruled with a Council of Regency. In 1928, a member of the council Sani Daudu was appointed second class chief in charge of the Emirate when Bahago proved incompetent and unacceptable.

From this unti the 1930s, the political history of the Emirate was one of frequent transfer from one province to the other. In 1922 for example, because of the size of the division in which Dabai and Illo were administered, it was suggested that the emirate of Zuru should be moved to Sokoto province. However, after some correspondence, the emirate was transferred to Niger Province which was carved out of the old Kotangora province then comprising Niger, Kotangora, Nassarawa and Zaria and with Zuru as a new division.[16] But this was not the final transfer, in 1924 Dabai or Zuru Emirate was once more transferred to Sokoto province. In 1927 it was separated from Sokoto Division and in 1930 it became part of Gwandu Division. In 1931, when it was found that the inclusion of Dabai and Yauri in Gwandu division could cause problems of supervision and related matters, it was once more reconstituted with Yauwuri, to form the Southern Division. Later in 1933, Dabai was transferred to Sokoto Division again. In 1939, again Zuru Native Administration was transferred to Kotangora Division of the Niger Province.[17]

The last transfer was greeted with resentment from Zuru Native Administrative area generally as it was viewed with apprehension by the people because of the type of treatment they might receive from administrators in Kotangora. However, when the British Assistant District Officer, one Mr. F. L. Parson assured them of protection from the supposed Kotangora oppression, the transfer was accepted with mixed feelings. Reasons given by the Zuru people against this transfer were; first, the fear of boundary revision in favour of Kotangora which might cost them the loss of some of their land and secondly, the fear of increases in tax and alteration of dates of collection which might make them pay another tax after they would have paid that under the

---

[15] Horold & Co., *Peoples of the Middle Niger, op.cit.*, P.33. See also *Annual Report on the Northern Provinces* 1927, Sokoto Pronvince, p.29.

[16] John Ralph Wills (ed.) *Gazetters of Northern Province op.cit. P.XV*, See Report on *Local Government in the Northern Provinces of Nigeria* Compiled by K.P. Maddocks & D.A. Pott 1950. p.39. See also Correspondence titled: *Zuru Native Administration: Proposed Transfer from Sokoto Province to Niger Province*. April, 1922 Between the Chief Secretary to the Government, Lagos and Secretary Northern Province in File No. 1387/92 Kaduna Archives.

[17] See the Correspondence in 16 above.

former division.[18] Soon, however, Zuru people got what they wanted when in 1943, they were transferred to Gwandu Division again.

Such were the experiences of Zuru Emirate during the colonial period up to the second World War. After the war, transfer and retransfer of the Emirate continued until finally it stayed under Sokoto Province. Such transfers, no doubt made it difficult if not impossible for the Emirate to develop its own political as well as administrative institutions and skills. As I said earlier, these oscillations between one administrative unit and another were not accidental. They were at best manifestations of the Emirate officials' intrigues and power squables to destabilize these chieftaincies for easy administration or were reflections of indigenous power tussle and politics among Hausa emirates for control over the chieftaincies. In spite of these transfers, however, Britain was able to maintain the peace that was required for easy and maximum exploitation of the natural and human resources of Zuruland especially with the missionaries penetrating their hearts to reconcile them with the philosophy of colonialism.

## Economic Reforms

Administratively therefore, with all the reforms examined in the previous section, British colonialism tried to improve the structure of the open economy. As this was being done, the British also pursued reforms in other fields especially in the economic sphere. Before getting into a detailed examination of the reforms in this area, however, it would be necessary to see the society in its totality.

The Zuru Native Authority, had a population of 93,700, situated in a land are of 3, 488 square miles with a population density of 27 persons to a square mile as at 1950.[19] The economic centre was Rijau. The people of the emirate looked to the Niger rather than Nortwards to Sokoto. The principal attraction about Rijau as economic centre of the emirate was its good communication with the river Niger and with the railway through Zungeru/Mokwa.

The chief occupation of the people was and still is farming. According to the 1920 annual report, however, there were a couple of important but secondary occupations, e.g. brewing, trading, weaving, dyeing blacksmithing, butchery, mat making etc. Of these, trading and blacksmithing need special mention. During the pre-colonial and colonial periods, Zuru Division was favourably placed in the Niger

---

[18] Correspondence between the A.D.O. Zuru and D.O. Gwandu Division on 19th June 1939 in File 187/8/92 Kaduna Archives, P.99.

[19] K.P. Maddocks & D.A. Pott, *Report on Local Government in Northern Provinces of Nigeeria*, Dec., 1950, See also *Gazetters of the Northern Provinces of Nigeria*, p. 39.

river trade system. Bena, Zuru, Isogogo, Diri, Sakaba etc. were some of the principal commercial centres lying on the caravan route tapping the externalities of this trading system.[20]

Similarly, Zuruland seems to have been richly endowed with iron ore. Preliminary excavation by some archaeological research reveals very interesting information about this. Just behind the mountain range lying north of Zuru town, lies the biggest furnance so far recorded in Zuruland. About 10 kilomitres from Zuru on the Zuru-Kotangora road, lies the largest iron ore mine in Zuruland. This mine is about ten metres deep. In Dabai, and in North-west and west of Zuruland, numerous iron slabs have been found by this team.[21] All these point to the conclusion that, during at least, the pre-colonial era, iron smelting was an important pre-occupation in Zuruland and with such important resources for military might, Zuruland must have played an important role in the commerce and politics of the middle Niger complex.

## Transport

To tap the resources of the land which were mainly agricultural, the British needed to improve the structure of the open economy by constructing roads. Before and during this time, however, river transport was extensively used by the Native Administrations of Argungu, Dabai and Gwandu divisions. This is evidenced in the 1927 annual report.[22] Security consideration also necessitated the construction of new roads, for the colonial government needed a certain level of security to maximize its exploitation of both the human and material resources of the land. Such security was guaranteed by the new roads along which punitive forces could easily be moved to "trouble" spots.

To achieve these objectives, Zuru Emirate was to be linked up with its neighbours with what started as seasonal roads but eventually developed into all season roads. In the North-East, Bena was linked up with Kotangora while Zuru town was placed on the Bokani-Kotangora-Zuru axis. Similarly, Zuru was further linked up with Sokoto on the Zuru-Kotangora-Sokoto road while Birnin Kebbi was connected with Zuru via Zuru-Sakaba-Gamba axis and with Bena and

---

[20] John Ralph Wills, *Gazetters of, op.cit.*, P.39.
[21] These discoveries were made by a team of archeologists involved in the Zuru History Project.
[22] *Annual Report on the Nothern Provinces*, 1927, P.40.

Yelwa.[23] In 1927, the Sokoto-Tureta-Zuru road was completed with a bridge constructed on the Zamfara river.[24] There is no doubt about the fact that one of the most obvious consequences of the road and infrastructure was the emergence of new settlement pattern as we shall see later.

Before this road network however, to give legal protection to her activities in the newly acquired territories, Britain made several proclamations. On the 1st of April, 1901, F. Lugard proclaimed that any child born after that date was free and immuned from slavery. This was a blessing for the subject people in Zuruland who were raided by their neighbours for slaves, while it deprived their own aristocrats of an important source of income from slavery and slave trade. The sale and gift of slaves was also prohibited. With these proclamations, more free labour could now be put into production from which the administration was to generate revenue. Another proclamation of Lugard was the prohibition of feudal lords from collecting any tax from traders, and merchants, passing through their territories.[25]

All these proclamations were to herald Lugard's numerous socio-economic reforms which were to have lasting effect on the people of Zuruland. These reforms were also to partially transfer privileges gradually from their traditional owners to Britain. In 1902 for example, chiefs were allowed to keep the tax collected from their subjects. From 1903 the government demanded one-third of this tax and in 1906 the Kotangora province and hence Zuruland, has to pay part of its tribute to the Government.[26]

So exploitative was the new tax system which replaced the tributary tax system of the pre-colonial era that it generated ill-feelings and hence protest from the people. This statement is substantiated in the 1940-1949 Zuru Native Aminustration Tax Assessment. In this assessment, Zuru Native Administration's tax jumped from £4,417 in 1948 to £12,728 in 1949.[27] This exploitative tax seems to have led to protest and migrations to areas of lesser tax of Sokoto and Plateau provinces. As has been said earlier, tax reforms were along the line of

---

[23] John Ralph Wills, *Gazetters* of *Op.cit*, P.39, see also *Annual Report on the Northern Provinces* 1927, P.40.

[24] *Annual Report, op.cit.* P.40.

[25] Lugard, F. *Annual Report, Northern Nigeria* 1900-1911 pp. 49-55, and pp. 293-295.

[26] Adamu, M., *op.cit.*, P.332.

[27] NAK, Minprof., 4353 *General Tax Assessment, Zuru Native Administrative.*

sharing traditional privileges with the colonial administration and so these and subsequent reforms were based on the same philosophy.

## Judicial Reforms

Before British occupation, the peoples of Zuruland maintained peace and tranquility in their societies through certain traditional institutions. In Dakarkari land for example, the *M'gilø* (men's secret society) settled disputes, cases of fighting, rape, poisoning, witchcraft and others.[28] With the coming of the British, things changed.

The British judicial reforms were basically intended to enable the administration to design "effective" ways of the dispensation of "justice", to maintain peace and order in the society as a prerequisite for exploitation and to share where possible, traditional privileges with the traditional elites. Thus, native or customary courts were created to handle traditional issues. These were purely native institutions as perceived by the colonial masters with predominant native membership. In addition there was the Alkali court presided over by the Alkali who treated cases outside the customary courts but inclined more to Islamic legal value. It should be said here that in addition to this, such courts entertained some criminal cases within the common law.

To dispense justice, according to the 1920 annual report, the following courts were established:

---

[28] Discussion at the August Workshop.

With these legal institutions, Britain could dispense justice the way she felt necessary and through them, was also able to generate revenue by means of fines, taxes and levies. With the new judicial system, the traditional system of dispensing justice was drastically reformed. This also saw the distortion of the value-system of the people and hence alienating them from their ancestoral legal institutions such as *Uhola* and *M'gilø* which has some regulatory effects on the social behaviours of the people.

## Populations, Settlement Pattern, Production and Commerce

To appreciate and understand human efforts of their process of survival, we need to know their physical environments and the characteristic ecological attributes of such environments. These determined largely the social formation in mind that we attempt to examine the physical setting of Zuruland and the transformation in this setting during the colonial era. Golden Childe's dictum that the environment makes the man applies very well to the experience of Zuruland.

Reports and participant observation corroborate the statement that the ecological zones of northern Nigeria and hence trans-human and production pattern have undergone tremendous transformation since the colonial era. Zuruland is not an exception to this rule. Within the span of the colonial era, however, there seems to have been no such drastic ecological changes and hence similar patterns, with slight variations, prevailed throughout the period. According to a report by Agency for International Development, compiled for the Federal Government in June, 1969, Zuruland and her neighbours are situated within the Niger-Benue river valley or ecological zone, II, known as Intermediate Savannah or Sudan Savannah zone. In this zone, a variety of crops and livestock could be grown and raised respectively. Most if not all of the grain varieties of crops could be grown and hence the predominance of agriculture in the area.

Topographically, Zuruland has the characteristic attributes of a region draining into a lower region, the Niger valley and other smaller rivers' valleys in the area. Generally, the land is undulating sandy plains with isolated tors and groups of bare steep-sided hills. These hills according to Fitzgeral writing in 1944, are of quartzite rock with very little soil above. These rise sharply to a height of 100-200 feet in the south and 200-400 feet in the North in Dakarkari area.[29] Here and there, there are mountains and inselbergs which, before the advent of colonial rule, used to provide shelter for people away from slave raiders, and other ecological vices.[30] In Dakarkari area of Zuruland, the plain to the east harbours the watershed which runs east and west across the centre of this area. This drains into the Gulbin Ka and to the South, into the Gulbin Boka and Malendo river systems. It is a well watered and attractive scenery dissected by a large number of small streams and fadama. According to McClintock writing early in this century, water could be found almost everywhere at a depth of fifteen to twenty feet and at forty-five feet, a fresh source of crystal clear water could always be tapped.[31]

The consequent settlement pattern to this topographical setting especially before colonialism is obvious. As has been stated, before "Pax Britanica", the settlement pattern was dense in and around the mountains and inselberge for spiritual and security reasons.[32] As a result of colonial "peace" however, new dispersal areas arose. These include:

1. Bangawa, north of the Zuru Federation,
2. Kelawa, including Isgogo, Gele, Fakai, Birnin Tudu, Kele, Zussun, Kulu and Kukun, and
3. Lilawa, Dabai, Isgogo, Tadurga, Rumu, Rikoto, Zuru, Kyabu, Ribah, Chonoko, Kanya, Kurumin Hodo, Penin Amana, Panin Gaba and Ane.

Dispersal appears to be caused by at least four factors: death among the older generations still living in villages with consequent weakening of both traditional and kinship ties; periodic removal of farms; the clustering of non-Dakarkari, particularly Hausa peoples into the

---

[29] Gunn, H.D. & Conant *Peoples of the Middle Niger Region of Northern Nigeria*, London, International African Institute 1960 P.34.

[30] Mountainous settlements throughout human history have been necessitated by security and spiritual considerations. Such considerations were very important in the settlement pattern of Zuruland before the establishment of Colonial administration. After, this is as a result of colonial policies coupled with the prevalance of peace, these environmentatl factors ceased to be important in determining settlement pattern.

[31] MaClintock in Gunn & Conant, *Peoples of the Middle Niger, op.cit.* p.34.

[32] Gunn & Conant *Peoples of the Middle Niger, op.cit.* P.35 *Report on Land Tenure Niger Province*. In African *Studies* Library Boston University, U.S.

villages and termination of war and raiding under the British administration.

In the old days, people would, and to some extent still, leave their hills to go out into the plains and valleys to cultivate their farmlands. In the part and especially during the colonial era, people could leave their hill settlement for a considerable part of the rainy season living on their farms. The old and the feeble would however remain on the hills engaged in terrace farming.

As the population increased and peaceful atmosphere continued to prevail, more and more people started to come down to the plains to settle. However, because of mass movement of people into the plains, the threshholds of the hills on the plains became chocked up and consequently people had to travel far and wide to cultivate patches of land for agricultural purposes. These men would go out as far as twenty or thirty miles as the case might be from their parent villages, coming in only for burials and religious ceremonies.[33] Village units had therefore traditional rather than political basis. With modernization, however, the custom of annual return to the parent village has been growing weaker. This is especially true as people come to settle by the newly constructed colonial roads to enjoy such facilities.

On the whole, however, there was no population pressure on the land. As stated in one colonial report, "the key note to land tenure conditions in Zuru is set by the fact that the overall population density is only 26.7 persons, per square mile (excluding nomadic Fulanis)."[34] This notwithstanding, in the days of Kotangora province, population density figure was highest in Dabai division that is, Zuruland with 13.5 and reaching 49 per sequare mile in the central Dakarkari land.[35] By the 1940s, due to reduction in infant mortality[36] the overall density reached the figure 26.7 quoted above. According to the 1920 report the population distribution in Dabai division was as follows:

---

[33] Wills, J.R. (ed.) *Gazetteers of the Northern Provinces of Nigeria, W.II The Central Kingdoms, Frank Cass, London, 1972 P.5-6* see also Maddocks, K.P *Report on Local Government in the Northern Provinces of Nigeria* 14the Dec. 1950, See also *Report on Land Tenure, Niger Province Kaduna*, 1948, P.41.

[34] Wills, J.R. (ed.) *Gazetteers op.cit.* P.5-6.

[35] Although the Colonial Medical care system was not adequate, it did eradicate some diseases which hitherto were fatal. This together with improved environmental sanitation reduced infant mortality thus leading to population growth.

[36] Wills, J.R. (ed.) *Gazetteers of the Northern Provinces op.cit*, P.39, see also *Report on Land Tenure Province Kaduna*, 1948, P.42.

| District | Population | No. of Villages |
|---|---|---|
| Dabai | 17,315 | 37 |
| Wasagu | 10,420 | 18 |
| Fakkai | 8,160 | 24 |
| Danko | 5,800 | 20 |
| Sakaba | 6,888 | 27 |
| | 48,583 | 126 |

By 1948, the number of villages had risen to 248 according to the village reorganization of June of that year.[37] By 1950, the overall population had grown from 48,583 in 1920 to 93,700. This represented an annual growth rate of 3% which is within the range of our national average. Based on this the estimated population of the entire emirate was about 123,480 by 1960. This was as follows from 1950:

| Year | Population |
|---|---|
| 1950 | 93,700 |
| 1951 | 94637.03 |
| 1952 | 97,476.14 |
| 1953 | 100,400.42 |
| 1954 | 103,412.43 |
| 1955 | 106,514.8 |
| 1956 | 109,710.24 |
| 1957 | 113,001.54 |
| 1958 | 117,391.58 |
| 1959 | 119,883.32 |
| 1960 | 123,479.8 |

Source: Figures computed on 3% annual population growth rate based on the 1950 figures found in *Report on Local Government in the Northern Provinces of Nigeria* compiled by K.F. Maddocks, Senior District Officer and D.A. Poot, District Officer on 14th December, 1950.

## Agriculture

Given the low level of technology, agriculture has been and still is the most important occupation of the people of Zuruland. In Dakarkari land, agriculture rested and still does on a system of shifting

---

[37] *ibid.*, p.35 See also *1920 Sokoto Province Annual Report.*

cultivation. The crops grown and the techniques employed conform to the general practices of central Nigeria. Crops grown included guinea corn, *Maiwa* or late millet, *gero*, maize, *acha*, tama rice, wheat, yam, cotton, onions, pepper, sugar cane, groundnuts, *Kwaruru*.beans, lalle, indigo, sweet potatoes, bananas and tobacco.[38] Many of these crops were inter-planted e.g. guinea corn with *gero*; guinea corn with maize; maize and beans, beans and yam, guinea corn and groundnuts etc. Crops such as guinea corn, millet, Masara, tubers(coco yam, yam and occasionally cassava) and rice were grown and owned by men while the women exercised their own monopoly in the growing of *acha*, (a variety of wheat), beniseed and beans.[39]

According to a report, the farming methods slightly differed between the Dakarkari and the Hausa farmers in Zuruland. While the Dakarkari tended to farm further and further away from his parent village, the Hausa, among whom immigration could only be caused by deteriorating conditions in the north, only farmed on the outskirts of the towns.[40] Similarly, while the Darkarkari did not use manure, presumably because there was vast unused land and hence who hardly moved away from the farm and whose land area was therefore limited and could therefore be easily exhausted, used manure to enrich their farms. The manure was got from Fulani cattle owners, household refuse and goat dung. They also practised crop rotation to improve the soil texture.

As regards labour for such activities, the two peoples also differed. According to the report quoted above, the Dakarkari and other "pagan" groups depended and still depend on traditional source of labour that is, the household and *gayya* according to tribal customs. Much of the farm work was done by young men who contracted to do so many seasons on the farms of their prospective fathers-in-law. They are known as *masu golmo* and the seniors among them elect two of their members to direct operations.[41] The Hausa on the other hand, hired and still hire casual labour when necessary and available.

Among the Dakarkari, farming was the chief occupation while a few of them has cottage industries to supplement their income. Indeed,

---

[38] Temple, G.L. *Notes on the Tribes, Provinces Emirate and states of the Northeern Provinces of Nigeria* Frank Cass 1965, P.89; Gunn & Conant *Peoples of Middle Niger Region. op.cit.*

[39] *Report on Land Teunre, Niger Province, op.*cit. P.43 also See Gunn & Conant, *Peoples of the Middle Niger Region, op.cit,* P.35.

[40] Temple, C.L. *Notes on the Tribes, op.cit.* P.90. See also *Report on Land Tenure Niger Province,* P.43.

[41] *Report on Land Tenure op.cit.,* P.43.

some of the older farmers would not even grow sugar cane and cotton but stick to what they called "real" farming, that is; guinea corn cultivation. A few of the cottage industries they had were: breweries, blacksmithing, mat making, smelting and pottery. The Hausa on the other hand, had some supplementary income from tailoring, trading, weaving, drumming, barbering, butchery, carpentary, dyeing etc.[42]

Other important sources of production were gathering and hunting. Such forest products as *doko, Kadanya* or shea butter tree and locust beans tree respectively, added to production from agriculture while hunting added to domestic sources of supply of meat and other animal products the surplus of which found its way into the trade system. Favourite areas for such games were in the direction of Kazuwa, North east adjacent to the then rich game centre of *Wabi* in Kwiambana District.[43]

## Ecology And Production

Although it has been said earlier that there was no drastic transition in the ecology and hence production during the colonial era in Zuruland, slight problems emerged here and there caused mainly by drought, insect visitation and other ecological disequilibriums. In some cases, these led to famine situation. As early as 1906 according to Abdullahi Sakaba in a commentary during the 1987 August symposium, there was famine in many parts of Zuruland. Similarly, the partial failure of the crops in 1926 resulted in a serious shortage of grains causing famine conditions in Sokoto Province generally. Consequently, grains were imported from other areas into the province.[44] During certain years, ecological factors were quite favourable and so was production. In 1931, for example, in spite of late rains, an excellent harvest of millet and guinea corn was registered throughout the province. Thus although there was locust visitation that year, there was hardly any famine situation in the province except in Dabai which was easily contained given the generally favourable harvest in the province.[45]

On the whole, however, while there were some ecological problems, the people produced surplus which went into the exchange system. As the report on proposed Dabai N.A. Reserve No. 2 of 1929 stated, some families averaging 4 to 5, could harvest as many as

---

[42] Correspondence between Reservation of Forests of the Northern Provinces of Nigeria and The Resident Sokoto Province on 20th March, 1929 on the subject proposed Dabai N.A. Reserve No.2 Preliminary Survey, p.3.

[43] Annual Report on the Northern Province of Nigeria 1931, PP.31-32 see also Annual Report on the Northern provinces, 1927, P.41.

[44] Annual Report on the Northern Provinces 1931, P.32.

[45] Correspondence & *Proposed Dabai Reserve No. 2 A Preliminary Survey*, of 1929, P.2.

one thousand bundles of corn each year. This no doubt left some surplus found its way into the trade system of the day.[46] Then, competition much more than necessity, promoted such intensive cultivation of land and hence production of surplus.

Other productive forces made some sizeable contribution towards producing surplus for exchange purposes. According to the 1920 annual Report, there were twenty breweries, sixty-five traders, thirty weavers, twelve dyers, thirty-five blacksmiths, fifteen butchers, three carpenters, twenty-five mat makers, two canoe builders, twenty-five potters and fifteen smelters in Zuru Emirate.[47] This no doubt added to the volume of production in the area and hence the gross domestic product of Zuruland.

## Mining Industry

As has earlier been said, the people of Zuruland were great iron workers in the pre-colonial times. During the colonial period, in spite of the importance of this economic pursuit in the life of the people, government policy was rather against it presumably because of the competition the product of such activities could wage against British iron bars, or because of the meagreness of the resources the government envisaged it could generate from it or because of the demand structure of British economy which favoured other colonial commodities more than iron, or also because of its labour supply to the more favoured sector, that is agriculture. Consequently, government response was discouraging to the iron smelting industry.

In addition to iron smelting, however, there were other mining activities in Zuruland. Several archival sources corroborated this statement. As early as 1934 for example, an application for mining leases over 29.5 acres of land on the river Ka, Donko District, was made by the Nigerian Mineral Development Company.[48] Late, similar demand was made and granted for exclusive prospecting licence over a land of 1.5 square miles south of Ruanjema Bukurun.[49] More conclusive statement on this industry may have to await the findings of our archaeologists and Doctoral works such as that of Shehu Lawal. Meanwhile, suffice it to know that Zuruland was not lacking in this vital sector of the economy during the time covered here.

---

[46] Wills, J.R. *Gazetteers of the Northern Provinces, op.cit.* p.35.

[47] NA, Files No.3402 titled *Application for Mining Lease over 29.5 Acres on the River Ka Donko District Zuru by Nigerian Minerals Development Company, 1934.*

[48] NAK, Files No.5373 & 5229 titled *Application for Exclusive License over 1,505 sq miles from miles South of Ruwan Jima Bukurun.*

[49] NAK File No.5920 titled *Application for Mining Lease in Kwiambana.*

## Commerce

As has earlier been argued, both during the pre-colonial and colonial eras, Zuruland was favourably placed in the middle Nigeria trading system. Towns such as Zuru, Bena, Rijau, Isogogo, *Diri* etc, were all very important trade centres on important trade routes. With the increase in production consequent to the prevelance of peace and order, some of these towns grew in importance while others declined due to changing settlement patterns and production activities, making way for the emergence of new ones.

The prevalence of peace during the colonial era; the new demands for tropical goods, e.g. cotton, groundnuts shea-nuts and other vegetable oil seeds in Europe, coupled with the monetary obligations of the colonial regimé on the people which forced them to produce more and more, no doubt led to increased production which also had some spill-over effect on commercial activities. With the various roads built by the colonial government as we have seen, more domestic markets were created for goods from other parts of this ecological zone or different ecological zones. This also necessitated expansion in production as simple rules of supply and demand would suggest. With all these, although we do not have quantitative data to illustrate growth in production and distribution in Zuruland, it could be safely concluded that colonialism saw growth in production and distribution in this area.

With the growth in output and expansion in distribution, thus wheeled cars were introduced and European merchant companies established stations. Wheeled vehicles started to come into use in the Sokoto region in the dry season of 1917. Hitherto, several horse-vehicles were in use throughout the year.[50] In Zuruland, park animals and camels were used along the routes and in the Niger respectively as earlier mentioned. Much earlier than the coming of wheeled cars, however in 1913, European trading firms that is, the London and Kano Trading Company and Messrs Ambrossini, the hide and skin trading company, opened branches in the region.[51]

As argued earlier, the opening up of more markets created more demand for local and foreign goods. Part of this demand was from these European companies. From this expanding production and commercial activities, the government and the various native administrations were able to generate revenue to lubricate their administrative machineries and at the same time appropriate surplus which was expatriated to Britain.

---

[50] Arnett, E.J. *Gazetteers of the Northern Provinces of Nigeria Vol.I the Hausa Emirates* Frank Gass 1972, P.55.
[51] *ibid.*, P.52.

In the early years before the depression, trade flourished. As reported in the 1927 annual report "trade appears to be flourishing and the people are certainly wealthier than they have been. Exports of hides and skins by European firms and the few big native traders (mostly Hausa in Dabai Emirate) who can furnish returns, rose from 163 tons and 255 tons in 1926 to 333 tons and 340 tons respectively."[52] These figures are not comprehensive, for probably as much again, or more was exported through other sources on which there was no reliable check.

During the same period, public finance seems to have been satisfactory in spite of the depression. According to the 1931 report, "the financial position of all the emirates, except Dabai, is reassuring considering the world-wide depression in trade and the consequent shortage of cash."[53] Needless to say, this must have been as a result of the extortionate tax, levies and arbitray fines which characterized government monetary policies of the time. During this year in Dabai, the Treasury reserve funds had to be realised to repay a loan from the Gwandu Emirate to buy food-stuffs and to inaugurate famine relief works.[54] In response to the depression, expatriate participants in the market tried to maximize their returns. According to the 1938 annual report, at Rijau, farmers refused to sell their cotton at the ridiculous price of 7/10th of a penny at the local market where expatriate companies, through market sharing, beat down the price. Instead, they took their commodity to Yelwa market in Sokoto province where prices were generally higher than in Niger province.[55]

When the depression set in, poor prices where paid by the trading firms for local produce and various depots opened up in the outstations especially in places like Argungu Emirate, have had to be temporarily closed down. Given its proximity to the Niger, one would assume that such depression period readjustment did not drastically affect Zuruland. With its monopoly, however, the Unite Africa Company, on the Upper Niger, established stations at three different places to employ local canoe services from Jebba. The idea was to use these canoes to bring sale goods and salts up the river and return laden wares and other produce bought at the revering depots.[56]

Dabai Emirate's experience in commerce during the colonial era was like those of other Emirates. From the start the demand by the

---

[52] *Annual Report on the Northern Provinces, 1931 Op.cit.* 31-32, See also, Annual Report on the Northern Provinces, .1927 P.41.

[53] *Annual Report on the Northern Province*, 1931, P.31

[54] *ibid.*

[55] NAK Min. Prof. M. 1863, Vol.6 Provinces Annual Report 1938.

[56] *Annual Report on the Northern Provinces*, 1931, P.32.

newly opened up centres and the transport network, all contributed to the growth in production and commerce. Like any economy at the time, however, this prosperity quickly turned into misery when the depression set in as from the 1930s. This continued throughout the inter-war period. After the war and before the end of the post-war boom in the early 1950s the commodity trade boom brought prosperity again to the various producers. Unfortunately however, the benefits of bouyant years quickly went to the colonial administration through taxes, fines and levies. These were more numerous and arbitrarily used during the depression of the inter-war period and during the Second World War. To this exploitation and oppression, Africans responded in may ways. Most important of these were protest migrations from Niger province where these seemed to have been worse than in many other provinces and other forms of defiance.[57]

## Zuruland during The Second World War

During the Second World war, Britain exploited her colonial territories both in human and natural resources to execute the war and to reinvigorate her battered economy. In Zuruland, like in other places, this exploitation took the form of war relief levies, forced recruitment to fight in the war and other services. In terms of human resources, about 20% of male population of recruitable age (17-25 years) were recruited to fight in the war.[58] This no doubt had negative impact on agricultural production and any other community services which needed the services of this segment of the population.

After the war, the ex-servicemen played very important roles in the life of post war Zuruland. They served as conduits through which Christianity and Islam were further spread, as messengers in government offices and Native Authority police while some served as promoters of Western education. Others played key roles in the post war politics in Zuruland.

In addition to the contributions above, Zuruland also contributed materially to the Win-the war relief fund. In 1944 the area contributed £523.12.6d.[59] During the war also taxes were unnecessarily stepped up, thus squeezing the people more and more. In 1939 the tax stood at £4,162.0d. This rose to £4,724 in 1941 and to £5,461 in 1943 and further to £7.797 in 1945.[60] All this instigated the tax payer into protest of one type or the other starting from Kotangora from where it

---

[57] NAK Min. Prof. 4353 General Tax Assessment Zuru Native Admin. NAK Min. Prof. M. 1863 Vol. 6 Provincial Annual Report, 1938.
[58] NAK Min. Prof. 5568 *Niger Province Annual Report 1944*.
[59] NAK Min. Prof. 668 *War With Germany, The Nigerian War Relief Fund*.
[60] NAK Min. Prof. 4353 *General Tax Assessment, Zuru Native Adimin*.

spread to other parts of the province. Needless to say this generated brutal suppression from the colonial state.

## Socio-Economic Changes

At this stage it becomes pertinent to examine the impact of the colonial experiences on Zuruland. Based on the broad British imperial policies and objectives, not much should be expected in the field of socio-political development in Zuruland during the colonial period. However, that there was some degree of transformation is not contestable. What is contestable is whether or not Zuruland got the equilibrium value of its investment in the colonial government both in human and material resources. In examining this issue there are two schools of thought, that is, those who believe that colonialism generally developed African human and natural resources, and those who contest this.[61]

To these might be added the category of those who feel that although the overall impact of colonialism was negative, one could see some superficial changes here an there whose overall impact on their host society was insignificant.[62] We therefore have the excavationists who condemn colonialism *in toto* and opposed to this, are those who glorify colonialism for having pulled the colonial territories out of their misery of barbarism and abject poverty. Finally, there are the moderates or liberals who maintain the middle road. To examine and illustrate these views, certain variables would be used. These include the provision of social services and the impact of these on the life of the people.

When we normally talk of social services, we always mean those services such as education, good drinking water, electricity, medical care and others that are considered to be necessary for the general upliftment of the society. In Zuruland, the colonial administration attempted to provide such but this fell much below expectations in spite of increased prosperity both in the private and public sectors of the economy and in spite of increased exploitation of the electorate in the form of taxes, fines and other levies the proceeds from which

---

[61] These schools are represented by A.G. Hopkins in his work *An Economic History of West Africa*, Longman, London, 1973 in which he sees European penetration of the Colonial Territories to be beneficial to the colonial people and Walter Rodney in his work, How *Europe Underdeveloped Africa*, 1975 in which he adapts a differeent approach from Hopkins, then came to the conclusion that contact between Europeans and Africans, representing the colonial territory, caused the backwardness of the continent today.

[62] Such position is maintained by liberal African historians who see the establishment of educational & Medical institutions, roads, and railway lines to be a mark of development for which credit should be given to Europe and colonizers.

should normally have gone to provide more and more of such services to the electorate.

In fact, on the contrary, the provision of such services seems to have squarely fallen on the shoulders of agencies related but outside the colonial administration that is, Christian Missionaries and other philanthropic organizations. Although this cannot be quantitatively ascertained due to unavailability of statistical data, given the predominance of Christians in this area and given the Missionary Philosophy of humanitarianism during the time in question, it would be safe to conclude that such services were provided more by such organisations than by the government whose main pre-occupation was structuring the colonial economies to serve British imperial interests.

As earlier pointed out, one missionary, the United Missionary Society alone, provided seven dispensaries; six day schools and a Bible school by 1943.[63] This Missionary first came to Zuruland in 1925 under the leadership of one Joseph Ummuel and Paul Ummuel.[64] By 1935, the missionary had established centres at Rikoto, Dabai, Tungan Magajiya and some other towns. Its educational works developed out of the necessity to spread the gospel as transmitted in the Bible and other religious books while medical works are supposed to have developed out of the "Christian compassion".[65] By the 1950s, this missionary alone had seventeen elementary schools, a teacher training college of one hundred and fifty enrolment; a secondary modern school, three Bible schools; a theological college, a one hundred bed hospital and a nurses training school within the K'otangora-Ilorin complex.[66] In addition, there were numerous dispensaries located in the rural areas to treat the numerous perenial and nagging diseases associated with rural Africa. By 1935, nineteen villages and towns, in Zuruland had churches. These churches were to serve as centres of Christian religions activities and other humanitarian services.

Given the magnitude of these activities, it would seem that the few educational and medical services provided by the colonial government, actually supplemented the efforts of voluntary humanitarian organizations instead of the other way round. In the field of education, the colonial government did very little in Zuruland. By 1927 there were nineteen Government schools in the whole of Sokoto Province

---

[63] Goddard, B.C. ed. *Encyclopedia of Modern Christian Missions*, Thomas Nelson & Sons N.J., P.665.
[64] A Document titled "History of Christian Missionaries in Zuruland" from 1925, By Sakaba and Zomi Rikoto.
[65] *ibid.*
[66] *ibid.*

and given the scepticism of the colonial administration in providing western-type schools in the Moslem area, especially at the initial stage of colonialism, one may safely assume that quite a number of these schools were located in the so-called "pagan" areas, that is Zuruland.[67]

Considering the need for western education at the time, however, nineteen schools to cater for the whole province was certainly inadequate. As this report says, "there is demand for more elementary schools and for something in the way of continuation classes and secondary school education which has to be left unsatisfied owing to lack of funds and staff". [68] This demand must have been met to some extent by missionary effort especially in places like Zuruland and as time went on, by the colonial government when its resources increased. As one source said, the United Missionary Society assisted Zuruland people in many ways - famine relief aid, medical care, schools etc.[69]

The prominence of Zuruland in the attainment of western education in the various sources mentioned, is substantiated by what could be called an unscientific (not quantifiable) assumption that in relative terms, there are more literate and possibly educated people from Zuruland today than there are from any other ethnic group in Sokoto State. This prominence certainly did not start over night but was developed over a long period of time, going back to those days of the vehemence of the Muslim areas to western education and the emphasis put on the so-called "pagan tribes" by the various missionary groups in Northern Nigeria generally. These missionaries were the United Missionary Society, Roman Catholic Mission Church, ECWA and the Christ Apostolic Church. All had the objective of spreading Christianity and western values in Zuruland.

Meanwhile Islam had made some impact on some parts of Zuruland especially the Hausa migrant groups from Katsina. With such migrants came Islam into Zuruland as far back as the 15th century. This Islamization of Zuruland gathered more momentum as from the Danfodio Jihad of early 19th century. This reached its peak in the 1960s when more and more Muslim scholars came to Zuruland to

---

[67] Initially the Moslem areas of Northern Nigeria were vehemently against Christianity and anything related to it such as Western education. As a result both government and private organizations activities in education was very mindful of this. Consequently, the non-moslems areas were left free to be opened up by Christian Missionaries. However, as time went by, the people of the Moslem areas came to see and appreciate the value of Western Education and thus started to acquire this as vigorously as their Christian counterparts.

[68] *Annual Report on the Northern 1927 Provinces*, op.cit., p.40.

[69] History of Emirate in Zuruland from 1925, p.4.

spread the religion. Prominent among these were late Mallams Dangurgu, Dogari and Balarabe.[70]

Like any other government policy, the educational policy and activities of the colonial government and religious organizations had tremendous impact on the traditional value system of the peoples of Zuruland. Directly or indirectly, certain values in the new educational system did come into contact with the values of the people. This interaction is usually seen in the day to day life of the people and their institutions e.g. marriage, worship, consumption pattern, habits etc. With time, through the process of disarticulation, the traditional value system was destroyed to prepare the people for the British capitalist market. In a sense some aspects of cultural mullatoism developed.[71]

## Medical Care

Like the provision of western education which was motivated by the desire of the colonial government to produce a class of collaborators (typists, messengers etc.) to assist them to plant the colonial establishment,[72] the provision of medical services except in the case of missionary medical care, was intended to reduce mortality rate so that a constant and more supply of virile labour could be guaranteed while the menace of diseases which caused incapacitation among the colonial labour force could be eliminated or contained. In the light of this, we should watch out against the popular bourgeois philanthropic view that such services were created purely out of humanitarianism. Although there could have been such in the consideration of the colonial government, it was secondary to the preponderant economic consideration of creating a virile labour force which was needed by imperial Britain to achieve its economic objective in the colonies.

Records on the provision of medical services in Zuruland, as scanty as they may be, seem to suggest that initially such services were intended or at least emphasized for government or related institutions and not for everybody. It also seems that from the beginning, western medicine was not popular among the electorate, for as the 1927 annual report reveals, "European medicine is now making appreciable strides in popularity. At Argungu, Birnin Kebbi and

---

[70] Interview and discussion at the August Workshop.

[71] British effort like any other colonizing power was to reorient the politics and economy of the colonial territory towards securing her domestic needs rather than the needs of the colonial peoples. This can be seen in the reorientation of the economy, for example, the emphasis on cash crop production at the almost total neglect of the food crop sector of the agricultural economy.

[72] Like notes 76 above, what Britain did in the medical sector was not of humanitarian drive to assist Africans rather it was out of the need to create a varile labour force which could be used to exploit the natural resources of the colonial territory.

steadily going upwards and at Zuru and Gusau, the people come in freely".[73] With more response from the public, the government provided more of this service. In 1930, the Zuru hospital was already fully operational. Statistical medical records reveal that there were 1669 out-patients in 1930, 1959 in 1931 and 1327 in 1932. In-patients were 217 in 1930; 191 in 1931 and 178 in 1932.[74] In 1931, the annual colonial report reported that, "work on the new African Hospital at Sokoto is nearing completion and dispensaries have been established at eight centres, all at District Head Quarters".[75] This pleasing picture seems, however, to have been interrupted by the depression of the 1930s which forced the government into taking the counter productive step of requiring people to pay for medical care. This no doubt pushed the hand of the clock back, for in 1931, when fees were introduced, people kept away from the medical institutions because they could not pay the fees.[76] In 1945, the United Missionary Society established a clinic in Zuru town and a hospital in Tungan Magajiya in 1950 to augment or complement government's effort in this direction.

According to the annual medical report of December, 1932, the commonest diseases treated among the European community were gonorrhoea, Muco-membearous colitis, syphilis and influenza. These diseases must have been imports into Zuruland thus rendering credence to the view that such diseases were introduced into the tropical regions by Europeans. Among Africans, the commonest were dysentary, which was due to poor drinking water and poor diet; a few outbreaks of small pox in January - April of that year; leprosy; guinea worm and related diseases. From the same report it is also gathered that Zuru had a big hospital with a capacity to serve its area for some more years before an expansion would be required. It could be said therefore that Zuru town and its environment were adequately catered for in terms of medical care for that period, thanks to the effort of missionaries in the area.

## Water And Electricity Supply

As regards pipe born water and electricity, there is no record of such before the 1950s. In fact as regards electricity, it would be safe to conclude that this was not provided except in Government Residential areas and Hospitals, until after independence. This is not surprising

---

[73] *Annual Report on the Northern Province 1927 Op.cit.* P.41, See also NAK 5.2583. *Zuru Annual Medical and Health Report for the year, Ending 31st Dec. 1932.*

[74] *Zuru Annual Medical and Health Report, op.cit.* p.2.

[75] *Annual Report on the Northern Provinces* 1931, *op.cit,* p.32.

[76] ibid *Zuru Annual Medical & Health Report, op.cit.* p.1-2.

given the urban-oriented development policies of Government of this country right from the colonial era to the present. Consequently, these social services continued to be unknown by the Zuruland tax payers most of whom were on the periphery of the Kotangora-Sokoto provincial administration until much later during the colonial period.

## Conclusion

On the whole therefore, the view of the school which contends that colonialism underdeveloped Africa, seems to apply to Zuruland in terms of the provision of social services which were intended to develop the people, and also in terms of the exploitation of both human and natural resources. At best what the colonial establishment seems to have done was to articulate the pre-capitalist economy of Zuruland to the level whereby it could lead to economic prosperity of the metropolis. This process involved economic, cultural, political and administrative reorientation. This explains the emphasis on agriculture to provide the necessary raw materials for British industries and also explains the philosophy which informed the various reforms treated earlier in this paper. The idea was to tune the native people towards and for the benefits of the British economy rather than for Zuruland and its people.

In areas where missionary presence was non-existent, these services were scanty. As has been argued, rural development was unheard of and so the bulk of the rural community continued to live at the mercy of their pre-colonial set up throughout most of the colonial era. Their benefits were incidental and not commensurate to their investment in the tax and court system and other levies characteristic of the colonial regime. Where such benefits were sizeable, they were due more to the efforts of organizations other than the colonial government, that is Christian Missionaries. Such were the experiences of Zuruland during the colonial era.

It should be said at this juncture, that, as stated in the opening of this paper, this is a first attempt at reconstructing the colonial history of Zuruland. The main purpose to be served with this work therefore is to ignite more interest in the examination of the past and present of this people who hitherto have been neglected in our historiography.

# Select Bibliography

## (a) *Oral Informants*

1. Bawa Bena, C. 105 years, Bena, 26/1/88
2. Dauda Iro, 35 years, Farmer, Bena 20/1/88
3. Marafan Dabai, 81 years, Dabai, 22/1285
4. Sarkin Wasagu, 55 years, Wasagu, 23/12/85
5. Mallam Karnso, Farmer, 80 years, Tudun Wada Zuru 26/12/85.
6. Sarkin Sakaba, 57 years, Zuru, 24/12/85
7. Mallam Rikoto Mai Anguwa, Tudun Wada Zuru, 65 years, Zuru, 26/12/85.
8. John Zome Rikoto, 75 years, Clergyman, Zuru, 16/9/85.
9. Sarkin Fakai, 49 years, Zuru, 27/12/85.
10. Mallam Salihu, 70 years, Zuru, 14/11/86.
11. Usman Gele, 55 years, Zuru, 14/11/86.
12. D.S. Magaji, 47 years, Zuru 14/11/86.
13. Group interview at the palace of Sarkin Wasagu, 23/12/85.
14. Group interview at the house of the village head of Ribah, 23/12/85.
15. Group interview at the house of the village head of Dirin Gari, 24/12/85.
16. Group interview at the palace of the District head of Fakai, 1987.

## (b) *Archival Sources.*

(i) *National Archives, Kaduna.*

| Reference | Description |
| --- | --- |
| NAK. SokProf/S.2524: | Annual Report, Southern Division, 1942 |
| NAK:Min/Prof/125/1926: | Achifawa-Historical and Anthropological Report by A.B. Mathews. |
| NAK:KON/Prof/2990/07: | Report on the Kontagora Province for quarter ended June 1907. |
| NAK:SOK/Prof 605/1913: | Sakaba District File by G.E. Boyd |
| NAK:SNP.17.8/K.2100: | Historical and Anthropological Report on the Katsinawa by A.B. Mattews. |

Bibliography 173

| | |
|---|---|
| NAK:SOK/Prof/Co446/4 | Despatch No.111 of 23rd March 1899. |
| NAK:SOK/Prof/1387/92: | Zuru Native Administration: Proposed transfer from Sokoto Province to Niger Province. |
| NAK:SOK/Prof/1387/8/92: | Correspondence between the A.D.O Zuru and the D.O. Gwandu Division, 9/6/33. |
| NAK: Min/Prof/4353: | General Tax Assessment, Zuru Native Administration. |
| NAK:MinDept/3402: | Application for Mining lease over 29.5 Acres on the river Ka, Danko District Zuru by Nigerian minerals Development Company, 1934. |
| NAK:MinDept/5373: | Application for Explosive License over 1,505 sq miles South of Ruwan Jima, Bukkuyum. |
| NAK:Mindept/5920 | Application for Mining lease in Kwiambana. |
| NAK:Min/Prof/M.1863, Vol.6: | Provincial Annual Report 1938. |
| NAK:Min/Prof/5568: | Niger Province Annual Report, 1944 |
| NAK:Min/Prof/668: | War with Germany, The Nigerian War Relief Fund. |
| NAK:Sok/Prof/S.2583: | Zuru Annual Medical and Health Report for the year Ending 31/12/32. |

(ii) *Sokoto State History Bureau*

*Reference* — *Description*

| | |
|---|---|
| SSHB:HIST/1/1/32/355: | Brief Historical Background of the Division/Districts, Zuru. |
| SSHB"HIST/1/1938: | Bukkuyum District Note-book |
| SSHB: HIST/1/1938.55: | Zuru Re-organisation 1938-55. |

## (c) *Unpublished Thesis:*

Abdullahi M. — "Political and Economic Development of Colonial Northern Nigeria: Case of Zuru", *Unpublished B.A. Thesis*, Univ. of Sokoto 1985.

Adamu, M., — "A Hausa Government in Decline; Yawuri in the 19th century" *Unpublished M.A., Thesis* A.B.U. Zaria 1968.

Adamu, M., — "The Hause Factor in West African History", *Unpublished PhD. Thesis* Univ. of Birmingham, 1974.

Ahman, H., — "Zuru - Dabai Relations: A Case study of the rise of political institutions in Zuru Emirate" *Unpublished B.A. Thesis*, Univ. of Sokoto 1983.

Alkali, M.B., — "A Hausa Community in Crisis: Kebbi in the 19th century" Unpublished M.A. Thesis, A.B.U. Zaria. 1969.

Anagbogu, I., — "Trade in 19th century Sokoto - Zamfara confluence Area", *Unpublished M.A. Thesis*, Univ. of Ibadan, 1980.

Augi, A.R., — "The Gobir Factor in the Social and Economic History of the Rima Basin C. 1650-1808 A.D" *Unpublished PhD. Thesis*, A.B.U. Zaria 1984.

Dandikko, Y.M., — "Traditional Medicine among the Dakarkari Speaking people in the 20th century", *Unpublished B.A Thesis*, Univ. of Sokoto 1986

Gonyo, J.I., — "The History of Zuru", *NCE Final Year project* Dept., College of Education, Sokoto nd.

Hamis, I.M., "Women's role in agricultural production: A case study of Dakarkari people in Zuru area, 1900-60", *Unpublished B.A. Thesis*, Univ. of Sokoto 1986.

Idris, M.B., "The Political and Economic Relations of the Bariba states", *Unpublished PhD. Thesis* Univ. of Birmingham, nd.

Lawal S.U., "Imperial policy, Capital Accumulation and Gold Mining in Colonial North-Western Nigeria, *Unpublished PhD. Thesis* U.D.U Sokoto, 1989

Makar, T.M., "A History of Political Change among the Tiv in the 19th and 20th centuries", *Unpublished PhD. thesis*, A.B.U. Zaria 1975.

Mary, S., "History of Christian Churches in Zuru Town", *NCE Final year project*, History Dept., College of education, Sokoto, 1981.

Mohammed, S., "Some Aspects of the Culture and Institutions of the Dakarkari people examined in the light of their contiguity with the Hausa people" *Unpublished M.A. thesis* B.U.k. 1982.

Nadama, G., "The Rise and Collapse of a Hausa State: Social and Political History of Zamfara", *Unpublished PhD. Thesis* A.B.U. Zaria. 1977.

Nagode, B, "The Development of Christian Churches in Zuru 1925-83", *NCE Final year Project*, History Dept. College of Education, Sokoto, 1986.

Rabecca, M.Y., "Development of Christian Churches in Zuru, 1920-83", *NCE Final Year project*, History Dept. College of Education, Sokoto, 1983,

Ribah, A.M.D. — "A History of Ribah", *NCE Final year Project*, History Dept., College of Education, Sokoto nd.

Sakaba, M.S. — "Themes in Lelan History in the 19th & 20th centuries", *Unpublished B.A. thesis*, A.B.U Zaria, 1974.

Usman, Y.B. — "The Transformation of Katsina, C.1779-1903: The overthrow of the Sarauta system and the establishment and evolution of the Emirate" *Unpublished PhD. Thesis* A.B.U. Zaria, 1974.

Watts, M. — "A Silent Revolution: The Nature of famine and the changing character of food production in Nigerian Hausaland ", *Unpublished PhD. Thesis*, Univ. of Michigan 1979.

(d) *Unpublished Papers:*

Abdulkadir, M.S. — "The Jihad in Igalaland,", *History Seminar*, B.U.K., Nov. 1985.

AbdulHakeen, M. — "Afro-American historians and the decolonisation of African and world History: A brief overview", *History Seminar, paper*, Univ. of Sokoto, 1983.

Bauta, J.B. — "A Brief Historical Origin of the Dakarkaris of Zuru and some of their cultural traditions," *Ms*, nd

Harris, P.G. — "Sokoto Provincial Gazetteer, *Mimeo*," 1938.

Last, M. — "Beyond Kano before Katsina: Friend and Foe on the Western Frontier" *Paper presented at the second International Seminar on the History of Kano*, B.U.K., Sept. 1985.

Lawal, S.U. — "The Use and Relevance of History", *Public lecture delivered to the History club*, College of Education Sokoto, April, 1987.

Modibbo, M.A. & A. Abba, "Roots of academic repression in Nigerian Universities: The role of the intellectual wing of the Northern oligarchy", Zaria 1982.

Mukhtar, M.I. "The significance of colonial labour policies in the Re-orientation of the Economy of Kano in the first half of the 20th century", *Paper presented to the second International Seminar on the History of Kano*, B.U.K. Sept. 1985.

Musa, I.U.A. "The rise of Muslim Sudanic historiography in Bilad As-Sudan, A tentative analysis", *History Seminar* A.B.U. Zaria nd

Sakaba & Zomi Rikoto "Tarihin Ekliseya a Kasar Zuru: Farkon Zuwan Maganar Allah a Kasar Dakarkari a Zuru Daga 1925", *Mimeo*, Nov. 1977.

Swai, B. "Fanon, contemporary Africa and relevance of the theory of historical expediency", *History Seminar*, Univ. of Sokoto, 1986.

Swai B. "How the past is politically inspected and Historically produced", *Lecture in honour of Prof. B. Pachai* Univ. of Sokoto, March 1985.

"In honour, remembrance and vindication of Frantz Fanon or on the apparitions, spectres and whimsies of critical criticism in African History", *History Seminar*, Univ. of Sokoto, 1987.

"Intellectualizing upon the National Nationality questions", *Mimeo*, Sokoto nd.

Temu, A.J. "Cults of facts and fetishism in professional African History", *Post-graduate Seminar papers*, A.B.U. Zaria, 1978.

Tukur, M.M. — "State-creation, the economy and the distribution of constitutional power in Nigeria", mimeo, Zaria 1983.

Wamba, E. — "History of neo-colonialism or neo-colonialist History? Self determination and history in Africa", *Mimeo*, Trenton, N.J., 1984.

Wrighley, C.C — "Historicism in Africa", Sussex 1970.

(e) *Articles:*

Arndt, W.W. — "The Performance of Glottochronology in Germanic", *Language*, 35, 1959.

Augi, A.R. — "Beyond the shadow of substance: The legacy of Gobir in the Sokoto Calipha", *Odu: Journal of West African Studies*, Forthcoming.

"The Significance of Hills and Inselbergs in the History of culture of the people of Hausaland", *Zaruma, A Cultural Magazine of Sokoto State*, Feb. 1982.

Bernstein, H. — "Marxism and African History: Endre Sik and his critics", *Kenya Historical Review*, 4, 1976.

Bhattacharya, S. — "History from below", *Social Scientist*, 11, 1983.

Blaut, D. — "Are puerto Ricans a National Minority", *Monthly Review*, 29, 1977.

Bradby, D. — "The Destruction of Natural Economy", Economy and Society, IV, 2, 1985.

Bright, W., "Glottochronological counts of Hokaltecan material", *Language*, 32, 1956.

Calvocoressi D. & B.N. David, "A new Survey of Radiocarbon Thermoluminescence dates for West Africa", *Journal of African History*, XX, 1, 1979

Effah-Gyamfi, K.. "Ancient Urban Sites in Hausa land: A Preliminary Report", *West African Journal of Archmelogy*, XVI, 1986,

Falola, T., "Presenting the evidence: A review of *A Little New light: Select writings of Abdullahi Smith*, Vol. I, Kaduna 1987, in *West Africa*, London, Sept. 1977.

Gibbon, P., "Imperialism and the National question: Some thesis", *Utafiti* IV, 1979.

Gudschinsky, S.C. "The ABC's of Lexico-statistics (Glottochronology)". *Word*, 12, 1956.

Gujiya, M.M. "The Dakarkari People (Lélna)", in *Zaruma*, 6th ed. nd.

Harris, P.G. "Notes on the Dakarkari people of Sokoto Province, Northern Nigeria", *Journal of the Royal Anthropological Institute*, LXVIII, 1938.

Hartle, D.D. "Preliminary Report of the University of Ibadan's Kainji Rescue archaeology Project 1968", *West Anthropological News-letter* 1970.

Jemkur, J.F., "Recent results of Thermoluminescence (Th) Tests on Nok Terracottas and Sherds",

Hoijer, H. "Lexicostatistics: A Critique", *Language*, 32, 1956.

Jaggar, P.J. "Kano City Blacksmiths: Pre-colonial distribution, structure and organisation", *Savanna*, 11,2, 1976.

Jones, G.S. "History: The Poverty of empirecism" in R. Blackburn (ed), *Ideology in Social Science*, London 1972.

Kaviraj, S. "On the status of Marx's Writings on India", *Social Scientist*, 124, 1983.

Lovejoy, P.E. "Plantations in the Economy of the Sokoto Caliphate", *Journal of African History*, XIX, 3, 1978.

& S. Baier, "The desert-side Economy of the central Sudan", *International Journal of African Historical Studies*, VIII, 4, 1975.

Mamdani, M. "The Nationality question in a neo-colony: an historical perspective", *Mawanzo*, 5, 1980.

Meera, et.al. "Karl Marx and the analysis of Indian Society", *Social Scientist*, 126, 1984.

Meillassoux, c. "From Reproduction to production", *Economy & Society*, I, I, 1972.

Musa, I.U.A. "On the nature of Islamisation and Islamic reform in Bilad As-Sudan up to Sokoto Jihad", *Dirasat*, vi, 1979.

Nzewunwa, N. "Recent archaeological works in the middle Niger Valley", *Proceedings of the 9th Pan African Congress of Prehistory and related studies*, Jos 1983.

*West African Journal of Archaeology*, XXI, 1986.

Obayemi, A., "A Note on Text excavations at Maleh and Toro, Sokoto Province", *Zaria Archaeology papers*, II, 1976.

"Aspects of field archaeology in Hausaland", *Zaria Archaeology papers*, 1, 1976.

"The Ulaira site and the History of the Yauri area, some questions", *Zaria Archaelogy papers*, 4, 1979.

"The Yoruba and Edo speaking peoples and their neighbours before 1600 A.D.", in J.F.A. Ajayi & M. Crowder (ed), *History of West Africa*, Vol.I (2nd ed.) Longman, 1976.

Priddy, A.J. "An iron age site near Yelwa, Sokoto Provinces: Preliminary Report", *West African Archaelogical Newsletter*, No. 10, 1968.

Rey, P., "The Lineage mode of production", *Critique of Anthropology*, No 3, spring No 1975.

Shaw, T., "Preliminary Report on Archaelogical Work in the Wushishi area, early 1976", *Zaria Archaelogy papers*, Vol 9, 1976.

Singh, S. et.al. "Subaltern Studies II: A review article", *Social Scientist*, 137, 1985.

Smith A., "Some considerations relating to the formation of States in Hausaland", *Journal of the Historical Society of Nigeria*, V, 1970.

Soper, R.C., "The Stone age in Northern Nigeria", *Journal of the Historical Society of Nigeria*, III, 2, 1965.

Sutton, J.E.G., "Kebbi valley preliminary Survey, 1975", *Zaria Archaelogy Papers*, Vol.5, 1976.

Swadesh, M., "Lexicostatistics dating of prehistoric ethnic contacts", *Proceedings of the American Philosophical Society*, 96, 1952.

"Salish internal Relations", *International Journal of American Linguistics*, 16, 1950.

"Towards greater accuracy in lexicostatistics dating", *International Journal of American Linguistics*, 21, 1955.

Today Sunday Magazine, "The idol Worshipers of Hausaland, *To-day Newspaper* Kaduna 20/7/86.

Troike, R.C., "The glottochronology of Six Turkic Languages", *International Journal of American Linguistics* 35, 1969

(f) **Books:**

Adamu, M., *The Hausa Factor in West African History*, A.B.C. Press, 1978.

Agh, A., *The Recent State of Imperialism and Non-alignment*, Dar es-Salaam, 1980.

Ajayi, J.F.A. & Crowder, M.(ed), *History of West Africa*, Vol.1, Longman. 1971.

Akinjogbin, & S. Osoba (ed), *Topics on Nigerian Economic and Social History.*

Arnett, E.J., *Gazetteers of the Northern Provinces of Nigeria*, Vol.1, London: Frank Cass, 1972.

Boyd, C.E., *Gazetteers of the Northern Provinces of Nigeria: The Central Kingdoms*, London: Frank Cass, 1967.

Bynon, Th., *Historical Linguistics*, C.U.P. 1977.

Clark, J.D. *World Prehistory*, London 1969.

Crummey, D. & C.C.

## Bibliography

| | |
|---|---|
| Stewart (ed), | *Modes of Production in Africa: The Pre-colonial Era*, London 1980. |
| Cohen, A., | *Custom and Polities in Urban Africa: Study of Hausa Migrants in Yoruba Towns*, C.U.P. 1968. |
| Deutscher, I. | *The Unfinished Revolution*, O.U.P. 1967. |
| Duff, E.C. & W. Hamilton-Browne, | *Gazetteer of Kontagora province*, London, 1920. |
| Fanon, F. | *The Wreteched of the Earth*, Harmondsworth, 1967. |
| Freund, B., | *Capital and labour in the Nigerian Tine Mines*, Longman, 1982. |
| | *The making of contemporary Africa*, Bloomington, 1984. |
| Giroux, H.A., | *Ideology, culture and the process of schooling*, London 1981. |
| Glynn, Maj. A.L., | *The Lower Niger and its Tribes*. |
| Goddard, B.C., | *Encyclopedia of modern Christian Mission*. Thomas Nelson & Sons, N.J. 1978. |
| Greenberg, J.H. | *Languages of Africa*, Bloomington 1963 |
| | *Studies in African Linguistic classification*, New Haven, 1955. |
| Gunn, H.D. & F.P. Conant, | *Peoples of the Middle Niger Region, Northern Nigeria*, London 1960. |
| Hopkins, A.G. | *An Economic History of West Africa*, Longman, 1971. |
| Ikime, O., | *The Groundwork of Nigerian History*, Ibadan, 1980. |
| Jaffe, H., | *A History of Africa*, London 1985. |
| Kani, A.M. | *The Intellectual Origin of the Sokoto Jihad*, Ibadan, 1985. |

Kirk-Greens, A.H.M., *The Emirates of Northern Nigeria*, O.U.P. 1966.

Kosambi, D.D. *The Culture and Civilisation of Ancient India in Historical outline*, Delhi, 1981.

Lehmann, W.B. *Historical Linguistics An Introduction*, Holt, Rhenehart & Winston, 1962.

Lovejoy, P.E. *Caravans of the Kola: The Hausa Kola Trade, 1700-1900*, A.B.U Press, 1980.

(ed), *The ideology of Slavery in Africa*, London, 1981.

Madauchi, I. et al, *Hausa customs*, NNPC, Zaria 1908.

Maddocks, K.P. & D.A. Pott, *Report to Local Government in Northern Provinces of Nigeria*, London, 1950.

Mamdani, M. *Politics and Class in Uganda*, London 1976.

Marx, K., *The Eighteenth Brumaire of Louis Bonaparte*.

*Pre-Capitalist Economic Formations*, New York 1965.

Mbiti, J.S., *African Religion and Philosophy*, London, 1972.

Mohammed, M.A. (ed), *A Giant of a Man: Tributes to professor Abdullahi Smith*, Kaduna 1986.

Netting, R.M., *Hill Farmers of Nigeria: A Cultural Ecology of the Kofyar of the Jos Plateau*, London, 1968.

Northrup, D., *Trade without Rulers: Pre-colonial Trade Among the Ibo*, London, 1976.

Onigu, O. & W. Ogionwo, *An introduction to Sociological Studies*.

| | |
|---|---|
| Perera, P.D.A. et al. | *Survey of Settlements in Sokoto State*, Sokoto, 1981. |
| Plumb, J.H. | *The Death of the Past*, Harmondsworth, 1970. |
| Prazan, C. | *The Dukkawa of Northern Nigeria*, Pittsburgh, 1977. |
| Rey, P., | *Les Alliances De Classes*, Paris, 1973. |
| Robinson, R. & J. Gallagher, | *African and the Victorians*, New York, 1962. |
| Shinnie, P.L., (ed), | *The African Iron Age*, O.U.P. 1971. |
| Sohn-Rethel, A. | *Intellectual and Manual Labour*, London, 1978. |
| Swai, B. | *Recovery of Local Initiative in African History: A Critique*, Dar es-Salaam, 1979. |
| Taylor, J. | *From modernisation to modes of Production*. New York, 1979. |
| Temple, C.L. (ed), | *Notes on the Tribes, Provinces, Emirates and States of the Northern Provinces of Nigeria*, London 1922, reproduced 1965. |
| Temu, A.J. & B. Swai, | *Historians and Africanist History: A Critique*, London, 1981. |
| Udo, R.K., | *Geographical Regions of Nigeria*. Ibadan 1967. |
| Usman, Y.B.(ed), | *Studies in the History of the Sokoto Caliphate The Sokoto Seminar Papers*, Sokoto 1979. |
| | *The Transformation of Katsina, 1400-1883*, A.B.U. Press, 1981. |
| | (ed), *Demystifying Nigerian History*, Ibadan, 1982. |
| Voegelin, C.F. & F.M. Voegelin, | *Classification and Index of the World's Languages*, Elsevier, 1977. |
| Watts, M., | *Silent violence: Food, Famine and peasantry in Northern Nigeria*, Univ. of California Press, 1983. |

# Index
Studies in the History of the People of Zuru Emirate

## A

Abandoned settlements; 30,31
Abba, A.; 14
Abdulhakeem, M.; 16
Acephalous societies; 8,17
Achifawa; 26
Adamu Mahdi; 147
Adeleye R.; 6
Administrative reforms; 149
Adulterer; 80
African; 12,18,19
  bourgeoisie; 2,16,21
  dilemma; 18
  history; 6
  languages; 49
  middle class; 12,16
  nationalism; 6
  neo-colonialism; 12
  perspective; 7
  political economy; 19
  renaissance; 16
  socialism; 16
  socialist; 19
  state bourgeoisie; 16,18
Africanist, alternative; 6
  euphoria; 9
  paradigm; 1,6,9,12,13,17,18,19
Age groups; 36
Agency for International Development (AID); 156
Agh, A.; 16
Agricultural production; 107,112
Agriculture; 35,36,3,64,66,159,160
Ajayi, J.F. Ade; 2,6,8
Ake, Claude; 1,2,4
Akilu, Ali; 14
Alkali court; 155
Alluvial material; 25
Almajiri (ita); 9
Ambrossini Messrs; 164

Ancestor worship; 115,116
Anglo-Saxons; 13
Animal domestication; 38
Architecture; 34
Archival sources; 172
Arewa House, Kaduna; 7,14
Arndt, W.W.; 53
Articles; 178

## B

Bahego; 151
Baiko, consanguine; 142
  fictive; 142
  putative; 142
*Baiko da Sarana*; 142,143
Ballard, J.A.; 23
Banganci; 46,47,54
Bangawa; 26
Banjanci; 55
Battacharye; 11,21
Bawa Bena; 43
Benue - Congo; 28,48
  languages; 47
Bernstein, H.; 10
Bethrothal; 135
Binary couplet; 8
Biological father; 141
Bitiyong Isa; 89
Blacksmiths; 75
Blaut, J.; 10,20
Borno Empire; 26
Borno-Kanem; 7
Bourgeoisie, African State; 18
  African; 2,16
  European; 11
  French; 20
  indigenous; 2,16
  petty; 20
  state; 2,12,17

Boyds and Hamlton; 4
Brama; 149
Bravmann A; 123
Bride (ladi); 137
Bright, W.; 48,49
British, Imperial agents; 148
    imperialism; 148
*Bude kofa*; 143
Burials; 44
Bynon, T.; 46,48

## C

*C'gamba*; 68
*C'lela*; 46,47,54
*C'rino*; 68
Capitalism; 11,16,20
Carbon; 14,46
Causes; 140,141,144
*Ch'ganga*; 37,44
*Ch'gongo*; 37,44
Ch'hwerke; 44
Ch'tage; 44
Cheik anta Diop; 16
*Chi'im chima;* 37
Childe Golden; 156
Christ Apostolic Church; 168
Christianity, influence; 146
    Zuruland; 146, 152,167,170,171
    entrance of; 114,126,127,128
Ciroma L.; 7,14
Civilised, culture; 8,18
    societies; 18
class, exploitation; 12
    oppression; 12
    question; 2,4,16
    differentiation; 114
Classlessness; 11
Clay pot; 41
Cognates; 48
Cold war; 12
Colonial, chauvinism; 6
    empires; 10
    historiography; 6,13
    mystagogy ; 6,10,20
    social relations; 111,113
    economic activities; 111,113
    historiography; 84
    restructuring; 149

Colonialism; 6
Colonization of Zuruland 1910; 113,114
Colonizing nations; 10
Commerce; 75,76
Common ancestor; 48
Communalism; 11,16
Comparison - Languages; 49-55
Compensation; 140,141
Conant F.P; 82
Cotton; 43
Council of Regency; 151
Cultural, institutions; 69,108
    nationalist; 14
    values; 115

## D

*D'biti;* 69,70,107,109,115,119,120,138
Dakarkari; 26
Danfodio Jihad; 168
Danouguzu; 148
Debche hill; 41
Defence mechanism-walls; 33
Democracy; 20,21
Demographic reproduction; 78
Dendchronology; 46
Depression; 164, 165
Deutsher, Isaac; 17
Dialectical relationship; 10
*Dibole*; 67
*Diganga drum*; 37
Divorce; 140
Dogal hill; 39
Dominated nationalities; 3,4,5,6,13,14,18,20,21
Drum and trumpet history; 18
Dukawa; 26
Dukes, P.; 18
Dukkanci; 46,47,54,55
Dye pits; 42,43

## E

Economic reforms; 153
Economies; 56
Economy; 35
    production organisation; 107

ECWA; 168
Endogamy; 142
Ethnicity; 11
Ethnocentric Eurocentric; 10
Eurocentrism; 10,11,15
European, bourgeoisie culture; 11
　capitalist formations; 10
Exhorbitant taxation; 113
Exogamy; 142
Extended communal labour;
　107,112

## F

Faceless rabble; 18
Fadamu; 59, 60
Fakawa; 26
Fakkanci; 46,47,54,55
Fallowing; 36
Falola T.; 7
Fanon, Frantz; 12,13,16
Festivals; 68
Feudal powers; 12
Fictive consanguine; 142
Fields, Daniel; 18
Financial independence; 145
Fitzgerald; 157
Fixed entities; 84
Flag independence; 20
Flood plains; 25
French, bourgeoisie; 16
　imperialist adventurism; 17
　revolution; 16
Freund B; 1,2
Fulani; 27
Funeral; 72
Furnaces; 39

## G

Gallagher, J.; 13
Gambo Andi; 150
Gayya; 67,160
Genetic Language relationship; 47
Germache shrine; 103
Gibbon P.; 20,21
Gift marriage; 141
Gipsies; 17
Giroux, H.A.; 19

Global monopoly capitalism; 20
Glotochronological estimates; 28
　investigations; 46,47,48,53,54
Glottochronology; 46,47,48
Gobir, Amuda Yusuf; 14
*Golmo*;
　36,37,68,69,115,120,121,136,
　137,140,146
*Gom-vu-menke*; 37,40
Gouro society; 79,80
Graves; 41,42,45
　kings, 45
Greenberg, J.R.; 48,49
Gudschinsky S.C.; 47
Guinea Savanna; 26
Gujiya Michael; 85
Gunn H.D.; 82

## H

Hamis Muhammad; 4,5,14
Harris, P.G.; 22,23,82,99,
　103,117,133,137
Hausa - Fulani; 9
Hausa; 26
Hausaland; 23
Hegemonic class; 1
Hierarchised political systems; 110
Hilly toprography; 29
Historicism; 15
Historiography, Africanist; 6
　Colonial; 6,13
　imperialist; 13
　Nigerian; 1
　Northern Nigeria; 9
　Sub-Saharan Africa; 1
History, Assumptions;
　83,84,85,86
　drum and trumpet; 18
　Iron Age; 89, 91
　Socio-political; 82,83
　Stone Age; 88,89
　Zuruland; 82,83
Hoijer H.; 47
Hunting; 72

# I

*Ibimo*; 41, 42
Idris Musa Baba; 91
*Igadu*; 41, 42
Igbo; 27
Imperial history; 20
Imperialised world; 20
Imperialism; 14,16,20
Imperialist, forces; 2,12,17
  historiograhpy; 13
Independence of choice; 145
Indigene or stranger sterotype; 85,86
Indigenous bourgeoisie; 2,11,16,17,18
Indigo; 43
Individual god; 114
Industry; 72,73
Inikori, J.E.; 13
Inselbergs; 25
Integral nation-states; 10
Inter-war period; 165
Interim Committee Services Agency (I.C.S.A.); 13
Internal migrations; 100
International Monetary Fund; 16
International order; 16
Iron, Age; 63
  smelting; 72,74
  technology; 38,40
*Iskoki;* 62
Islam; 141, 142
  entrance of; 114,122,123,124,125
Islamic influence; 109
Islamization, Zuruland; 168,169

# J

Jaffe, H.; 11
Jones, G.S.; 18
Judicial reforms; 155

# K

*Kashilu*; 109
Katsinawa; 26
Kaunbari; 26
Kaviraj, S; 11
Kawi, A.M.; 4
Kebbi Empire; 23

Kinship; 11
Kisra legend; 91,101
Kosambi D.D.; 8,9
Kuba Joseph; 128

# L

Labour; 36
Land and labour policies, 113
Land sharing; 107
Land; 36
Languages; 28,48,55
  comparison, 49-55
Last, Murray; 95
Late Stone Age; 28,62,63
Latoritic residual hills; 32
Lawal S.U.; 1
Lélna; 26
*Lefe* ; 142
Lehman; W.P.; 47
Lenin V.I.; 21
Leonard Glyn; 117
Lexicostatistics; 46,47
Liberal scholarship; 12
Lineage mode of production; 78
Linguistic classification; 28
  date; 28
  history; 53
Logow; 44
Lovejoy, P.E.; 78
Lugard, Lord; 154

# M

*M'bimo*; 41,42
*M'gilø*; 65,68,101,107,109,117,118,120
Macarthy John; 128
Magaji; D.S; 118
Mahdi Adamu; 4,8,22,23,123,125
Mahogany; 26
Majiro Eave; 27
Mamdani Mahmood; 8,11,18
Manufacturing activities; 107
Marriage, changes; 145
  continuity; 145
  definition of; 135
  dowry; 136,142,146
  systems; 132,135,141
  traditional; 132,135

Marx, Karl; 10,15,17
Marxism; 14
Mary, S.; 95
*Masu golmo*; 160
Material culture; 83
*Mazuganci*; 77
Mbiti J.S; 117
Mecrav; 10
Metal pots, 41
Migration; 26,29,63,64,65
  internal; 100
  significance; 100,101
  the Achipawa; 91
  the Bangawa (Dankawa); 98
  the Dakarkari; 94,95,96
  the Dakawa; 99
  the Fakawa; 100
  the Kambari; 92
  the Katsinawa Laka; 99
Missionaries; 152,157,170,171
Mode of Production; 78
Modibo, M.A.
Monetarist economics; 16
Muffet, D.J.M.; 11
Muhammadu Kanta; 23
Murderer; 80

# N

Nation Building; 12,13
National question;
  2,4,12,16,18,20
Nationalism; 17,20
Nationalist predilections; 2
Nationality question; 2,3,4,12,18
Native court; 155
Natural econocmy; 81
Negritude; 15
Negro races; 13
Neo-colonies; 19
Neo-colonial history; 12
Neo-colonialism; 16,20
Neutrality; 12
Niger-Congo, languages; 28,48,89
Nigerian, Historical Scholarship; 2
  Historiography; 1,13
  Middle Belt; 25
Nigerian Mineral Development
  Company; 162

Nok terrucotta; 42
  tradition; 40
Northern, Hausa-Fulani oligarchy;
13
  History Research Scheme; 7
  Nigerian historiograhpy; 9,20

# O

Obayemi, Ade; 28,30,82,83,91
Occupational sophistication; 114
Ogionwo, W; 116
Oppressed, classes; 18
  nation; 20
Oppression; 20
Oppressor nation; 20
Oral Informants; 172
Ore; 38
Ottite, Onigu; 116

# P

Parson F.L. 151
Patrilineage; 66
Patriliny; 14
Peasant, agriculture; 35
  population; 27
Pedestrian logic; 19
Penin, Amana; 105
Petty bourgeoisie; 20
Phonetic similarity; 48
Phonological correspondence; 48
Plumb J.H.; 17
Political instability; 147
Polities in Zuruland;
  101,102,103,105
Popper, Karl; 15
Population; 23,26,29,63,64,65
  distribution; 30
Positivist interpretation; 10
Pottery; 41,75
Pre-Social relations; 111,113
Pre-colonial economic activities;
  111, 113
Pre-histories; 46
Price mechanism; 113
Production of use; 112,113
Putative consanguine; 142

# R

Racism; 11
Rainfall; 25
Reactionary; 17
  culture; 21
Regional interests; 2
Related Languages; 54
Relief; 29,32
Religiosity; 16
Religious ethnics; 113
Rethel, Sohn; 9
Revolutionary movement; 8
Robinson, R.; 13
Rodney, W.; 10
Roman Catholic Mission; 168
Russian Revolution; 17

# S

Sacrifices; 116
Sahara; 29
Sakaba Emirate; 149
Sakaba, M.S.; 95
Samuel, R.; 12
*Sarakuna*; 67
*Sarkin Golmo*; 138,139
Satist developmentalism; 3
Sayen Baki; 144
Second Republic; 3
Self-determination; 3
Self-reliant; 20
settlement; 26,29,30,31,33
  walling; 33
Shifting cultivation; 107
Singh, S; 17
*Skeme*; 68
Slaves; 76,77
Smith, Abdullahi; 7,8,14
Social, engineering; 19
  father; 141
  groups; 109
  husband; 141
  institutions; 115
  self-determination; 3
  self-emancipation; 3,21
Socio-economic conflict; 114
  reforms; 154,166
  transformation; 147

Socio-political evolution; 101,110
Soil; 59
Sokoto Caliphate; 7
Sokoto Jihad; 105,123,124
Soper, R.; 23
State bourgeoisie; 2,13,17
Stateless Societies; 17,82
Statelessness; 11,17
Statist developmentalism; 20
Stone Age; 27
  axes; 27
  tools; 43
Strangers; 26
Sub-cultural groups; 134
Sub-Saharan Africa; 1
Suitor; *(tuku)*; 137,139
Surplus value; 113
Swadesh, Morris; 46,47
Swai, B.; 12,13,16,18,20

# T

*Talakawa*; 9
*Tama*; 62
Tax system; 154
Temperature; 26
Terracing; 35
Terracotta Vigumines; 42, 44
Topograhpy; 25, 59
Toure, Sekou; 16
Trade; 75, 107, 108
Traditional belief systems 132, 133
  forces; 16
  marriage systems 132, 135
  worship; 113, 114
  powers; 12
Traditionalism; 16
Transport; 153
Tribal gyrations; 9
  statistics; 66
Tribalism; 16
Tribe; 11
Tribes of Northern Nigeria; 5
Troike, R.C.; 47,48,49,53
Tukur, M.M; 3

## U

*Uhola*;
69,70,107,109,115,119,120
Ummuel Joseph; 167
Ummuel Paul; 168
Uncivilized culture; 8
Undulating plains; 29
Unequal exchange; 113
United Africa Company; 164
United Missionary Society; 68,126
Universal God; 114
Unpublished Papers; 176
Unpublished Thesis; 174
Urbanisation; 145
Usman, Y.B.; 76

## V

Value - freeism; 12
Vegetation; 26, 59
Victorian wisdom; 13
Voegeling, C.F.; 48,49

## W

*Waliyai*; 142
Walls - defence mechanism; 33
Wamba, E.; 3,18
Win-the war relief fund; 165
*Wøh*; 71,108,115, 121
*Womo (Ahifa)*; 101
Working people; 12,14,16,17,18
World Bank; 16
Wriggely C.C.; 14,15

## Y

*Yadato*; 139
Yam cultivation; 37
*Yan Golmo*; 138,139
*Yawon gudu*; 143

## Z

Zamfara; 26
*Zoge;* 37, 40
Zuru, Club; 88
  cultural and religious
    dimensions; 108
  economy; 106
  external influence; 105
  internal influence; 105
  settlements; 106
  social groups; 109
  native administration; 151
  region; 23,29
zuruland, administrative reforms; 149
  agriculture; 159,160
  Anglo-Zuru relationship;
    150,151, 165, 166
  British imperialism, 148,149
  Christianity;
    146,152,167,170,171
  colonial restructuring; 149,157
  colonialism - impact of; 166
  commerce; 163
  during second world war; 165
  ecology and Production;
    161,163
  history; 82,83
  Islamization of, 168
  land tenure systems; 158
  medical care; 169,170
  mining industry; 162
  production patteern; 156
  settlement pattern; 156
  socio-economic changes, 166
  socio-economic transformation; 147
  underdevelopment of; 170
  water and electricity supply; 170
  Western Education;
    145,146,167,168